T0365643

"61 Minutes"

Reflections and Homilies for the Year of Matthew

by

Rev. Michael W. Rothan

authorHOUSE®

AuthorHouse™ LLC
1663 Liberty Drive
Bloomington, IN 47403
www.authorhouse.com
Phone: 1-800-839-8640

Published by AuthorHouse   12/23/2013

ISBN: 978-1-4918-4597-4 (sc)
ISBN: 978-1-4918-4596-7 (e)

Library of Congress Control Number: 2013923185

Front Cover: *The Anxiety of Saint Joseph (L'anxiété de Saint Joseph)*[1]

Betrothed, but still unmarried, Mary and Joseph do not yet live together, making the news of her unexpected pregnancy a cause of deep concern for Joseph. Ordinarily industrious, as the curled wood shavings around his feet attest, the carpenter hunches over his bench, lost in thought and unable to work. In the hope of catching a glimpse of Mary, he gazes out at the street as women pass, carrying jars filled with the day's water.

Although traditional representations of Joseph show a man of advanced age, Tissot painted him as younger and more robust, arguing in his accompanying commentary that "Rabbinical doctrine" would have regarded the union of an old man and a young girl as a "profanation." He further asserted that the rigorous demands placed on the Holy Family, required a man of vigor.

---

1   James Tissot, French, 1836-1902. Portfolio/Series: *The Life of Our Lord Jesus Christ (La Vie de Notre-Seigneur Jésus-Christ)* Description taken from the Brooklyn Museum of Art.

CONTENTS

This is dedicated to my loves: Rose & Lily, Xavier, Michael, Sophia, Celia, Kyle, Eliana, Logan, Mason, Krystopher, and others who will sometimes refer to me as "Uncle Mike."

It is in the children that Jesus offers us example; it is in the childlike, that the humanity of Jesus can be seen most clearly. Who's your favorite uncle?

FOREWORD

As I write these words, we move toward the completion of our "Year of Faith." We received the gift of this "Year of Faith" from Pope Benedict XVI. We began this journey on October 11, 2012 and continued to the Solemnity of Christ the King on November 24, 2013.

Our Diocese of Harrisburg encouraged parishes to present the work, "Catholocism," by Fr. Robert Barron, as an opportunity to strengthen and eepen our faith together. I remember very well the scene that Fr. Barron presented when Pope John Paul II visited Poland in 1979.

Fr. Barron wrote, "On June 2, 1979, Pope John Paul II came to Victory Square in the heart of Warsaw and celebrated Mass in the presence of hundreds of thousands of people and the entire Polish Communist Government. During his homily the pope spoke of God, of freedom and of human rights—all topics frowned upon by the Communist regime. As the Pope preached, the people began to chant, 'We want God; we want God; we want God.' The pope continued and the chant went on, 'We want God; we want God,' and did not stop for an astounding fifteen minutes."

As this book has found its way into your hands, you probably also 'want God.' I assure you that as you use this book well, the presence of God that you desire to experience will flow into your life again and again.

I have read both editions of "61 Minutes" as they presented homilies from the Liturgical years which feather the evangelists, Luke and Mark. I have been waiting for this edition that features the evangelist, Matthew. Finally, the long wait receives its reward.

In this Third Edition of "61 Minutes" we encounter some homilies in Spanish. We hear some of the experiences of Fr. Rothan's days during a summer program in Mexico. We encounter a homilist who has grown in faith, hope and love.

1

Saint Jerome wrote, "Ignorance of Scripture is ignorance of Christ." I thank Fr. Rothan for exhorting us to read and reread the Sacred Scripture texts that inspire these homilies. I publicly confess that I have not always done this. I enjoy his writing so much that at times I fail to read the Word of God first.

I'll try to do better with this Third Edition. Certainly, I joyfully anticipate the fruit of Fr. Rothan's prayerful reflection on these Scriptures and his experiences, but he tells us to read the Sacred Scriptures first. Thank you, Fr. Rothan, for your instruction and inspiration. With the combination of God's Word and your words, certainly our faith deepens and increases. We come to know Christ better and deeper.

Saint Matthew, pray for us.

Saint Anthony of Padua, pray for us.

All you Holy Men and Women, pray for us.

Fr. Daniel Mitzel
Pastor, Saint Anthony of Padua Parish
Lancaster, PA

November 1, 2013 . . . the Feast of All Saints

INTRODUCTION

Read this first!

The person of Christ Jesus was far closer to us than we might imagine. He was a person you know. Yes, he is God; but a person. Now, I'm not speaking of "three persons in one God" (that's a homily for Trinity Sunday). I'm speaking of a person . . . people . . . a person.

An obstacle that keeps so many from scripture, is a false belief that the people in these stories are characters within a drama, or just pawns in an elaborate mythological game of chess. These assertions could not be further from the truth. The reality, is that scripture is composed of sacred words about people. And not people who were invented for a novel, let alone a "made for TV movie." The book begins with a promise, and concludes with fulfillment. That is the story I'm talkin' about!

What about you? Ever get up with a headache? See the person coming down the street and try to find a way out? Receive news of a tragedy or a sudden death? Ever know someone who was deaf or blind or lame or sick, and once, just once, wanted to hear or see or walk or feel good? Ever dislike someone, but feel sorry for them? Ever feel like you are absolutely alone? Ever feel like no one understands you? No one listens to you? No one loves you? Ever feel that giddy sense in your stomach when your love or crush smiles in your direction? Ever feel the wrenching in your stomach over rejection? Ever way too hot, or cold to the bone? Ever wish you had never been born; or at least question the conditions into which you were born? Ever want a second chance? How about a third? Ever feel such remorse, that you change your life (by the way, that's not remorse but repentance)?

If you answered yes to any of the above, then keep reading, because so did they. Who are they? *They* were the *Am segulah*; they were the *anowim*; the *hoi palloi*; the *God-fearers*; the *Christians*. The Bible is not a life history or a biopic, as much as it is a love diary, and a faith journey of people, just like you and me, who were trying to do what they could to grow closer to the One from whom they came. Matthew's Gospel shows us the humaness of Jesus in a way that goes far beyond the other evangelists. And yet, through and through, his Gospel has a Jewish flavor that does not exclude the non-Jews in the group. His, is a gentle story, of the Christ who came into the world as all of us do. Of a God who could have chosen to enter into history in any other way. And yet he chose *this* way.

Matthew begins his story with a genealogy. He opens with the formidable family tree of Jesus, represented by the good, the bad, and the ugly. We come to understand that God chose to enter the world, not just as a baby, but a poor baby; not just a poor baby, but a poor baby born in a barn; not just a poor baby born in a barn, but a poor baby born in a barn who had a price on his head! And that bounty would never be revoked. This theme of the meek and humble Messiah, would cycle throughout the Gospel, until he gave up his spirit as humbly as he was first *in-spired*.

The person of Jesus, was just that . . . a person, who *did not deem equality with God as something to be grasped, but emptied himself taking the form of a slave . . . being in the likeness of man (Philippians 2:6 ff.).* So God who created us in His image and likeness, now takes on the image and likeness of the *created* . . . so that *He* might save *us*.

I imagine that some days Jesus got up with a headache. I mean, after all, he did sleep in the desert for the most part, and I'm sure had some allergies. He stubbed his toe, and yes, it hurt. He was without sin, but he was *not* perfect. Imagine him trying to tie a fisherman's knot, having never done that before. We know he could be sad, because he cried at the death of Lazarus. We know he could be frustrated at times, for he actually states to the Disciples and people at one point, *"How much longer must I be with you and you still do not understand!"(Mark 9:19)* We know that he could suffer from human ailments; I mean he was scourged and crucified. We know that he could get angry, or as scripture is sometimes translated, *"perturbed."* We know that he could be anxious or grievous, lest we forget the garden of Gethsemane. He is one of us. As St. Athanasius said, "He became what we are so that he might make us what he is."[2]

When we begin to see Jesus as a person . . . as one of us, then we can relate to him as one of us. Only then is he one who understands *my* struggles, because he had struggles. Only then is he the one who comforts me in my loneliness, because he felt that at times. Jesus is the *consoler* in my betrayal, because he was once betrayed. He is my Savior, because he *CAN* save only what he assumes. And because he assumed our lowly nature in his humility, then ***even I*** can be saved.

This book is the last in the series of ***61 Minutes***, but the first in the cycle of the readings used in the Liturgical year for the Roman Catholic Church. We all grow and change over time. St. John Neumann once said: "To live is to change . . . to live perfectly is to have changed often."[3] It has now been over four years since I have published a book, and in those four years (almost half of my priesthood thus far) I have grown and changed immensely. I'm sure that will be reflected in part through these last homilies.

A note to the reader: there are some homilies you will find in English and Spanish. The homilies in Spanish include some homilies from the other two books, which had never been offered in Spanish. Under the title, will be the designation of "Year B" or "Year C" if they are not for the current year. For three of my nine years, I was in a wonderful Spanish and English parish. It is only appropriate that I include those reflections in the hopes that they drew some of my people there to Christ; or if they didn't, that they at least gave the congregation a laugh at my inept Spanish. ¡Lo siento mis amigos en Cristo!

As always, read; re-read; reflect and enjoy. I encourage you to read the readings for the Sunday first; then to reflect on that homily at your leisure. We have little enough time to reflect, so speed-readers, slow down! Now, having said that, I am not so naïve as to believe many of you will do so. And you know what? I don't care. It's the

---

2   St. Athanasius. *On the Incarnation. (ca297-373)*
3   John Henry Newman, (21 February 1801-11 August 1890).

third book, and you paid good money for it; so read all you want! Know, however, that the only reason I can write anything, is because I reflect on everything. Speed-reading is fine if you're focused on the destination; but reflection is for those who are on the journey.

Rev. Michael W. Rothan
Written at Pangaea, 29 September 2013
(Feast of the Archangels)

OUR LADY OF GUADALUPE
(MICAH 5:1-4; PSALM 13; ROMANS 8:28-30; MATTHEW 1:1-16, 18-23)

You know the story. But I will tell you my own. I arrived at the Basílica of our Lady of Guadalupe early in the morning. The vendors were just setting up their goods. It was very easy to walk the sidewalks, but the night before they were full of vendors. I entered the gates to the grand basílica, and already, the people were walking up the slate sidewalk . . . on their knees. I saw a woman carrying her sick child . . . I saw old men and women, on their knees . . . together, holding hands as they approached the church. Each had a prayer. Perhaps it was something they wanted for their family or friends; perhaps it was something for which they were thanking God; perhaps they wanted forgiveness of sins; or perhaps, it was purely in praise for God's glory . . . through *this woman.*

She is the greatest of humanity; and the humblest of humanity. The god of the sun is behind her; the goddess of the moon is under her feet; the two great gods of the *aztecas* are small, when compared to this princess who is pregnant. And **that** is the point. The center of the image is not our lady of Guadalupe, but a child in her womb . . . Jesus, who comes to us in a few days. He was the center of Her life; and she desires that He is the center of ours.

I saw the humility; the reverence of these Mexican people and some tourists, as well, as they approached the Basílica. Like our Lady, however, they would not be the center . . . they would not leave empty, but would carry Jesus within . . . as we do today. Then we also, may walk on our knees, thanking God for the greatest gift. The gift we are preparing to receive . . . the gift of his Son.

For the full story of my experiences in Mexico and the Basilica, see appendix IV.

LA FIESTA DE SEÑORA DE LA GUADALUPE

(MIQUEAS 5:1-4; SALMO 13; ROMANOS 8:28-30; MATEO 1:1-16, 18-23)

Ustedes conocen la historia. Pero te diré la mía propia. Llegué a la Basílica de Nuestra Señora de Guadalupe por la mañana temprano. Los vendedores eran sólo la creación de sus productos. Fue muy fácil de caminar por las aceras, pero la noche antes de que se llena de vendedores. Entré en las puertas de la gran basílica y ya, la gente caminaba por la acera de pizarra . . . de rodillas. Vi a una mujer cargando a su hijo enfermo . . . Vi a hombres de edad y mujeres, de rodillas . . . juntos, cogidos de la mano mientras se acercaban a la iglesia. Cada uno tenía una oración. Tal vez era algo que quería para su familia o amigos, tal vez era algo que estaban dando las gracias a Dios, tal vez ellos querían el perdón de los pecados, o tal vez fue simplemente en alabanza de la gloria de Dios . . . a través de esta mujer.

Ella es la más grande de la humanidad, y el más humilde de la humanidad. El dios del sol está detrás de ella, la diosa de la luna bajo sus pies, los dos grandes dioses de los aztecas son pequeñas en comparación con esta princesa que está embarazada. Y ese es el punto. El centro de la imagen no es nuestra señora de Guadalupe, pero un niño en aquélla a quien . . . Jesús, que viene a nosotros en unos días. Fue el centro de su vida, y ella desea que él es el centro de la nuestra.

Vi la humildad, el respeto de esta gente mexicana y algunos turistas, así, mientras se acercaban a la basílica. Al igual que la Virgen, sin embargo, no sería el centro . . . no van a dejar en blanco, pero llevar a Jesús dentro de . . . como lo hacemos hoy. Entonces también, puede caminar de rodillas, agradeciendo a Dios por el regalo más grande. El regalo que se preparan para recibir . . . el don de su Hijo.

First Sunday of Advent

(Isaiah 2:1-5; Psalm 122; Romans 13: 11-14; Matthew 24: 37-44)

Now is the Time

"Brothers and sisters: You know the time; it is the hour now for you to awake from sleep. For our salvation is nearer now than when we first believed; the night is advanced, the day is at hand . . . Let us put on the Lord Jesus Christ, and make no provision for the desires of the flesh." The hour is at hand.

There is a shadow looming over the world. We in the United States, often have this attitude that nothing affects us; that we, as the *land of the free,* aren't plagued by the misguided attitudes of the world . . . we are wrong. This shadow has been slowly infecting us for years, and now it accelerates each day that we do nothing.

Over the course of the last fifty years, our country has gone through a transformation, and few places have been untouched. This transformation began with something called the *Sexual Revolution,* but that is a misnomer. It should have been called the sexual *de-evolution.* The one to whom this revolution is attributed, is one of the founders of *Planned Parenthood,* Margaret Sanger. I quote her here:

> Greater understanding and practice of planned parenthood, through the use of contraceptive measures prescribed by doctors and clinics, will mean that there will be more strong and healthy children and fewer defective and handicapped babies unable to find a useful or happy place in life.[4]

---

4   Margaret Sanger, *Women and the New Race* (Eugenics Publ. Co., 1920, 1923).

9

This is a woman who would go on to say: "The most merciful thing that a large family does to one of its infant members is to kill it."[5] Sounds like someone interested in creating a master race or who did not have the best family situation. These attitudes, however, were just the beginning pangs. This *revolution* would lead to an epidemic of fatherlessness; epidemic of STDs not to mention HIV; it would lead to abortion and eventually to the acceptance of civil unions. Why? Because it replaced "commitment" with "liberation"; "Family" was replaced by "choice"; And Marriage became relegated to a legal contract.

We cannot easily conquer this monster, nor reclaim what was lost; we can only prevent further degradation of this sacred gift from God. We hear of a plague that hit Europe in the beginning of the last millennium: the *Black Death*. Millions died from that black death, but I would suggest many more have already perished from this one. As long as secular humanism, that holds the person as the center of the universe, prevails, we are at risk, and our children are the most vulnerable. We don't feel the pressure right now, because we have become subject to the "boiled frog syndrome." Try to boil a frog by placing it in a pot of hot water, it will hop out. But place it into the cool water, slowly turn up the heat, and the frog will remain there and slowly die.

This is happening now! If you doubt this for a minute, ask yourself if you would have even seriously considered *civil unions* thirty years ago. Would you have thought abortion would ever be legal, let alone, promoted in the middle of the last century? If anyone had told you that children would be able to watch movies in public with suggestive scripts or nudity; or that schools would be teaching our children how to use contraception!

Jesus says: *"Therefore, stay awake! For you do not know on which day your Lord will come. Be sure of this: if the master of the house had known the hour of night when the thief was coming, he would have stayed awake and not let his house be broken into."*

---

5   Ibid.

We have been asleep way too long. My nephew, Xavier, was being held in the arms of my sister (his mother), while she climbed the stairs to put him to bed. Half-way up the stairs, there is a crucifix, and Xavier grabbed it off the wall and yelled, "Wake up! Wake up!" That's not exactly what I had in mind, but perhaps he understands the urgency.

What has happened in that slumber? Marriage is no longer between a man and a woman! Wow . . . I *was* asleep a long time. When did this happen? While we go along with our daily lives, insidious powers are at work. Many states in New England have passed amendments allowing for *civil unions* (let the reader understand). They have made it law, that marriage is no longer between a man and woman, a complementary pair. Okay, so how does this affect me?

In New Jersey, where this is the case, a Methodist Church was sued, and subsequently lost their tax-free status when they refused to witness a civil union in their outside pavilion. Now THIS is an issue of Church and State. They couldn't go through that means, so they cited them on an environmental issue. True!

In California, Gov. Schwartzanegger enacted a law that changed the content of textbooks used in schools. Textbooks must now be all inclusive, reflecting civil unions, which means; no more mention of a "mother" or a "father" just "parent." It means that their story books will have, perhaps, two "moms" or "dads" and depict this as *normal*. Bear in mind that most of our textbooks, are produced in California. The instruction and promotion and glorification of birth control and casual sexual encounters has continued to dull the moral compasses of our youth, let alone our parents. Our abortive mentality has created a "Hollywoodesque" landcape where we can make mistakes without consequences.

These circumstances, among many others, have contributed to the dismantling of the family unit, which for thousands of years has held civilizations together. Now, don't misunderstand, this is not about condemning "lifestyles of the rich and famous," nor is it about supporting a particular party. This goes much deeper than that! This is about PROTECTING AN INSTITUTION . . . something we call a SACRAMENT, because it is Sacred. About protecting the family because it is sacred! It has nothing to do with discrimination; on the contrary, it has to do with a loud minority, trying to force a silent majority, into believing something contrary to natural law! This is yet another nail in the coffin of this sacred domestic church we call the family. The attack against the family is insidious, because it attempts to break down the domestic church in an effort to cripple the Church as a whole.[6]

What can we do? Twenty-seven States west of Pennsylvania, have already enacted this *Marriage Protection Act*, which states: "Only Marriage between one man and one woman shall be valid or recognized as a marriage in this State . . ." Many states have pulled funding from the organization Sanger instituted long ago. Many churches have yielded under pressure from wealthy congregants, or have decided that they are tired of fighting. The Catholic Church has remained firm.

It is not enough to write a letter to your state representative; but if that is all you can do, then do it. We must call them personally, or better yet, visit them personally. We are the people who are responsible for shaping this country through our right to vote. We must educate others on what's happening and encourage them to write and call as well, because many of us are just the frogs, who have been heated up slowly over a long time; that we are asleep. WAKE UP! Now is the time to act. We are not lobbying for a Catholic country. But we are lobbying for a country that will not take what is against objective truth, and make it right. We do not want a country that not only allows evil things to occur, but promotes them as "good" and garnishes them with words like "diverse" and "freedom" to make them palatable.

6   Since this homily was given, the Supreme Court ruled that the *Protection of Marriage Act* was unconstitutional. States are currently responding to this ruling.

They have taken the sacred and made it profane; they have capitalized by exploiting the young; they are stealing this world from our children, and **by God** we must take it back! And you . . . . you are the ones who will do this. YOU ARE the Church. And Jesus said, *"On this rock I will build my Church and the gates of Hell will not prevail against it."*(MT 16:18) Prevail against it . . . that means that Hell is on the *defensive*, which means **we** are on the *offensive*; and if we are on the offensive we are going to **offend**! Most of us will say . . . "but I am a *good person*" . . . . evil has persisted . . . . it has continued to infect our world for so long, because *good people* have done nothing.

Brothers and sisters: You know the time; it is the hour now for you to awake from sleep.
For our salvation is nearer now than when we first believed; the night is advanced, the day is at hand . . . . Let us put on the Lord Jesus Christ, and make no provision for the desires of the flesh. The hour **is** at hand.

Note to the reader: *I know that was a tough one, but just run with me here for a little bit. I think you'll be glad you did.*

PRIMER DOMINGO DE ADVIENTO AÑO "C"

(JEREMÍAS 33:14-16; SALMO 25; I TESALONICENSES 3:12-4:2; LUCAS 21:25-28, 34-36)

¿En que corres tu?

Qué sería si una respiración fuera todo lo que necesitamos para toda la vida? Años pasarian, y el unico requisito sería una respiración? (Quizas seria un aliento muy malo). Qué sería si todo lo que necesitaríamos fuera una bebida para toda nuestra vida; para nuestra vida entera? Qué sería si solamente fuera necesario comer una sola comida y seríamos alimentados para siempre? No se a cuantos de ustedes les gustaría eso, pero se que a mi no me gustaría. Somos seres vivientes, no una especie sin vida: y por eso necesitamos un suministro consatante de aire, comida, y bebida. No dudamos esto, porque somos creados de tal manera que si nos negamos estas cosas, nuestro cuerpo protestará. Entonces porque pensamos que una cantidad minima de espiritualidad es suficiente para nuestra vida? Porque pensamos que una oración rezada una vez al año, una vez por mes, o hasta una vez al día es suficiente? Nosotros comemos, bebemos, y respiramos varias veces al día. Necesitamos esas cosas para nuestra existencia física . . . pero que pasa con nuestra existencia espiritual?

Escuchen a Jeremías: *"Se acercan los días, dice el Señor, en que yo cumpliré la promesa que hice a la casa de Israel y a la casa de Judá."* **Yo cumpliré**, quiere decir que todavía no lo ha cumplido. Significa que en nuestra vida, nuestro ser espiritual es la sombra de nuestro cuerpo que necesita alimento constante. Jesús advierte: *"Estén alerta, para que lo vicios, con el libertinaje, la embriaguez y las preocupaciónes de esta vida no entorpezcan su mente y aquél día los sorprenda desprevenidos, porque caerá derrepente como una trampa."*

Tenemos un hueco basío, ese ruido en nuestro estómago cuando tenemos hambre; y la boca seca cuando tenemos sed; y nos quedamos sin aíre y tenemos que descansar cuando no respiramos bien. Pero quizás hay otro dolor . . . otro vacío; ese algo que nos falta, y no hemos logrado resolver que es. Entoces empezamos a comprar obsequios para nosotros mismos y para los demas; hemos leído libros o empezados programas, y nada parece ayudarnos. A aque señala ese anhelo?

A un hombre se le quedo el coche al lado de la carretera. Una grúa llego a recogerlo, y se lo llevo al taller del mecánico. Ellos pasaron horas trabajando en el coche, tratando de averiguar cuál era el problema. El mecánico trató el filtro de aíre, cambio de aseite, todas las cosas básicas, pero no les resultó. Despues se volvio mas costoso. El comenzo a deshacer el motor y a reconstruirlo; le coloco nuevas bujías de encender y un arrancador, y aún así nada sucedio. En su ultima visita, el hombre estaba listo para llevar el coche hasta el deposito de fierro viejo, y lo acompaño su hijo. Su hijo le pregunto: "Papi, tu coche tiene gasolina?" De mala gana los dos revisaron el tanque y, efectivamente estaba basío. Ellos llenaron el tanque y el coche se prendio . . . despues de unos cuantos miles de dólares.[7]

A veces, necesitamos evitar de solucionar el problema por medio de colocar nuevas piezas, o intentar nuevas experiencias, y fijarnos en lo evidente. Esta vacío el tanque? Ha estado vacío? Antes de deshacerse del aparato completo, revise lo que hay dentro del tanque. Permita que esto sea una oportunidad de llenar el tanque con gasolina para la jornada; y estaremos en camino a satisfacer el hambre que Dios puso en nuestros corazones desde el principio.

Feast of the Immaculate Conception
(SEE APPENDIX I)

---

7   Internet Forward.

SECOND SUNDAY OF ADVENT
(ISAIAH 11:1-10; PSALM 72; ROMANS 15:4-9; MATTHEW 3:1-12)

Stay Awake!

The people were in the doldrums. And why shouldn't they be? It seemed as though they were born into slavery, or enslaved throughout their life at some point, or even when not enslaved, persecuted. These were the *Am segulah* (chosen people). These were God's chosen people? Man; I'd hate to see the people he hadn't chosen. Poor Isaiah is preaching to a people who are destined for exile. Now granted, they are slaves, but to their own kings at this time. Isaiah is telling them that they're gonna be enslaved to another Pharaoh, who will take them away from their land . . . yep, that's the promised one with milk and honey. Can you see why Isaiah is among a good bunch of people at the wrong time and the wrong place? This good bunch of people we call the "prophets."

At this juncture, God's chosen people are dead. They are like the stump of a tree. They are just there! They aren't happy or sad; rejoicing or despairing. The attitude seems to be one of indifference, or apathy, if anything. Which is why Isaiah is saying "get ready!" From this dead stump, life can still arise. The shoot that shall sprout from a stump is the hope if Israel. The people are asleep, just going through the motions; caught up in the machine. They are so into themselves and their condition that they are unaware of the great thing that is about to happen in their midst. The prophecy speaks to us of hope . . . the God of *second chance* is about to do something great, but if we are not ready, we might miss that opportunity.

John the Baptizer is the last in the line of these prophets, but his message is consistent with theirs. Something great is happening among us, as subtle as the silence before the storm. For those whose hearts are ready, a "way" must be paved. For those who are asleep in the daze of *acedia*, the time to wake up is here!

Just yesterday, I was playing paintball with my nephews. My younger nephew broke his finger and was unable to play. So in my compassion, I gave him a paintball gun and had him sit on the side. If he saw us from the front, he could fire at us (for it was unlikely that he would hit us.) I got into position behind a wide tree, and was pretty safe from the possible onslaught that lay before me. Much of this game was just waiting. So as I sat there, safe from my enemies, my mind began to wander. I began to feel smug at how clever this hiding place was. I had almost lowered my gun, when all of a sudden, pain exploded on the side of my neck. I was almost speechless, as much out of surprise, as I was because of the pain. I looked from where the shot had come, all the while thinking to myself, "How could anyone have hit me?" As I looked over, my eyes rested on my nephew with the gun held loosely in his hands, and face filled with fear. He stuttered an apology as he dropped the gun and ran. So I stand before you today with a bruise on my neck. Having seen that bruise, I knew that today I would have to explain what happened; lest you think the bruise on my neck was something else!

We all have our moments of indifference or *acedia*[8]. We have those times when we go through a dry time of prayer; or don't feel the presence of God; or are walking through the doldrums. We get caught up in the machine. We lose our sense of purpose or meet our midlife crisis, or just get stuck. It is in those moments that we need the pinch; we need to get the little shake to wake us up in time for renewal. We are in Advent. Advent is the beginning of the Church year. The old is past, and now this renewal will begin with a preparation for the greatest event our universe has known: the Incarnation. Advent then is that time to wake from sleep. To prepare a way for the Lord, means that we awaken to possibility. To live in hope that as the psalmist says: "*In Him shall all the tribes of the earth be blessed; all the nations shall proclaim his happiness.*"

---

8 *Acedia* is a spiritual apathy or depression. Originally one of the seven deadly sins as *per* St. John Cassian

Segundo Domingo de Adviento Año "C"

(Baruc 5:1-9; Salmo 126; Filipenses 1:4-6, 8-11; Lucas 3:1-6)

Escuchen al profeta Baruc. El menciona la palabra "*gloria*" cinco veces en nueve versos. La palabra gloria viene del Hebreo "*shekinah,*" que significa la presencia de Dios. Baruc dice: "*vistete con la gloria de Dios; con la diadema de la gloria; gloria en la piedad; Dios te los devuelve llenos de gloria; para que camine seguro bajo la gloria de Dios.*" Baruc no habla de tristeza, sino de una esperanza jovial de alguien grande. La misma esperanza que nos acompañó cuando eramos pequeños en los dias antes de la navidad. Con la gloria siempre viene la alegría.

El salmista dice: "*El Señor ha estado grande con nosotros, y estamos alegres.*" Es cierto! A menos que no tengamos esa esperanza. A menos que se haya perdido la magia. Si fuera magia, sí la hubieramos perdido; porque la magia se trata de engaños; momentos en el tiempo de moviemientos ligeros con la mano o una ilución. Pero algo que es verdadero, algo que continúa: algo que es eterno. Si creemos en esto, entonces tenemos esperanza. Y el fruto de tal esperanza, es la capacidad de amar . . . incluso a los que no nos parecen.

"*Mi oración es que su amor siga creciendo más y más . . . que ustedes sepan valorar las cosas que son importantes,*" dice Pablo. Y cuales son esas cosas que realmente son importantes? Recuerden, la semana pasada Jesús dijo, no permitan que sus corazónes sean perozos en "*las ansiedades del mundo*" sino sean vigilantes. Tal vez ya no sentimos la anticipación que sentíamos alguna vez, porque no hay que anticipar. Quizas nos sentimos deprimidos con las condiciónes de las cosas; tal vez estamos agoviados con el mundo; quizas hemos perdido las esperanzas en los demas . . . quizas, quizas, quizas.

Y sin embargo . . . la voz del heraldo clama en el desierto: "*Preparen el camino del Señor. Hagan rectos sus senderos*" porque aquí viene.

Lo que sigue esta afirmación de Juan, es algo interesante: *"Todo valle será rellenado, toda montaña y colina rebajada."* Esto es lo que llamamos la divinidad pasíva. No hay quien actue . . . Dios es quien cumple el hecho. Por lo tanto, Dios es quien rebajará las colinas y rellenará los valles. El es quien se encarga de estos obstaculos que parecen insuperables. Estos enormes muros y fronteras, el Señor los rebajará . . . pero, que debemos hacer? Preparar el camino.

Para hacer un camino, tenemos que despojar las malas hierbas y las espinas; debemos quitar lo que nos tropieza; y debemos andar una y otra vez por ese mismo camino, para hacerlo plano y firme. Seguimos en ese camino, y lo enderecemos. Eso es lo que debemos hacer. Porque? Por que el no esperara más que nosotros vayamos hacia el . . . el vendra hacia nosotros. Nosotros debemos preparar el camino y sacar la alfombra roja para el . . . y el rebajará todo lo que se encuentra entre nosotros. Pero eso depende de nosotros.

Me pregunto si la gente compredio a Baruc, cuando el profetizaba el Cristo. Me pregunto si cuando el llego; si ellos sabían que el sería quien rebajara las montañas con sus sermones y rellenaría los valles con su fuente. Me pregunto si ellos sabían lo que tenían, si hubieran dejado todas la distracciónes atras para estar con el un día . . . una semana con el. Me pregunto si nosotros sabemos lo que tenemos . . . me pregunto si estamos preparados para su regreso. Por que si estamos listos, resonarán las palabras de Baruc; y comenzaremos a amar como Pablo nos aconseja. Y pasaremos algun tiempo este adviento, preparando el camino, haciendo rectos sus senderos, para cuando el venga . . . y vendrá, podamos vivir su gloria, y con ella . . . una gran alegría!

THIRD SUNDAY OF ADVENT
(ISAIAH 35:1-6,10; PSALM 146; JAMES 5:7-10;
MATTHEW 11:2-11)

Happy Holidays or Hoildays or Holy days?

The desert and the parched land will exult; the steppe will rejoice and bloom. They will bloom with abundant flowers, and rejoice with joyful song.

Why? What is all the anticipation about? *"Desert exult!"* *"Steppe, rejoice?!"* What can be that great that all of these things, which are seemingly inanimate, are rejoicing? What is it that they are anticipating? In the Gospel it's much the same. John wants to know, *"Is this the one who is to come?"* Is this what we're waiting for? It seems that nature knows what the anticipation is about. It appears that John the Baptizer knows what the anticipation is about . . . but do *we*? He wants us to be prepared and not wait until the last minute.

When I was first a seminarian, we had a Christmas party with the Bishop (at that time, Bishop Dattilo). I was on my way to the party, but forgot to get a card for him. So I stopped at the dollar store and saw they had a sale on cards. A whole box of twenty cards was only a dollar. I grabbed the box, and when I got to my car, filled out the card and was now prepared for the party. All was well when I left, but I used the same cards for my family that year and each called, not only to thank me for the card, but to inform me that the card read: **"Happy Hoildays."** I guess there is no such thing as a free lunch. Our bishop had a great sense of humor . . . I was ordained as a priest, in case you were wondering. We can't wait until the last minute, but we also must understand what it is that we are celebrating.

Over the last two weeks, I polled grade school students at St. Joan of Arc in the CCD program here, and high school students at Lebanon Catholic. And I would like to give you now, the test that I gave to them. It is a word association test. I will give you a word, and remember the first word or image that pops into your head:

St. Patrick's Day
Easter
End of October or beginning of November
Christmas

It's interesting, that when I asked the kids what the first word was that came to mind, most of them for St. Patrick's day said: shamrocks, leprechauns, green, gold, rainbow, etc. most for Easter said, bunnies, candy, and eggs. Only one or two said, the Resurrection or crucifixion of Christ. When I said end of October, beginning of November, practically everyone said, Halloween; candy; fall; costumes; ghosts. Finally, what did they say for Christmas? Most said: Santa, stockings, trees, gifts (high on the list) and a few, Jesus' birth.

What am I getting at? Christmas was originally set on the date of December 25, because that was at the time, a pagan feast. It was the feast of the unconquered sun or *Sol Invictus.* In his first encyclical, Pope Francis says this:

> The pagan world, which hungered for light, had seen the growth of the cult of the sun god, *Sol Invictus*, invoked each day at sunrise. Yet though the sun was born anew each morning, it was clearly incapable of casting its light on all of human existence. The sun does not illumine all reality; its rays cannot penetrate to the shadow of death, the place where men's eyes are closed to its light. "No one—Saint Justin Martyr writes—has ever been ready to die for his faith in the sun."[9]

We made it the birthday of Christ and called it the feast of the unconquered *SON.* All of these days I previously mentioned, are Catholic Christian feast days. They are days to commemorate some great moment in the history of our Salvation and our Church. What has happened over time, however, is that the "World" has taken our

---

9   Pope Francis. *Lumen Fidei*, 1.

"holy days" and made them into "holi days." And for what? Profit. Not Prophet, but profit!

Ask this question: Would they have decorated so early for Christmas if there was no money to be made? I mean, let's face it, if there were not money to be made, they would decorate right before the feast, and take the decorations down the day after it was over. If they did at all. Don't believe it? These are the same ones who are trying to take "One Nation under God" out of the pledge of allegiance. There is money to be made on presents. The decorations will come down the week after to make room for Valentine's day; then St. Patrick will be in competition with Easter, because we need to buy, buy, buy.

I believe it was said best in the paper a few weeks ago. "Many industries count on the Christmas season to make their bottom line." What is Christmas about . . . do they know? How can they know, when we have taken the name of *Christ* out of it and put an "X" in its place. *X's* are typically used to cross things out. Have we done that? What would our children say Christmas is about? Might they say, "It's the one time of year we go to Church?"

We are looking forward to the miracle that "He, whom the heavens could not contain, she now contains within herself."[10] Our God who could have chosen any way to be manifest in the world, chose to be born as a baby . . . and not just any baby . . . a poor baby; and not just a poor baby, but a baby born in a barn; in a foreign place, under the reign of a King who was not satisfied by simply denying God, but sought to destroy Him. THIS is what we celebrate. And to those who would X out Christ . . . those who don't understand, the only proper response is pity. Because if they did understand, they would celebrate it as we do . . . every Sunday.

---

10 Bishop Fulton J. Sheen, *The World's First Love*, (New York, NY: McGraw-Hill Co., 1952), 71.

Tercer Domingo de Adviento
Año "C"
(Baruc 5:1-9; Salmo 126; Filipenses 1:4-6, 8-11; Lucas 3:1-6)

"Si Dios no interviene por nosotros a través de los sacramentos, quizas algun día dejaremos nuestras pasiones pecaminosas . . . pero ellas no nos dejarán."

Esta ya es la tercera semana de Adviento. Pero, hemos cambiado? Dijimos que lo hariamos . . . dijimos que esto sería diferente. Sólo necesitaríamos un nuevo comienzo, y el Adviento sería la oportunidad perfecta. Pero, qué hemos hecho? Eso no ha terminado . . . todavía hay tiempo para dar ese paso y prepararnos para la venida del Señor. Sólo necesitamos desearlo. Pero sepan esto, si no hacemos algo ahora, quizas nunca lo haremos. Si esuchamos hoy su voz, y edurecemos nuestro corazón, talvez no habra otra oportunidad. No porque Dios nos abandonará, o no este dispuesto a perdonarnos; sino porque talvez nunca regresaremos.

Hay una historia que viene de Alaska.

Cuando a un lobo lo encuentran devorando al rebaño y a los perros, el dueño tiene la obligación de actuar para deshacerse del lobo; no lo caza. El lobo se le escapa por semanas. En lugar de cazarlo, el tomará un cuchillo y empapará la hoja con sangre de una matanza reciente y lo dejará afuera para congelarse. Despues lo empapara denuevo con más sangre y denuevo lo dejará afuera para congelarse. Finalmente, entierra el cuchillo en el hielo, con la hoja hacia arriba, y despues espera.

El lobo puede oler la sangre y finalmente encuentra esta "paleta" en el hielo y comenzará a lamerla. Mientras lo lame, el sabor ha creado en él un frenesí, y continua a lamer la sangre frenéticamente. Mientras la lame, la hoja del cuchillo eventualmente será expuesta y comenzará a cortarse la lengua.

Ahora, probando su sangre caliente con la otra, no puede detenerse, hasta que porfín; se cortará tanto la boca que él sangrará hasta morir. El cuerpo del lobo se puede encontrar junto al cuchillo.[11]

"Si Dios no interviene por nosotros a través de los sacramentos, quizas algun día dejaremos nuestras pasíones pecaminosas . . . pero ellas no nos dejarán."[12]

---

11 Internet forward, author unknown.
12 Bishop Fulton J. Sheen. *Lift Up Your Hearts*. (New York: McGraw-Hill Book Company, Inc., 1950), 200.

FOURTH SUNDAY OF ADVENT
(ISAIAH 7:10—14; PSALM 24; ROMANS 1:1-7; MATTHEW 1:18-24)

The Lord Himself will give you this sign.

This whole section of Luke speaks about Joseph and his dilemma. Here is St. Joseph, one of the most highly revered saints in the Church, and yet within all of scripture, he doesn't say a single word. Some wives might say "Maybe if my husband didn't speak he would be a saint too," but I digress. Here is Joseph, his whole life ahead of him. He marries this woman because she is so good, and probably makes him want to be a better man simply because of her witness.

And then the plans change. She becomes pregnant. This was not in his ideal dreams. In an instant, his life is in a tailspin. The embarrassment; the scandal, and no choice but to leave the woman he loves . . . and then, the dream.

Isaiah says to Ahaz: *"The Lord Himself will give you this sign."* It is not through Joseph's ***words*** that he witnesses to his faith, but through his actions. Despite his worry, his fear, he listens to the voice of the Lord, and walks into what appears to be his greatest fear. And because he does this, he becomes the foster father of the Christ!

We often find ourselves at a crossroads; kinda in a rut, and we cannot seem to move. We're just stuck here with seemingly no way to get out. And yet, the Lord speaks to us in ways that are beyond our senses, and through people we would never have suspected could be prophets in our lives. There is a painting by the artist James Tissot called *L'anxiété de Saint Joseph* or *the Anxiety of St. Joseph* (This is the painting on the front cover of the book). This is my new favorite painting. Reflection on saints or biblical characters can often leave us feeling frustrated or disconsolate, because we can never reach the level of sanctity that they did during their lifetime. They are so high up on a pedestal that we almost must view them as divine, or far beyond anything we could even strive for. That could not be farther from the truth. Which is why this painting offers us a true picture of the foster father of Jesus.

Joseph, is half slumped forward over his workbench, with a knife carelessly resting in his hand as he stares out into space. This picture could have been created at two moments in his life, and depending on your imagination, quite a few others as well. I perceive this as the moment he found out Mary was pregnant, and not knowing what he should do, being that he was a righteous man. The other possibility is that this is the day after the dream, where he is told he is to be the foster father of Jesus. What qualified him, a lowly carpenter, to be the father of the Messiah? Joseph was stuck; but not without hope!

If we are at a crossroads; if we don't know in which direction to turn, we need to look at our fears, and often that is the direction in which the Lord is inviting us. I don't mean fear of heights or spiders or snakes, etc. Fear of forgiving, and asking forgiveness; fear of opening ourselves to another—to our God; fear of loving someone, when that love might not be returned. If we have the faith we say we have, then we can certainly *hope* for something better than this world. And if we can hope for something better than this world, then we are no longer insecure or fearful, because we know this is not the end. And if we are no longer fearful, then we can love, as we were meant to love.

Joseph was directed to a foreign place, with a woman who was pregnant with a child not his own; he walked in the direction of his fears, and because of that, he is remembered in the Gospel today. We wait for the Christ in this fourth Sunday of Advent, and if we journey toward those fears . . . those things we have avoided for so long, it is there, where we will find *He has been* all along.

Cuarto Domingo de Adviento
Año "C"
(Isaías 7:10-14; Salmo 24;
Romanos 1:1-7; Mateo 1:18-24)

"El Señor mismo les dará una señal"

Toda esta parte del Evangelio de Lucas habla sobre el dilema de José. Allí se encuentra José, uno de los santos más venerados en la iglesia y, en toda la escritura, no dice ni una sola palabra. (Algunas esposas dirían "si mi esposo no hablara, también sería un santo") pero yo opino diferente. Aquí esta José, tiene su vida entera por vivir. Se casa con una mujer porque es tan buena, y quizás esto lo motiva a ser mejor persona, simplemente por su testimonio de fe.

Y después los planes cambian. Ella queda embarazada. Esto no era parte de su sueño. De repente, su vida se ha convertido en un torbellino. La vergüenza; el escándalo, no le quedaba otra opción, más que dejar a la mujer que ama. Y después tiene un sueño.

Isaías dice a Ajaz: *"El Señor mismo te dará una señal."* No sucede por medio de las palabras de José, que él es testigo a la fe, sino por medio de sus acciones. A pesar de su preocupación, su temor, él escucha la voz del Señor y camina hacia lo que parece ser su temor más grande. ¡Y, porque él hace esto, llegar a ser el padrastro de Cristo!

A veces, nos encontramos en una encrucijada, nos sentimos atrapados y parece que no podemos movernos. Nos encontramos en un lugar del cual parece que no podemos salir. Y aún así el Señor nos habla en maneras que van más allá de nuestros sentidos por medio de personas quienes nunca sospechamos fueran profetas en nuestras vidas. Si nos encontramos en una encrucijada; si no sabemos cual dirección seguir, es necesario mirar hacia nuestros temores, y muy seguido, esa es la dirección que el Señor nos invita a seguir.

No me refiero al miedo de las alturas, o de arañas, o víboras. Hablo del miedo de perdonar y pedir perdón; el miedo de ser abiertos con nuestro prójimo—con nuestro Dios; el miedo de amar a alguien sin que esa persona nos ame en retorno. Si nosotros tenemos la fe que decimos tener, entonces ciertamente podemos esperar algo mejor en este mundo. Y si podemos esperar algo mejor en este mundo, entonces ya no sentimos inseguridad ni temor, porque sabemos que esto no es el fin. Y si ya no sentimos temor, entonces podemos amar, como debemos amar.

José fue dirigido hacia un lugar extraño, con una mujer embarazada con un hijo que no era suyo; camino hacia sus temores, y a causa de esto, se le recuerda en el Evangelio de hoy. Esperamos a Cristo en este cuarto domingo de adviento y si nos dirigimos hacia esos temores . . . esas ocasíones que hemos evitado por tanto tiempo, nos daremos cuenta que allí es donde siempre ha estado.

CHRISTMAS VIGIL
(ISAIAH 62:1-5; PSALM 89;
ACTS 13:16-17, 27, 29; MATTHEW 1:1-25)

The <u>Real</u> Christmas

Just a week before Christmas, I had a visitor. This is how it happened. I just finished the household chores for the night, and was preparing to go to bed when I heard a noise in the front of the house. I opened the door to the front room, and to my surprise, Santa himself stepped out from behind the Christmas tree. He placed his finger over his mouth, so I would not cry out. "What are you doing?" I started to ask him.

The words choked in my throat, as I saw he had tears in his eyes. His usual jolly manner was gone. Gone was the eager boisterous soul we all know. He then answered me with a simple statement, TEACH THE CHILDREN! I was puzzled: What did he mean? He anticipated my question, and with one quick movement brought forth a miniature toy bag from behind the tree.

As I stood there bewildered, Santa said, Teach the Children! Teach them the old meaning of Christmas. The meaning that a now-a-day Christmas has forgotten!

Santa then reached in his bag and pulled out a FIR TREE and placed it on the mantle. Teach the Children that the pure green color of the stately fir tree remains green all year round, depicting the everlasting hope of mankind. All the needles point heavenward, making it a symbol of man's thoughts turning toward heaven.

He again reached into his bag and pulled out a brilliant STAR. Teach the Children that the star was the heavenly sign of promises long ago. God promised a Savior for the world, and the star was the sign of fulfillment of that promise.

He then reached into the bag and pulled out a CANDLE. Teach the Children that the candle symbolizes that Christ is the light of the world, and when we see this great light, we are reminded of He who displaces the darkness.

Once again he reached into his bag, and then removed a WREATH and placed it on the tree. Teach the Children that the wreath symbolizes the eternal nature of love. Real love never ceases. Love is one continuous round of affection.

He then pulled out from his bag an ornament of HIMSELF. Teach the Children that Santa Claus symbolizes St. Nicholas and the generosity and good will we feel during Advent.

He reached in again and pulled out a HOLLY LEAF. Teach the Children the holly plant represents immortality. It represents the crown of thorns worn by our Savior. The red holly berries represent blood, shed by Him.

Next he pulled out a GIFT from the bag and said, "Teach the Children that God so loved the world that He gave His only begotten Son. Thanks be to God for His unspeakable gift. Teach the Children that the wise men bowed before the holy babe and presented Him with gold, frankincense, and myrrh. We should give gifts in the same spirit as the wise men."

Santa then reached in his bag and pulled out a CANDY CANE and hung it on the tree. Teach the Children that the candy cane represents the shepherd's crook. The crook on the shepherd's staff helps bring back strayed sheep from the flock. The candy cane is the symbol that we are our brother's keeper.

He reached in again and pulled out an ANGEL. Teach the Children that it was the angels who heralded in the glorious news of the Savior's birth. The angels sang 'Glory to God in the highest, on earth, peace and good will.'

Suddenly, I heard a soft twinkling sound, and from his bag he pulled out a BELL. Teach the Children that as the lost sheep are found by the sound of a bell, it should bring people to the fold. That as the bell is rung at Mass, heaven joins earth and God comes among His people to change lowly bread and wine into his very self!

Santa looked at the tree and was pleased. He looked back at me, and I saw the twinkle was back in his eyes. He said, "Remember, teach the Children the true meaning of Christmas, and not to put me in the center, for I am but a humble servant of the One who is, and I bow down and worship Him, our Lord, our God."[13]

---

13 Internet Forward

Homilia para la Navidad

(Isaías 62:1-5; Salmo 89;
Hechos 13:16-17, 27, 29; Mateo 1:1-25)

Algunas veces nosotros invitamos a
Dios en nuestras vidas, pero no hay lugar.

Hay una historia navideña que les aseguro no han escuchado todavía. Esta historia no la verán en la television, ni en los teatros . . . es muy sutil para eso.

El hombre, y la mujer encinta, caminaban despacio por las calles angostas de Belén. Habían viajado muy lejos y no se detuvieron durante la noche. Era tarde y la mujer estaba cansada y enferma. Ella estaba en los últimos días de su embarazo y habia montado el burro por varios días. El hombre vio una posada a lo largo de la carretera, y se acerco con el acontecimiento de lo major. Tocó la puerta fuerte, pero nadie se movia en el interior. Dio vuelta y miro a su esposa, ahora sudando y adolorida, y tocó denuevo: no estaba dispuesto a aceptar el rechazo. Denuevo, nadie hizo ruido por dentro. Por fín, despues de ofrecer una oraicón en silecio, tocó por tercera vez. Finalmente, había un ruido por dentro, y derrepente había un abierto pequeño en la puerta por donde se veía el rostro de un hombre.

"Que quieren? Ya es tarde." El hombre contesto: "Por favor, necesitamos un lugar para descanzar. Tuvimos un viaje muy largo y estamos muy canzados." El posadero respondio: "Yo tambien estoy cansado! Muchos han viajado para llegar aquí, pero no hay cupo. Lo siento." El posadero intento cerrar la abertura en la puerta, pero el hombre le atravesó la mano. "Por favor . . . mi esposa está apunto de dar luz a nuestro primer hijo. Nos dormiremos en el suelo, en la ventana, donde sea, pero necesitamos un lugar. No importa si solo puede acomodar a mi esposa . . . por favor."

El posadero se estaba enfadando, y aún así comenzo a sentir compassion. (Sera esta la primera vez en años que sintio compasíón.) "Esta bien. Hay un pajar en el cerro. Hay un buey, un burro, y algunos ganzos. Ustedes se pueden reposar alli. Pero no prendan lamparas o incendios . . . eso sera todo lo que necesito, que toda el pajar se prenda en lumbre!"

El hombre estaba muy agradecido, y el y su esposa viajaron en camino hacia el lugar de descanso. Mientras sucedia eso, el posadero estaba muy enojado. "Porque sera que todos dependen en mi para darles algo. Siempre estoy hacienda algo para otras personas . . . me la paso trabajando todo el dia y para que? Mi familia nunca me ve; mis amigos ya no me conocen. He dejado mi fe . . . me he alejado de mis seres queridos. Y tú, Dios . . . he esperado tanto que hagas algo pero nunca hces nada! Pido muy poco y nunca contestas mis oracionés!" Se fue a recostar, y las ultimas palabras que dijo antes de dormirse fueron las siguientes: "Cuanto he esperado para que tu entraras a mi vida, a mi mundo, y nisiquiera has tocado mi puerta" . . . y despues penso.

El penso en su vida y el rumbo que seguia. Era un padre y esposo joven, y se dio cuenta que estaba viviendo para trabajar, no trabajando para vivir. Entonces penso en la pobre mujer apunto de dar a luz. Se levanto de la cama y su esposa pregunto: "Simon, a donde vas?" Pero salio del a casa sin decir ni una palabra. El queria ver como estaba la pareja. Se puso su bata y salió al aire frio de la noche. El escuchaba el ruido de los grillos y el susurro del viento a traves de los arboles de olivos. Escucho el arroyo que fluía a lo largo del camino y una cascada pequeña por delante. Miro hacia el pajar y vio que estaba oscuro. Quizas sentian mucho frio. Y despues sucedio algo azombroso.

De pronto el mundo se quedo inmóvil. Las hojas estaban en silencio, y el agua quedo helada en su camino. Las creaturas no hicieron mas ruido y todo el mundo se detuvo, como en temor de un gran acontesimiento. Y entonces, de repente el mundo se movia de nuevo. Las criaturas siguieron con sus ruidos y el agua fluyo y la brisa soplo, y ahora mirando hacia el pajar, vio una luz.

"Les dije que no prendiaran una lampara!" El se enojó y camino mas rapido hacia el pajar. Mientras se acercaba, escucho unas ovejas (el no tenía ovejas) y vio una multitud alrededor del pajar. Cuando llego, las palabras que estaba pensando en decir eran en un momento sofocadas en el momento que sus hojos gozaron la vista de ese momento unico. Se quedo mudo. Un niño, recostado en las manos de su madre y la luz parecia venir de todas partes. No había fuego, sino luz. Entonces el niño lo miro como si lo hubiera conocido desde mucho antes. El posadero se quedo tan mudo que simplemente estaba quieto.

Un pastor que cargaba una oveja le dijo: "carga esto", y estaba tan sorprendido que lo hizo. (Y hasta este dia, en realidad es el posadero quien esta cargando la oveja, no el pastor). El pastor, entonces se arrodillo y adoro al niño. Y el nombre del niño era Jesus.

El se fijo mientras el padre del niño tomo un viejo pesebre para alimentar a los animals, cual tenía su marca, y le puso paja, y lo uso como cuna para el niño. Simon no se recordo de cuanto tiempo se le quedo mirando. Pero sabía que Dios estaba con el esa noche . . . y su vida cambio para siempre. El nunca más penso en ese niño y la familia . . . hasta que.

Treinta años despues, desde esa noche hace años, puso a su familia en segundo lugar, porque Dios ocupaba el primero . . . el Dios quien le había tocado la puerta y le pedio un cuarto . . . en eso días no habían cuartos. Simon estaba en Jerusalen con su familia para celebrar la pascua. Y mientras caminaba por la calles había una comocion. Quería ver lo que sucedia y se acerco a la multitud y fue empujado a la calle por un soldado Romano. "Ayuda a este prisionero. Morirá antes de llegar a la colina." Simon le rogo que no tenía nada que ver con lo sucedido, que el estaba con su familia, pero el soldado no le permitio continuar y lo empujo hacia el hombre condenado. El cargo la madera, y mientra lo hizo, sus ojo reconocio una marca en la madera. Esta madera, esta cruz le pertenecía a el. Y Simon miro al hombre condenado, el hombre lo miro a el, y Simon vio al niño que le salvo la vida. El niño que una vez fue cargado por esta Madera, ahora el cargaba la madera ; y entonces Simon el Cirineo comprendio que el estaba en Jerusalen para Dios . . . y Dios llego a Belén para el.

Algunas veces nosotros invitamos a Dios en nuestras vidas, pero no hay lugar. Algunas veces debemos viajar a lugares donde no queremos estar; algunas veces debemos cargar cosas que preferemos no cargar. Simon cargo una oveja por fuera del pajar y se le entrego la vida. El ayudo a cargar una cruz, dentro de una marcha hacia la muerte y fue entregado la salvación.

La Fiesta de la Sagrada Familia
(Eclesiastés 3:2-6, 12-14; Salmo 128; Colosenses 3:12-21; Mateo 2:13-15, 19-23)

La fiesta de Navidad es sobre de la familia

Me maneje a casa de mis padres de dia de la Navidad. Mientras maneje, vi muchas señales. En los signos fueron las palabras, "Los servicios de vísperas de Navidad. No hay servicios el día de Navidad. Tener tiempo ser con su familia." Así que lo que estamos diciendo es, " abierta los regalos; come las comidas, hacer fiestas, pero no adorar al hijo de Dios."

La fiesta de Navidad es sobre de la familia, pero mas sobre de traer a la familia a la Iglesia. Todos los domingos llegamos a la misa, pero muchos no vienen en el dia de Navidad. La Navidad es el motivo de la misa!

María, José y Jesús, la sagrada familia, no dejó que las amenazas de Herodes, el mal tiempo, o incluso su pobreza evitar que adorar a Dios. Todos podemos tener una familia santa . . . sino el comienzo de ser santo está trayendo a nuestra familia a la Misa El principio de ser santo, es enseñar a nuestros hijos que Cristo es el centro de nuestra vida.

"Journey to Bethlehem"
sketched in the desert of General Cepeda MX.

FEAST OF THE HOLY FAMILY (SUNDAY IN THE OCTAVE OF CHRISTMAS)

(SIRACH 3:2-6,12-14; PSALM 128; COLOSSIANS 3:12-21; MATTHEW 2:13-15, 19-23)

All in the Family

For the most part, I was a child of the "eighties." However, the "seventies" were a big part of my life as well. I recall a show we used to watch called "All in the Family." I'm sure many of you recall this show as well, if not when it was running, then years later in syndication. It was the years later in syndication that I really appreciated and began to understand all the innuendo and some not-so-innuendo. The head of the family was not only racist, but a bigot. The wife was the classic submissive, obedient housewife, while the daughter and her "meathead" husband were the classic liberal hippies of the age. It's hard to imagine such a show being so popular in this day and age with our political correctness, but I'm sure you are aware there are worse things on TV and the internet these days than could ever have been conceived by the creators of *that* show. The idea of the family in this show was so entertaining, because the viewers could perhaps see nuggets of this comedy that applied to their own families.

Families are not perfect. Quite to the contrary, they can be literally cannibalistic at times. We don't choose our families. However, if our goal within a family is to be perfect, or at least to look perfect, then we are missing the point completely, or at the very least setting ourselves up for disappointment. We are not called to have a perfect family, whatever that means! We are called to have a holy family. And sometimes, it is well within our power to affect that; while at other times, despite our mightiest efforts, our family only ever might approach the shadow of holiness.

The dream of a perfect family probably comes from a misunderstanding of that family we hold in high regard. The 2.5 kids (however you come up with that!) living in the house down the street with the picket fence, the dog that never barks the parents who never fight and the bills that always get paid. I use the word *dream* intentionally. Remember, even the holy family in the Gospel today, was not perfect. What! Did he just say that? Yes, hold your gasp a moment as I say, the holy family, within which is Jesus our Lord and Savior, was not perfect. Without sin? Yes. At least the Blessed Mother and Jesus. But perfect? Why should we think that?

Maybe it's because all of the statues or paintings we see of Mary and Joseph, for the most part, appear so ordered and pristine. They have their hands folded or their eyes closed and are at such peace. If the artists who had lived at the time of Mary and Joseph created their renditions of what they observed from this couple, I imagine the picture would be quite different. These were human beings; not gods.

There were times, I'm sure, when Mary did not stitch a straight line, or when Joseph was chiseling away and split the wood by accident. Can you imagine a fourteen or fifteen year-old girl, getting pregnant without a husband with whom she was living, and trying to tell her parents that it was through the power of the Holy Spirit? Really? Her mother probably would have struck her for blasphemy. Later they would understand, but not then. What about the village gossips?

Joseph was a righteous man. The word in Greek (*diakasoonā*) is a word that could only be ascribed to a person by another. It was a legal term which means the person was guilty of nothing. Don't you think he agonized over this decision, and what it could mean, before he had the dream? And after the dream, don't you think he worried what kind of life he could offer to this child, when he himself could not read; was not a Pharisee or priest; and had no power in the kingdom?

In Luke's story for the feast of the Holy Family, he tells the story of Mary and Joseph losing Jesus in Jerusalem. Now come on people! You who are spouses and parents know how this conversation probably went. Mary: "Have you seen Jesus? I'm getting worried. I haven't seen him for two days." Joseph: "He's probably with the cousins or his aunt and uncle." Mary: "I thought he was with you. You mean you don't know where he is? Joseph, we talked about this, he was going to be with you. This was going to be your 'quality time' with him." Joseph: "I'm sorry, I forgot about that. I thought he was with you." Mary: "Well that's great! We lost the Son of God!" And the arguing probably went on for awhile until they both went to find him. Perfect? No. Without sin? Yes.

When they do find him, Mary says, in our English translation, "Your father and I have been searching for you anxiously." The Greek word translated as "anxious" is *splagatzo*. Literally it means "twisted in the bowels." Ever feel that when you looked around in the mall and suddenly your child is gone?

I know there were times when Mary was probably frantic or stressed out. Are you kidding? Running to Egypt (where they had never been before) because an insane king wanted to kill their baby. Do you not think there were times that Mary would grab Jesus by the arm, if she saw him playing in the dirt road, and give him a little smack with the exhortation: "Don't you ever go out into the street! You'll get hit by a . . . . well . . . a camel or a horse or something!" These were real people. These were holy people. But they were not *perfect* people.

St. Paul says in his letter to the Colossians, *"You who are wives be submissive to your husbands."* Sub misso means "sent under" or "ordered under." This is not a term to enslave the wife, but if the husband is Christ, as St. Paul calls him to be, then he is the head of the family in the faith. And those families in which the father practices the faith and prays and leads, the family most often follows. He goes on to break this down by saying: *"Husbands love your wives and avoid any bitterness toward them. Children obey your parents in everything as the acceptable way in the Lord."* There is nothing in here about perfection . . . just sanctity. Sirach goes into more detail, but says the same thing.

Sanctity comes from peace, and perhaps that is why the statues we see of the Holy Family *are* so peaceful. Not perfect, but *saints*. And in the end, isn't that the most important thing?

Solemnity of the Most Blessed Virgin Mary, Mother of God
(SEE APPENDIX I)

Día de los Tres Reyes
(Isaías 60:1-6; Salmo 72;
Efesios 3:2-3, 5-6; Mateo 2:1-12)

Él proveera para sus hijos queridos, y con exceso.

Nosotros no podemos hacer tratos ni negocios con Dios. No podemos hacer ningun trato ni negociar con Dios porque en realidad no temos poder en la situación. Sería como tratar de negociar con alguien, y no tener nada que ofrecerle. O, aún mejor, sería como hacer un trato con alguien para darnos lo que deseamos, cuando, al final, Él terminará dandonos lo que nescesitamos. El único negocio que podríamos hacer con tal persona, sería intentar de conseguir lo que no sería mejor para nosotros, sino lo que deseamos. No es necesarío pedirle alimentos, porque ya nos ha entregado a si mismo! Y, aún así, continuamos intentando de hacer tratos.

Los tres reyes se acercaron a Jesús para adorarlo. La palabra griega en el Evangelio es *proskenesthai*, que significa someterse a algien de alto nivel, o con quien hacemos tratos. Ellos vienen ofreciendo regalos, no para Dios, o para un dios, sino para un rey. Un rey que quizas podría ser competencia en los días por venir. Como la mayoría de las personas en esa epoca, ellos no compredían la monarquía de Cristo. Un rey verdadero es uno que cuida de sus sujetos . . . de quienes se someten . . . quienes lo adoran. Un rey verdadero pone en práctica el dominio.

Nosotros no podemos hacer tratos con Dios, "Señor, si yo hago esto, entonces tu has esto . . ." pero lo bueno es que que no es necesario hacer tratos con Dios. Porque Él proveera para sus hijos queridos, y con exceso, TODO lo que ellos NECESITAN. Todo lo que ellos necesitan, no necesariamente para hacerlos feliz en esta vida, sino para que sean felices junto a Él en la próxima vida.

THE FEAST OF THE EPIPHANY
(ISAIAH 60:1-6; PSALM 72;
EPHESIANS 3:2-3, 5-6; MATTHEW 2:1-12)

We cannot bargain with God . . . and why would we?

We cannot make deals or bargains with God. We cannot make a deal or bargain with God, because we really have no power in the situation. It would be like trying to bargain with someone, and we have nothing to offer in return. Or, better yet, it would be akin to trying to bargain with someone to give us what we want, when He will ultimately give us what we *need* anyway. The only bargaining we would need to do with such a person, is in trying to get what might not be the best for us, but what we *want*. We do not need to request that God do us no harm, because ultimately He will not. At times He will allow it, and, let's face it, we are in a world that is sinful, so evil will occur. We do not need to convince Him that we are lovable, because He already loves us more than we could ask or imagine. We do not need to beg Him for food . . . He has given us His very self! And yet . . . we continue to make deals.

The three magi approach Jesus to do homage. The Greek word in the Gospel is *proskunesthai*, which means "submit to someone higher," or "make a treaty with." They are coming, bearing gifts, not for God, or a god . . . but a king. One who might quite possibly be competition in the days ahead. Like most people of the time, they didn't understand Christ's kingship. A true king is the one who cares for those who are the subjects . . . those who submit . . . those who offer homage. A true king exercises *Dominion*.

We cannot bargain with God, "If I do this God, then you do this . . ." but the good news is, we don't *need* to bargain with God. Because He will provide for His dear children, with extravagance, all they *NEED*. All they need, not to make them happy in this life necessarily; but to be happy with Him in the next.

THE BAPTISM OF JESUS
(ISAIAH 42:1-4; PSALM 29;
ACTS 10:34-38; MATTHEW 3:13-17)

The Man . . . the Mission

The baptism of Christ meant three things: mission; message; miracles. His *mission*, consisted of a strong *message* and resulted in many signs and wonders we call *miracles*. Jesus' mission was to show the face of God to a people who was lost; to bring the lost back to the fold, and to leave others to do the same, once he returned to his Father.

The message was the **hesed** of God: his abiding mercy and love for one who was repentant. What was the second part of the message? . . . repent! Things are not going well. You are not living as I created you to live; you are not loving as I created you to love . . . repentance.

Finally the miracles. He gave sight to the blind; to those who were not seeing or perceiving, he gave an opportunity: *"What do you want me to do for you?" "I want to see."* He raised up those who were dead. Even so dead, they were buried. Martha says about her brother Lazarus, *"Lord there will be a stench . . . he's been dead four days."* He cured those who were decaying and covered with sores . . . alienated from humanity. He cast out demons from those who were tormented. He made food for crowds where there was little to none; He calmed the storms . . . and the fears. He rose from the dead.

The baptism of Jesus was not just a validation of his mission, but the proclamation of his message, paving the way for miracles about which even the pagans would talk. Okay . . . fine. End of story, right? Well . . . aren't you baptized? You are? Then what does it mean to you? That is the question, right? Does it mean anything? Or maybe you really don't know . . . so let me tell you what it means.

Your baptism means three things: Mission; Message; Miracles. I know, I know . . ."But I am not the Messiah." Well neither am I. As my friend in the Seminary informed me, "That job's already taken." But we do have a mission, and it is much the same as the mission of Jesus: To show the face of God to people who are lost . . . even if they have not left the fold. And to bring the lost back to the fold; and to leave others to do the same, so that when we are gone, the mission will not cease.

Our message is also the mercy and love of God; most often proclaimed clearly through our actions. That if we can forgive and accept and forget and excuse and pardon and welcome, then they will be led to the **one** who has taught *us* how to do those things. But our message is also that "Not everything is acceptable; and if you are living in a way that is not good, I should help you to change that." Most often, by the way I model my life, not by the voice in which I correct another.

If we are possessed by this mission and proclaim the message, miracles will follow. Sometimes the miracles begin with us. We begin to see the lepers as cured; we begin to give a new perspective to the blind and ignorant; we begin to raise up those who were bowed down and even dead; and we anticipate our own resurrection.

This mission is not for the lazy or faint of heart. This purpose is not for the sleeping. What if this sleeping giant awakes, imagine the possibilities! You are baptized, right? What does it mean to you?

EL BAUTISMO DE JESUS
(ISAÍAS 42:1-4; SALMO 29;
HECHOS 10:34-38; MATEO 3:13-17)

El hombre . . . la Misión

El bautismo de Cristo significa tres cosas: la misión; el mensaje; los milagros. Su misión, que consistía de un mensaje fuerte y esto resulto en señales y maravillas que llamamos milagros. la misión de Jesús fue para mostrar el rostro de Dios a un pueblo perdido, a restituir a los perdidos al rebano y ensenar a los otros hacer lo mismo después que regresó a su Padre.

El mensaje era el *hesed* de Dios. *Hesed* en Hebreo significa la misericordia y amor permanente de Dios, para uno que estaba arrepentido. Esto fue la segunda parte del mensaje . . . arrepientense! Dios dice "Su vida no esta bien. No vive como yo deseo que vives. no se amas como yo he creado que amaras . . . arrepentimiento."

Finalmente, los milagros. Él dio la vista a los ciegos, una otro oportunidad . . . Se resucito a los que estaban muertos . . . Los que estaban enterrados, Curó a los que estaban en descomposición y cubierto de llagas . . . alienada de la humanidad. Exorcismo fuera a los demonios de los que fueron atormentados. Alimento a las multitudes, donde había poca o nada; Él calmó la tormenta . . . y los temores. Él resucito de la muerte.

El bautismo de Cristo, no era simplemente una validación de su misión, sino la proclamación de su mensaje.

Muy bien . . . muy bien. Fin de la historia, no? . . . Acaso no son bautizados? Usted está, verdad? Entonces, ¿qué es el significado para usted? Esa es una buena pregunta? O quizás no significa nada para usted? O realmente no lo sabe . . . así que déjame decirte lo que significa.

BAUTISMO DE JESUS

Su bautismo significa tres cosas: misión; mensaje; milagros. Yo sé, yo sé . . ."Pero yo no soy el Mesías." Bueno, yo tampoco." Pero tenemos una misión, y es semejante a la misión de Jesús: Para mostrar el rostro de Jesús a las personas que se pierden . . . incluso no han salido del rebano. Y restornar el perdió al rebano, y ensenar a otros hacer lo mismo.

Tambien, nuestro mensaje es también la misericordia y el amor de Dios. proclamamos más claramente a por de nuestras acciones. Que si podamos perdonar y aceptar y olvidar y disculpar y dar la bienvenida, entonces les dirigimos a Dios.

Pero también, nuestro mensaje es que "No todo es aceptable, y si usted está viviendo en una manera que no es bueno, me ayudará a cambiar eso."

Si, pues, estamos poseídos a esta misión y proclamar el mensaje, los milagros siguen. A veces, los milagros comienzan con nosotros. Comenzamos a ver a los leprosos ya curados, empezamos dar una nueva perspectiva a los ciegos e ignorantes; comenzamos a sanar a los que están infermo, o muertos de espíritu; y anticipamos nuestra propia resurrección.

Esto no es para los perezosos o débiles de corazón. Esto no es para ellos están durmiendo. ¡Qué si este gigante dormido despierta, imagina las posibilidades! Usted está bautizado, ¿verdad? ¿Qué significa para usted?

SECOND SUNDAY IN
TEMPUS PER ANNUM[14]

(ISAIAH 49:3, 5-6; PSALM 40;
I CORINTHIANS 1:1-3; JOHN 1:29-34)

What makes a "Sosthenes"?

Who was Sosthenes? Paul writes this letter, one of his most famous letters to the people in Corinth, and mentions that Sosthenes also gives greetings. But who was he? Obviously the people of Corinth knew who he was, and probably were wondering how he had been. These letters didn't travel nearly as fast as ours do today, and perhaps months passed between the correspondence being written and being received. He isn't mentioned in any of the other letters of St. Paul, and yet, he must have had an important part in the evangelization of the world . . . right? I mean, after all, Paul *does* mention him by name.

Who was John the Baptizer? We know what is written in the Gospels, and that's about it. His early life is as hidden as was Jesus' life. Some think he might have been an Essene, but there is not clear proof of that. Others think he modeled himself after the prophet Elijah, and, although that might be true, there is not enough evidence to convict him of that either. We know what he ate in the desert, and where he lived. We know what his message was, and that's pretty much it. And yet, he too is mentioned by name; a martyr and a saint.

So what is it that connects this guy Sosthenes, a Greek, with John the Baptizer, a Jew? The first reading. Listen to the words from the prophet Isaiah:

---

14 *Tempus per Annum means* "Time through the year." *Ordinary time* in common language not referring to anything "ordinary," but something that is "ordered." Much like the "cardinal numbers" these times are "ordinal."

48

The LORD said to me: "You are my servant, Israel, through whom I show my glory. That Jacob may be brought back to him and Israel gathered to him; and I am made glorious in the sight of the LORD, and my God is now my strength! It is too little, the LORD says, for you to be my servant, to raise up the tribes of Jacob, and restore the survivors of Israel; I will make you a light to the nations, that my salvation may reach to the ends of the earth."

The servant doesn't **need** to be named! The servant doesn't **need** to be recognized for what he has done, because that is the whole point. God's glory shines *through* him. Sosthenes was just a servant, not nearly as interested that his name was known, as he was that the Gospel was proclaimed. John decreases as he realizes the one who he was to announce, increases. That was the way it was supposed to be. There was no confusion or doubt. And yet the Lord says through the prophet: *Is that job too little for you?* Do you need recognition? Do you need to be revered . . . at my expense?

Our job is to be a light to the nations; and a light does not illuminate itself! Our job is to present the *Other*. Isn't it Paul who says: *"It is no longer I who live, but Christ who lives in me?"* So it is with us. We are called to be the prophets to the nations; contrary to what the world might say it's not "all about me." It's about the One who created me. Well for some . . . that *is* too little. And yet, it is only in presenting our God to a waiting world, that we experience his glory.

A story is told of a successful business man who was growing old and knew it was time to choose a successor to take over the business. Instead of choosing one of his directors or his children, he decided to do something different. He called all the young executives in his company together.

He said, "It is time for me to step down and choose the next CEO. I have decided to choose one of you." The young executives were shocked, but the boss continued. "I am going to give each one of you a seed today—one very special seed. I want you to plant the seed, water it, and come back here one year from today with what you have grown from the seed I have given you. I will then judge the plants that you bring, and the one I choose will be the next CEO."

One man, named Jim, was there that day and he, like the others, received a seed. He went home, and excitedly, told his wife the story. She helped him get a pot, soil, and compost, and he planted the seed. Every day, he would water it, and watch to see if it had grown. After about three weeks, some of the other executives began to talk about their seeds and the plants that were beginning to grow. Jim kept checking his seed, but nothing ever grew. Three weeks, four weeks, five weeks went by, still nothing. By now, others were talking about their plants, but Jim didn't have a plant, and he felt like a failure.

Six months went by—still nothing in Jim's pot. He just knew he had killed his seed. Everyone else had trees and tall plants, but he had nothing. Jim didn't say anything to his colleagues, however, he just kept watering and fertilizing the soil—he so wanted the seed to grow. A year finally went by, and all the young executives of the company brought their plants to the CEO for inspection.

Jim told his wife that he wasn't going to take an empty pot. But she asked him to be honest about what happened. Jim felt sick to his stomach; it was going to be the most embarrassing moment of his life, but he knew his wife was right. He took his empty pot to the board room. When Jim arrived, he was amazed at the variety of plants grown by the other executives. They were beautiful—in all shapes and sizes. Jim put his empty pot on the floor, and many of his colleagues laughed, a few felt sorry for him! When the CEO arrived, he surveyed the room and greeted his young executives. Jim just tried to hide in the back. "My, what great plants, trees and flowers you have grown," said the CEO. "Today one of you will be appointed the next CEO!"

All of a sudden, the CEO spotted Jim at the back of the room with his empty pot. He ordered the Financial Director to bring him to the front. Jim was terrified. He thought, "The CEO knows I'm a failure! Maybe he will have me fired!" When Jim got to the front, the CEO asked him what had happened to his seed, Jim told him the story. The CEO asked everyone to sit down except Jim. He looked at Jim, and then announced to the young executives, "This is your next Chief Executive Officer! His name is Jim!" Jim couldn't believe it. He couldn't even grow his seed. "How could he be the new CEO?" the others said.

Then the CEO said, "One year ago today, I gave everyone in this room a seed. I told you to take the seed, plant it, water it, and bring it back to me today. But I gave you all boiled seeds; they were dead—it was not possible for them to grow.

All of you, except Jim, have brought me trees and plants and flowers. When you found that the seed would not grow, you substituted another seed for the one I gave you. Jim was the only one with the courage and honesty to bring me a pot with my seed in it. Therefore, he is the one who will be the new Chief Executive Officer!"[15]

You see, as far as being an apostle, "God doesn't ask us to be successful . . . he asks us to be faithful."[16] To try our best with what we have been given. If we can do that, then we are fulfilling our purpose and growing the seed we were entrusted with, from the beginning. The ability to show **His** glory through our work as His apostle!

---

15 Internet Forward
16 Blessed Mother Teresa of Calcutta

Segundo Domingo del Tiempo Ordinario

(Isaías 49:3, 5-6; Salmo 40; I Corinthios 1:1-3; Juan 1:29-34)

¿Quién fue Sóstenes?

¿Quién fue Sóstenes? Pablo escribo esta carta, una de sus cartas más famosas de la gente en Corintio. El, menciona que Sóstenes también saluda. Pero, ¿quién era? Obviemente el pueblo de Corinto sabía quién era, y probablemente se preguntaban cómo era. Estas cartas no viajan tan rápido como el nuestro correo hoy. Quizas meses pasaron entre la communicacion. El nombre de Sosthenes, no es mencionado en cualquiera de las otras cartas de san Pablo y sin embargo, mi parece, que era una persona importante en la evangelización del mundo . . . ¿no? Pablo lo menciona su nombre.

¿Quién era Juan el Bautista? Sabemos lo que está escrito en los Evangelios y eso es todo. Sus primeros años de vida son ocultos como era la vida de Jesús. Sabemos lo que comieron en el desierto, donde vivió, sabemos lo que su mensaje fue, y eso es todo. Y sin embargo, también menciona a su nombre; un mártir y un santo.
Entonces, ¿Que conecta este Sóstenes (un griego) con Juan el Bautista (un judio)? La primera lectura. Escucha las palabras del profeta Isaías:

> El Señor me dijo: "Tú eres mi siervo, Israel, por medio del cual puedo mostrar mi gloria. que Jacob se podrá interponer de nuevo a él e Israel se reunieron con él; y yo estoy hecho glorioso ante los ojos de Jehová, y mi Dios es mi fuerza! Es muy poco, dice el Señor, para que seas mi siervo, para levantar las tribus de Jacob, y restaurar a los sobrevivientes de Israel; Te haré una luz para las naciones, para que mi salvación alcance hasta los confines de la tierra."

El serviente no tiene por qué ser llamado! El serviente no es necesario que sea reconocido por lo que ha hecho. Ese es el punto. La gloria de

Dios brilla a través de él. Sóstenes era simplemente un sirviente. No interesado en que su nombre era conocido, El queria que el Evangelio fue proclamado. Juan disminuye a medida mientras el que anunciar aumenta. Es correcto. Y, sin embargo el Señor dice: ¿Es el trabajo demasíado poco para usted? ¿Es necesario el reconocimiento por tu trabajo? Qué se necesita para ser venerado . . . a mi costa?

Nuestro trabajo es ser una luz para las naciones, y nuestro trabajo es presenter el Dios; el otro; a quien. San Pablo, dice: *"no soy yo quien vive, sino Cristo quien vive en mí"*? Lo mismo ocurre con nosotros. Somos llamados a ser los profetas de las naciones, contrariamente a lo que el mundo podría decir no se trata de mí. Se trata de aquél que me ha creado . . . Pero para algunos . . . eso es muy poco. Y, sin embargo, es sólo en proclamando nuestro Dios a un mundo que espera, que expeimentamos de su gloria.

Un hombre de negocios estaba envejeciendo y sabía que era tiempo de anunciar un sucesor para hacerse cargo de la compania. En vez de escoger uno de entre los directores o su hijo, el decidio hacer algo diferente. Reunió a todos los ejecutivos jovenes en su compania. Les dijo, "Para mi, ha llegado el tiempo de renunciar mi puesto y escoger uno de ustedes. Los jovenes ejecutivos se quedaron sorprendidos, pero el jefe continuo. "Les voy a dar a cada uno hoy una semilla—una semilla muy especial. Quiero que siembren esta semilla, la den agua, y regresen aquí dentro de un año con lo que han crecido de la semilla que yo les he dado. Juzgaré las plantas que ustedes traigan, y el que yo escoja sera el próximo jefe de la compania."

Un hombre, llamado Jim, estuvo presente ese día y el, al igual que los demás, recibio una semilla. Se fue a su casa muy contento y le conto la historia a su esposa. Ella le ayudo a conseguir una maceta, la tierra, y el fertilizante y sembro la semilla. Cada día, le daba agua y se fijaba a ver si había crecido. Después de tres semanas, algunos de los ejecutivos comenzaron a hablar de sus semillas y las plantas que empezaron a crecer.

53

Jim continuo revisando su semilla, pero nada crecia. Pasaron tres, cuatro, y hasta cinco semanas . . . y nada crecía. A este tiempo, los demás hablaban de sus plantas y como habían crecido, y Jim no tenía ninguna planta y se sentía como un fracas ado.

Pasaron seis meses, y aún no había crecido nada en la maceta de Jim. El supo que había dañado su semilla. Todos los demás tenían árboles o plantas grandes, pero el no tenía nada. Jim no les conto nada a sus compañeros, sino que siguio dandole agua y fertilizante a su maceta . . . quería tanto que su semilla creciera.

Por fin paso el año y todos los ejecutivos de la compania trajeron sus plantas al jefe para que el las revisara. Jim le había dicho a su esposa que el no podia llevar una maceta basía. Pero ella le dijo que fuera sincero sobre lo que había pasado. Jim se sintío muy molesto, porque iba a ser el momento más vergonzoso de su vida, pero sabía que su esposa tenía razon. El llevo su maceta basía a la sala de conferencias. Cuando llego, se quedo sorprendido al ver las plantas que sus compañeros habían cultivado. Eran hermosas—de todos formas y tamaños. Jim puso su maceta basía en el suelo y algunos sus compañeros se reieron de el, y algunos sintieron lastima por el.

Cuando llego el jefe, el se fijo en las plantas y saludo a los ejecutivos. Jim trato de esconderse. "Que grandes son sus árboles, plantas, y flores; dijo el jefe. "Hoy uno de ustedes sera nombrado el nuevo jefe!" Derrepente, el jefe notó a Jim en el fondo de la sala con su maceta basía. El ordenó uno de los directores de finanzas que llamara a Jim hacia el frente. Jim estuvo muy espantado. Pensaba, "Mi jefe sabe que fallé, y quizas me va a despedir."

Cuando Jim llego hacia el frente, el jefe le pregunto lo que había pasado con su semilla. Jim le conto la historia. El jefe pidio que todos se sentaran, menos Jim. Lo miro, y después anuncio a los jovenes ejecutivos, "Este es su nuevo jefe! Su nombre es Jim." Jim no lo pudo creer. El nisiquiera podia cultivar su semilla.

"¿Como puede ser que él es el nuevo jefe?" preguntaron los demás. Después el jefe les dijo, "Hace un año, les di una semilla a cada uno de ustedes, Les dije que tomaran la semilla, la sembraran, le dieran agua, y me la trajeran hoy. Pero a todos les di semillas cocidas; estaban muertas—no era possible que crecieran. Todos ustedes, menos Jim, me han traído árboles, y plantas, y flores. Cuando ustedes se dieron cuenta que la semilla no crecía, sustituyeron la que yo les di, por otra. Jim fue el único con el valor y la sinceridad de traerme una maceta con mi semilla. Así que, el es quien sera el nuevo jefe de la compania."[17]

Vean ustedes, cuando se trata de ser apostoles, Dios no quiere que seamos exitosos . . . Dios nos pide que seamos fieles. Nos pide que intentemos hacer lo major con lo que nos ha dado. Si podemos hacer esto, entonces estaremos cumpliendo nuestro proposito y cultivando la semilla que se nos ha confiado, desde el principio.

---

17 Internet Forward

Third Sunday in
Tempus Per Annum
"Catholic Schools Week"
(Isaiah 8:23-29,30; Psalm 27;
I Corinthians 1:10-13, 17; Matthew 4:12-23)

. . . that's what we taught them from the beginning; and that's what we teach them today.

"Catholic Schools light the way." This is the theme for *Catholic Schools week* this year. It should be, "We Continue to light the way, as we have for centuries."

We are a light; a sign in the world to our child. We are either a sign that leads them to want to be better; to want to see this God, who created them unlike any other; or a sign of contradiction. Whichever sign we are, they will become. Our children do not have to believe what we say, but they must believe what we do.

I remember my Catholic education very vividly. It was an old building, with those steam radiators. The teacher had to pound them every morning with a wrench to get them going. And then we would hear, "bang, bang, clang" for the first hour. By 10:30 it was so hot, we had to open the windows in winter time. It was a sampling of what hell would be like (we were told). I remember Friday Masses, and the students doing the readings and gifts and singing. I remember, one day a week, going over to the church so Fr. Geiger could give us a lesson. I remember we didn't just celebrate Christmas, but Advent. We didn't just celebrate Easter, but Lent. And in my family, during Lent and Advent, we prayed the Rosary. We went to the Church on Friday nights to eat during Lent. We paraded around as Saints on November first and had a May procession to our Lady. Our religion wasn't something tagged onto life . . . but was our life. That *is* Catholic Education.

And despite what later life gave to us, we were ready. We may not have understood at the time, memorizing the prayers, the devotionals, and attending Mass every week, but later on in life there was some foundation, by which we were able to weather the storms and realities that come with adulthood. This is what Catholic Schools do. We light the way in a world that continues to compromise itself. The Catholic Church has remained consistent in its *kerygma* and morals since the beginning; even when most other Christian churches have acquiesced to the popular opinion.

What does this love demand? Sacrifice. A "sacred doing" or a "making sacred." When we think of the many sacrifices we make for our children, isn't this one of the most important? I know personally of the numerous sacrifices our teachers, both in the school and the religious education program, make for our children. Those sacrifices, however, are minimal compared to a true *giving* love; a love that gives the faith that **can** save, what we cannot.

Love always leads to God; if it does not, then it is not love. And we equate many things to love in our life. We give our children things; we offer them opportunities; we take them on vacations; and yet, amidst all these things, sometimes the greatest sacrifice is also the simplest; to share the faith. This necessarily requires that we first believe. We cannot give what we do not have.

"Our children do not always listen to what we say, but they are experts at imitating us."[18]

I once told the students a story about a boy I had befriended in grade school. He didn't have many friends, and so, due to my guilty conscience I decided to hang out with him, and eventually we became friends. He grew confident and began to do better. Over time we lost touch. I went to college, and when I was trying to start a business went to the bank for a loan. When I went in without collateral or a home, the officer laughed at me. Then the door of the branch manager opened and there was my friend from grade school, who

---

18 Anonymous quote.

instructed the loan officer to give me whatever I needed. I then asked the boys and girls, "What is the point of this story?" A little girl replied, "We should always be nice to everyone . . ." I smiled because she got it! Then she added, "Because later on in life they might give us money." Well, what can you say? It's a journey, not a destination!

This boy, who was not a branch manager, was certainly a prophet to me . . . and taught me a great lesson in "gift." Our children will often be prophets to us, humbling us. And at times, we might be tempted to deny that; to say "they're only children"; to discredit what they say. And yet Jesus will say elsewhere: "What He has hidden from the wise and the learned, he has revealed to the merest children."

What we do through Catholic Education, can only build on what is given by the parents and adults in the life of the child. And so the future of your child depends on what type of teacher *you* are, and the sacrifice you are willing to make . . . because that's what we taught them from the beginning; and that's what we teach them today.

TERCER DOMINGO DEL TIEMPO ORDINARIO

(ISAÍAS 8:23-29,30; SALMO 27; I CORINTIOS 1:10-13, 17; MATEO 4:12-23)

Pro-vida y la Unidad Cristiana

Nuestra voz se está ahogando rápidamente en este mundo. Hay tantas voces que claman en el desierto, pero el problema es que no estan unidas en su grito. En el inicio del siglo, las denominaciónes cristianas de este país, apesar de la diferencia en sus puntos dogmáticos, permanecieron unidas, por la mayor parte, cuando se trataba de la moralidad. Esa union comenzo a derrumbarse durante la decada de 1930 (mil novecientos treinta) cuando ciertas denominaciónes decidieron, en un intento por no excluir a nadie, debilitar su creencia moral, y ese firmamento pronto sería una bajada tan resbaloso y demasíado precipitosa, que no se podia mantener firme en cualquier cosa.

Mientras miraba las noticias, vi una historia que se trataba de una mujer y su compañero en una compañia que se dedica a hacer embriónes y tenerlos disponibles a cualquier pareja que desea tener uno implantado. Tienen resumenes para cada embrión, como si estuvieran aplicando para Harvard. Tienen los resultados del examen de conciencia intelectual de sus padres, sus claificaciónes, sus atributos físicos, y dicen que todo esto es un esfuerzo para dar a los padres el hijo que ellos quieren, en vez de simplemente aceptar lo que reciban.

Nuestra voz se está ahogando rápidamente en este mundo. Estos noticieros estaban felicitando a esta mujer y su compañia por utilizar la tecnología para ayudar a los demas . . . . Ayudarles a que? Diseñar a sus hijos . . . sin la ayuda de Dios? Su voz es la que se escucha. Que pasa con la nuestra?

Este fin de semana se considera el domingo de la Unidad Cristiana. Aunque existen muchos temas dogmáticos que nos separan de otras denominaciónes cristianas, no podemos arriesgar el perjuicio que nuestra division presenta en cuestiones morales. Tenemos que estar unidos. Como este fin de semana es el fin de semana de la Unidad Cristiana, tambien es el fin de semana despues de "la marcha por la vida" en Washington, D.C. Tuvimos un autobús lleno de estudiantes quienes representaron nuestra iglesia y escuela superior en esta marcha. Estabamos unidos con miles de personas en un esfuerzo para protejer la vida . . . toda la vida.

El evangelista Lucas escribe: *"Yo tambien, ilustre Teófilo, después de haberme informado minuciosamente de todo, desde sus principios, pensé escribirtelo por orden, para que veas la verdad de lo que te he enseñado."* El nombre Teófilo significa amador-de-Dios. Aquí, Lucas quiere asegurar que todos comprendan lo mismo. El no vacila con las palabras. El quiere que nosotros tengamos una sola voz, y como dice Pablo: *"Un cuerpo, aun cuando hay muchas partes."* Cada parte es necesaria para que el cuerpo unido, actue.

Jesus dice, en medio de críticas y persecuciónes en la sinagoga: *"El Espíritu del Señor está sobre mí, porque me ha ungido para llevar a los pobres la buena nueva."* El unico año aceptable es cuando porfin podamos unir nuestras voces y nuestros corazones y quizas poder clamar mas fuerte que aquéllos quienes, por causa de nuestra división, desean ver persistir el mal.

En su libro "Castillo Interior", Santa Teresa de Avila escribe: ". . . he aquí los diablos muestran una vez más al alma estas viboras—es decir, las cosas de este mundo—y ellos pretenden que los placeres terrenales son casí eternos."[19] Que trágico al ver que vidas estan sacrificando como accesorios dañados por las diviciónes en el Cuerpo de Cristo. Pero, si estuvieramos unidos? Que pasaría si aceptamos nuestro llamado? Pues, entonces nosotros seríamos los que "llevariamos la buena nueva a los pobres" . . . especialmente los que no tienen voz, sino la nuestra.

---

19 St. Teresa of Avila, *Interior Castle*, trans. E. Allison Peers (New York, NY: Doubleday, 1989), 48.

FOURTH SUNDAY IN TEMPUS PER ANNUM

(ZEPHANIAH 2:3, 3:12-13; PSALM 146; I CORINTHIANS 1: 26-31; MATTHEW 5:1-12)

There are no volunteers in the Church, only Disciples

God could've created the world without you in it, but He didn't . . . why? I'll say it again. God could've made the world without you in it, but he didn't . . . why? He must have created you to do something that no one before you could ever do; and no one after you would ever be able to do. Something that is so special and so sacred, that when you fulfill this task for which He has created you different from any other, the world will be changed forever, because of you. A great part of this purpose in life, is to belong to something greater than our-self. To be in community with others who are striving toward the same end. That is what we call, "the Church."

Paul often speaks of the *Body of Christ,* and in doing so, emphasizes again, and again, how important each part of the body is. He tries to make us understand that none of the parts can independently "do" anything. It is only *as a part* of the body that we fulfill our function. This is most clearly expressed in the body of the Church. We are all called to full, active participation in the Church.[20] Otherwise, the body is to a certain extent handicapped or impaired. There are many opportunities to do this within our own parish community.

Right now in most parish churches, a small percentage of the whole parish is actively involved in the work of the Church. The work of the Church is to bring the Word and Sacraments of Christ to the World. We do this in a number of ways, some more subtle than others. One of these ways is through youth ministry.

---

20 Pope Paul VI, Constitution on the Sacred Liturgy, *Sacrosanctum Concilium*, #14.

I don't know whether you noticed this or not, but we are all getting older! I know when I get a haircut more and more of the bristles falling to the floor are gray in color. Of course, some of you will never have "gray hair," but you *will* age. Many of our youth are already taking the responsibility to be active members of the Church community, but they are not nearly enough. There are many, many high school students in the parish. There are slightly less Junior-High students in the parish . . . . where are they?

Perhaps a better question is: "Where are we?" You see, a Church is supposed to be different; countercultural to society and yet we are much *on par* with how many operations work. A few good people do the work of the many. A few people will volunteer for twenty jobs within the parish, and what happens is, the other eighty percent either think that the job is taken care of; or that they are unneeded. Some will think themselves inadequate or overloaded already, so that they don't want to do anything extra. Well let me assure you, there are no "volunteers" in the Church; there are only active members. Let me say that again: There is no such thing as a volunteer in the Church; there are only those who are doing what they were obligated to do.

Listen to the letter of Paul to the Corinthians. He could just as well have said: "A letter from Paul to the people of St. Joan of Arc Church."

> *"Consider your own calling, brothers and sisters. Not many of you were wise by human standards, not many were powerful, not many were of noble birth. Rather, God chose the foolish of the world to shame the wise, and God chose the weak of the world to shame the strong, and God chose the lowly and despised of the world, those who count for nothing, to reduce to nothing those who are something, so that no human being might boast before God."*

You see, I think we don't see many of the youth in the parish helping to build up the community, because, like their guardians, they come to Church; do their duty; and that's it. Ask yourself: if a tourist comes in; sits through Mass; gives to the collection; receives communion, and leaves. What is the difference between them (a tourist) and you (a parishioner)? It's a valid question. And if there **is no** difference, perhaps now is the time to change that situation. If we are active in the Church, our children will be active in the Church, and if our children are active now, there is a great probability that they will continue to be active once they are out of the house. Even those children of active parents who leave, as is common through the college years, will more often return than others who have had no such direction.

There are so many opportunities to participate in the Church. It doesn't require a weekly commitment or even monthly, but a commitment. Our world is not so big on commitment. But to a God who is so committed to us, we should make every effort.

If we want the children to be involved, we need the adults to be involved. This is a great opportunity for you to have an effect on a young life. Getting involved is also a type of stewardship. This does not take the place of your monetary stewardship. When I first became a priest, I thought I shouldn't tithe or give ten percent of my income to the Church. I figured since I was a priest, I already served the Church. But when I saw other priests, priests I respected, doing it, I followed suite, and I have learned. The more I worry about money, and don't give it, the less I have. The less I worry about it and offer it . . . well . . . there's always enough.

There is no such thing as a volunteer in the Church; only those doing what they are called to do. We can only do this if we understand the beatitudes. The beatitudes speak of incompletion. "This life is an incomplete symphony. It will always be incomplete because we were not made for this world."[21] Often, however, we invest ourselves so much in the "worldliness" of this world, we are not nearly ready for the next. We are so saturated with the things and activities of this world, that we can't foresee anything better. What we need to do is dry ourselves out; we need to look toward the next life and offer everything we have to the Lord; we offer what little gifts we possess. Then in the next life, our Beatitude awaits!

---

21 Karl Rahner, as quoted in: Ronald Rolheiser, *The Restless Heart*, (New York, NY: Doubleday, 2004), x.

CUARTO DOMINGO DEL TIEMPO ORDINARIO AÑO "C"

(JEREMÍAS 1: 4-5, 17-19; SALMO 71; I CORINTIOS 12:31-13:13; LUCAS 4:21-30)

"El amor nunca fallá"

No lo podemos creer! No puede ser cierto. Que existe algo tan "abnegado." No podemos creer que exista algo tan perfecto y tan poderoso y omnipotente como Dios, que nos amo a la existencia. No podemos creer que alguien pudo haber creado el mundo sin nuestra existencia . . . pero no lo hizo. No estamos dispuestos a creer que alguien nos conocía aun antes habernos formado en el seno, y nos puede consagrar como profetas para las naciones; nos puede hacer una ciudad fortificada, y estará a nuestro lado para salvarnos. Uno quien nos ama como si fueramos la única criatura.

Qué queremos decir con "amor"? Qué es lo que Pablo nos quiere decir? Pablo nos dice todo tál y como es: Si tu eres el el presidente de una compania, si eres un gran artista, si eres un gran músico, si eres muy inteligente en los temas más dificiles del mundo, si hablas varias lenguas, si eres el jugador más valioso de tu equipo, si eres la persona más fuerte del mundo; incluso cuando tu fe en Dios haya pasado la prueba . . . pero si no tienes amor . . . todo es inútil! Qué es este amor?

En el mundo antiguo, habían cuatro palabras en griego que significan "amor." Quisiera hablar sobre tres de las cuatro que se utilizaron. La primera es *"Filios."* *"Filios"* se utilizaba par describir un amor entre amistades. El nombre *"Fila delfia"* viene de *"Filios"* y *"Adelfos"* (hermano)—por eso se llama "la ciudad del amor fraternal." La segunda palabra es *"Eros"*, cual significa una amor romántico entre esposos o amantes. De este palabra tenemos la palabra "erotico."

Estas dos palabras tienen en común el hecho que significan un amor por algo que es deseable. La tercera palabra es diferente. La tercera palabra, *"agape,"* es un amor incondicional; un amor por algo, aún cuando no es deseable. Este amor, es el amor del Creador. Este es el amor que nosotros debemos ofrecer, siendo que fuimos creados en su imagen y semejansa.

Dos de mis sobrinos, Krystopher y Mason, eran muy activos cuando tenían cuatro y seis años de edad. Cuando iba a su casa para jugar con ellos y despues dejarlos muy exitados con mi hermana y su esposo, (es broma, nunca haría eso, . . . no es cierto) tocaba el timbre en una cierta manera cada vez. Mientras esperaba, escuchaba los gritos y la estampida en el suelo. Cuando entraba a la habitación, ellos brincaban sobre mi.

Estabamos jugando uno con otro, simplemente disfrutando la vida. No habían requisitos, solamente "juega con nosotros." Me daban un beso y decian "Te quieromucho, tio Mike." ESO ERA TODO! Piense en sus propios hijos; o si no tienen hijos, piense en los hijos de los demás. Ese fue el amor expresado plenamente y sin dudas ni inseguridades ni impedimentos . . . un amor verdadero.

Escuchen al salmista: *"Porque tú, Dios mío, fuiste mi esperanza y confianza, Señor, desde mi juventud. En el vientre materno ya me apoyaba en tí, en el seno, tú me sostenías."* Me imagino que eso es lo que Dios acuerda también. El acuerda las veces que nosotros fuimos tan facíl de amar, y El disfrutaba nuestra apertura y nuestra necesidad por El. "Todos necesitamos más amor de lo que nos merecemos."[22] El gran pecado de la gente en el Evangelio, fue que rechazaban el amor de Dios; el don de Dios. "Porque tanto amó Dios al mundo que nos dio a su Hijo únigenito . . ."

Esto es lo que celebramos en la educación Católica. Que nuestra fe en Dios es lo más importante que tenemos. Lo proclamamos . . . en nuestros salones de clase, en nuestros retiros, y dentro de

---

22 Peter, Van Breeman, S.J., *The God who won't Let Go*, (Notre Dame, IN, Ave Maria Press, 2001), 21.

nuestros grupos. Lo enseñamos: a nuestros padres y nuestros hijos. Lo promovemos, porque en una escuela Católica si podemos. Lo vivimos: porque detras de todas la clases, deportes y actividades que forman parte de cada escuela, existe una fe en algo más que este mundo puede proveer. Nuestra fe en Dios.

Sin embargo, al igual que todos los niños, me imagino que mis sobrinos creceran. Comenzamos a dudar la posibilidad que alguien nos ame tanto, de una manera incondiciónal, aún cuando pecamos. Por causa de esto, nos negamos a permitir que el amor de Dios nos toque. Y así como la gente en el Evangelio, seremos incapaces de vivir la experiencia de cualquier milagro. Quizas, si seguimos la receta que Jesús nos ofrece una y otra vez, quizas por primera vez en nuestra vida, tal vez podamos experimentar el milagro, quizas podamos apreciar el amor agape que Nuestro Padre tiene por nosotros. *"Deben ser como los niños pequeños. Quien no llega a ser como un niño pequeño, nunca entrará al reino de Dios."*

FIFTH SUNDAY IN TEMPUS PER ANNUM

(ISAIAH 58:7-10; PSALM 112; I CORINTHIANS 2:1-5; MATTHEW 5:13-16)

"To be or not to be" isn't the question.

In all our dreams and fantasies of a future; whether that is a future with someone, or without; whether it involves a particular place or livelihood; as we ponder where we will be led over the years, I would wager that none of us pictured ourselves as a prophet. Have you ever thought about that? But, that is what we are. We are all prophets! You've heard it said that people do not have to believe what you say, but they will believe what you do. By our very actions, we proclaim a message and give an indication of what is to come to pass. Whether we want *to be or not to be* (that is the question?). We are a city on a hill, like it or not! We are a lighthouse, illuminating the way for ships which are lost at sea or just coming in to moor. To be a prophet isn't something we ask for; it just is. So because it's not within our power to deny such a roll (as Charles Barkley tried to do at a point in his career) we must decide what we will do with that responsibility.

Jesus uses two metaphors: salt and light. Not ironically, both are essential for life. But what he says about salt seems to be a contradiction if not a naïve hypothesis: *"What if salt loses its saltiness?"* The only way this could occur is if the salt went through a chemical change.

A little chemistry for you today . . . a physical change is when a substance changes its phase but retains its chemical makeup. For instance, ice and steam are both water, but in different phases. They retain their chemical makeup. However, when you have something like an egg, and you boil it, you can never get the boiled egg back to the liquid substance. A chemical change has occurred.

For salt to lose its saltiness or its *property*, a chemical change would have had to occur. It's a great commentary on how we can get so far away from God, that it seems we can never go back again . . . that as much good as salt can do to flavor and preserve, and as necessary as it is for life; if it changes too drastically, it neither adds flavor, nor does it preserve, nor does it give life. However, even in this state, we can still be a light in the world; still be a city on a hill. The difference is we are no longer leading ships out of the stormy seas into safe harbor, but leading them into our world, where salt is no longer of use.

Jesus says that *"your light must shine before men so that they may see,"* what does he say, *"<u>goodness in your acts</u> and give praise to your heavenly Father."* He is the one for whom you prophecy. In Paul's letter to the Corinthians he tells us that as a prophet he was not the most eloquent or wise, but he came upon them in weakness and fear.

No one would choose to be a prophet, because we become the one who can lead others to God, or away from God by what we say or do . . . but it is not a choice. The choice is in how we accept this as a part of who we are; and live as we were created to live. You see, we are free.

> But independence is conditioned upon dependence. Our Declaration of Independence affirms certain basic freedoms, such as the right to life, to liberty and the pursuit of happiness. But in a previous sentence it ascribes this independence to the fact that all of these are the endowments of a Creator.[23]

What we sometimes forget is that the prophets in scripture, chosen by God, were prepared over the years to be prophets. And having been open to the Holy Spirit, were prepared to act, when called upon. We cannot forget, however, that there were many more "false prophets" than true ones, both in the Old and the New Testaments. The true prophets lead others to God. The false ones, lead only to themselves. We will be one of the two. Which will you be?

---

23 Fulton J. Sheen, *The World's First Love*, (New York, NY: McGraw-Hill Co., 1952), 84.

Quinto Domingo del Tiempo Ordinario Año "C"

(Isaías 6:1-2, 3-8; Salmo 138; I Corintios 15:1-11; Lucas 5:1-11)

"La gente se agolpaba en torno suyo para oír la palabra de Dios."

"Soy un hombre de labios impuros, que habito en medio de un pueblo de labios impuros." ¿No les parece asombroso que la lengua es uno de los musculos más pequeños del cuerpo y aún así muy pocas personas la puden contener. Le hacemos tanto daño al Reino con nuestras palabras; a veces mucho más daño, yo creo, que con cualquier otro aspecto de nuestra persona.

Una palabra puede cambiar el estado de alguien; lo puede condenar a muerte; puede clamar ayuda o ofrecer amor; puede perdonar o acusar; puede construir o derrumbar. Hay tanto poder en una palabra que muy seguido en el Evangelio, Jesus puede sanar desde una distancia, simplemente con una palabra. Eso fue lo que hizo con la palabra . . . por eso Él ERA la PALABRA.

En el mundo antiguo, la palabra dicha nunca se podia recaudar. Si tú ofreciste una bendición, duraría parasíempre, pero si ofreciste una maldición, tambien duraría parasíempre. Ellos creían que el mismo acto de eschuchar quería decir que la palabra entraba a su cabeza por medio de los oídos, y se convertía en parte de tí. La palabra tambien se convertía parte de quienes la escucharon, y por ese motivo lo que dice una persona tuvo gran efecto, lo quisieran o no.

Pablo esta compartiendo lo que él recibio . . . quiero decir . . . lo que escucho a través de lo que decian los demás. Él se siente obligado a compartir estos dones y bendiciónes con otras personas, para que la Palabra nunce se deje de escuchar. El Evangelio de San Lucas comienza: *"La gente se agolpaba en torno suyo para oír la palabra de Dios."* Sus palabras formaron parte de ellos, cual resulto en eque ellos dejaran todo atrás para seguirle a Él. Nuestras palabras son tan poderosas, pero ¿qué es lo que hacemos con ellas?

Lamentablemente, lo que sucede es lo que no debe ocurrir, es que utilizamos nuestras palabaras en una manera que nunca fue la intención de Dios. Ahora que obviamente estamos en buena compañia con Isaías, fue necesario para él purificarse la lengua con una brasa caliente. ¿Y la nuestra?

Hay una historia de un monje en el monte athos.

> Un hombre se acerco a él y le conto de su problema con las murmuraciónes. "Cuando hablo, solamente murmuro o digo infamias cotra mis vecinos", le dijo. El monje le ordeno: "Para tu penitencia, ve a la cima del monte más alto con esta almohada llena de plumas. En cuanto se llegue la hora, abre la almohada y suelta las plumas al aire, y despues regresa a mí con la almohada basía." El hombre hizo esto y cuando regreso al monje, le pregunto si había algo más por hacer. El monje le contesto: "Ve y junta todas la plumas de los cuatro vientos." "Eso es imposible" le contesto el hombre. "Así de imposible es que tú puedas recaudar todas las palabras que les has dicho a tu projimo." No las podemos recaudar . . . pero . . . si podemos hacer las paces.[24]

Quizas usted ha tenido uno de esos días cuando todo les parece salir mal, y una palabra amable de una persona puede cambiar el resto de nuestro día. Tal vez una palabra cariñosa de su pareja, cual no fue solicitada, le da sentido a su semana. Vea usted el gran poder que tiene en la lengua para construir, para alumbrar, y fortalecer, para promover . . . si tan sólo podriamos utilizarla para esas cosas. San Pablo dice: *"Digan solo las cosas buenas que la gente necesitan escuchar."* Les quiero ofrecer un mecanismo que mi director espiritual me enseño y que ha sido muy útil cuando hablo.

---

24 Story about 16th Century Saint.

Hablen sólo en la bondad. La caridad en la verdad. Si debes decir algo negativo, dilo en caridad. Si no tienes que decir algo negativo, entonces no lo hagas! Y si te encuentras en una situación donde sólo se hablan murmuraciónes y tú no puedes decir nada bueno de esa persona, entonces no digas nada. Pero intenta un experimento. Esta semana, cuando te encuentres con alguien, busca lo más positivo que puedas decir, y dilo. Especialmente si es una persona a quien le has hecho daño en el pasado. Creo que nos quedariamos sorprendidos. No es que podamos recaudar todas la plumas que estaban dentro de la almohada, eso es imposible. Sino que podamos soltar diferentes plumas alrededor del mundo, que no solamente seran elevadas por el viento, sino tienen el poder de elevar los oyentes tambien.

Sixth Sunday in Tempus per Annum

(Sirach 15:15-20; Psalm 119; I Corinthians 2:6-10; Matthew 5:17-37)

Above and beyond

The scribes and the Pharisees followed the letter of the Law: no more and no less. Jesus is quite happy with the law, and he assures us that he will not change it, but he is more interested in the *spirit* of the law . . . the "Why is the law here in the first place?" Throughout his ministry in Galilee and beyond, this will be the struggle. There will be almost constant persecution regarding the Sabbath, when Jesus happened to perform many of his miracles; about washing before meals; about sinful people speaking with him or touching him and finally that one should die, so that the many in the nation of Israel might survive.

Very often, we can get caught up in the *letter of the law*, and forget the spirit. There is a story of a bank robber trying to escape a police chase. The police quickly caught up with the man because the man, never once exceeded the speed limit. While they were arresting him, the officer asked why he didn't speed away. The man replied, "Speeding is against the law!" That is a true story. So let's look at the spirit of the law, through the words of Christ, and find out just what this demands of us.

The first had to do with murder. Now to make sure we're on the same page, he doesn't say "kill" but "murder." The original commandment in Hebrew means also *to murder*. Well, what's the difference? Murder is the killing of an innocent person. According to that law, then, you cannot murder someone, but you can abuse people, exact vengeance on people, and sue your opponent, amidst many other uncharitable acts. Jesus is taking it a step further and says, "Listen . . . before it comes to murder, there are things we can do to avoid getting to that point!"

What about adultery? We see how the Sanhedrin would address such a thing in chapter eight of John's gospel, where the woman is caught in the very act of adultery. Since that story is only in John's gospel, we don't know whether it occurred before this speech of Jesus or after. Regardless, Jesus is breaking this commandment down in a way that even the Pharisees might find challenging. The law, as it is written, was that one could not commit adultery, but they *could* look at a woman with lust, right? (which was challenging due to the amount of clothing they wore to cover up). Furthermore, although it was illegal to speak to a woman who was not your wife, I'm sure people found a way to do that, amidst other lesser degrees of infidelity. Jesus is telling us that to objectify anyone is wrong. If he lived today as he did back then, he would have to walk with his eyes to the ground most of the time.

This leads to the discussion in the last case which involves marriage. To place this in context, Jesus is living in a time when you had strict followers of the law, and those who took a more relaxed approach. For those who were more liberal or relaxed, a man could divorce his wife for burning the toast; for those who were more strict, it took a great deal more in order to divorce. Jesus wants them to take this covenant seriously. It is not a *civil union*, or a *sale of one to another*, but a covenant relationship. He has a clause in Matthew's gospel where the word **porneia** is used. This word was most often used to denote incest. In other words, this marriage so close in the family would be an *unlawful marriage* anyway, so divorce would be permissible. This also presumes that the marriage was a valid one, where both parties offered free consent, and had full knowledge of the other.

Finally, the false oath. His whole point is, why do you have to take an oath at all, unless you lie. It's true! God never lies, for if he doesn't like something he can just change it. Which is why Jesus says in the last part of the Gospel, you have no power at all regarding the things of this world. So just tell the truth.

Jesus says, "*take up your cross and follow me.*" Paul says that the men of this age are headed for destruction. Maybe he was writing to us! Maybe *we think* a crucifixion might be easier than living by these codes. The truth, however, is that we are made in the likeness of God. These codes are not so much laws to follow, but guides to the peace that we all seek. Anything worth having is not easily obtained. Perhaps that is why Jesus warns, we're gonna have to be better than the Pharisees (just following the letter of the law) if we wish to enter the kingdom of heaven. But the choice is ours. "*If you choose you can keep the commandments; it is loyalty to do his will. There are set before you fire and water; to whichever you choose, stretch forth your hand. Before man are life and death, whichever he chooses shall be given him.*"

Sexto Domingo del Tiempo Ordinario Año "C"

(Jeremías 17:5-8; Salmo 1; I Corintios 15:12, 16-20; Lucas 6:17, 20-26)

Las Bienaventuranzas

Me parece que la mayoria de la gente no se decide de manera positiva: "Qiero mi mediocridad; no deseo mejorar." T.A Sparks escribe:

> La espíritualidad no es una vida de represión. Eso es negativo. La espíritualidad es positiva: es una vida nueva y adicional, no es la vieja lucha por obtener el dominio de si mismo. Si continuas haciendo lo que simpre has hecho, continuaras recibiendo lo que siempre has recibido.[25]

Es cuando deseamos cambiar que hay pruebas positivas que El Espíritu Santo está trabajando en nosotros.

¿ Y como es que trabaja El Espíritu Santo dentro de nosotros? Quizas podríamos haber tratado diferentes typos de auto-ayuda o incluso la psiquiatría. Y para ciertas cosas, es la manera que debemos solucionar nuestros problemas, pero lo que sucede a menudo, es que borramos lo invisible con las cosas que si podemos ver. Escuchen al profeta Jeremías: *"Maldito el hombre que confía en el hombre, que en él pone su fuerza y aparta del Señor su corazón."*

Jesus nos da una sugerencia en el Evangelio de hoy como es que El Espíritu Santo nos acerca a Dios. Él nos ofrece cuatro recetas para la

---

25 T.A. Sparks, in Kollar, Charles Allen, *Solution-Focused Pastoral Counseling: An Effective Short-term Approach for Getting People Back on Track,* (Grand Rapids, MI, Zondervan Press, 1997), 53.

felicidad, y cuatro advertencias cuando no estamos donde debemos estar. Estas recetas a menudo pueden ser un poco confusas, así que espero ponerlos en contexto, y hacerlos un poco mas facil de seguir. Nosotros le podemos decir la "actitud de ser."

"Dichosos son los pobres." Esto quiere decir: Preocupense y sean determinados. Uno de los atributos de la gente mediocre es que se sienten comodos con su "enfermedad." Los que no se preocupan por lo que comeran el día de mañana; donde estarán; lo que haran; pueden estar cómodos; sin la nesecidad de recursos. No es así con los pobres. Si nos encontramos preocupados por donde estamos y a donde vamos, haremos un esfuerzo constante para correjirnos. Si mostramos preocupación, entonces seremos determinados, y El Espíritu Santo trabajará con esa determinación para bendecirnos con el Reino.

"Dichosos los que tienen hambre." Sean motivados y comprometidos. El aburrimiento y el gozo no se puden comparar. Jesus no dice, "dichoso el que tiene hambre." El lo dice en la forma plural. Somos motivados y comprometidos a nuestra fe cuando la podemos compartir. Aúnque nuestro mensaje sea bueno, si el que lo escucha encuentra que el mensaje es repugnante, o falso, ese mensaje no tine esperanza . . . llega descolorido por el olor de quien lo pronuncio.

"Dichosos los que lloran, porque al fin reirán." Sean humildes. Dense cuenta que nuestras pertenencias son un regalo. No hemos hecho nada para que se nos entreguen estos dones, y pueden fallár o nos los pueden quitar a cualquier hora . . . todo es gracia. La humildad es una oración que, si se dice con devoción, siempre se escucha.

Finalmente, *"Dichosos serán cuando los hombre los aborrescan y los expulsen; y cuando los insulten y maldigan por causa mía."* Sean perseverantes. Podemos llevar acabo nuestras resoluciónes de Año Nuevo, y nuestra penitencia Cuaresma durante la primera semana con facilidad; pero despues de ese tiempo nos damos cuenta por que es una resolución o una re-solución y penitencia. Cuantas veces hemos escuchado de los tiempos que han encontrado a gente perdida, y sucede que los encuentra a sólo unos metros de la civilización. Si nosotros podemos ver la luz, podemos sobrevivir casí cualquier evento. Si logramos preocuparnos por los demas y somos determinados; si nos podemos motivar y comprometer; si podemos ser humildes, entonces la luz brillará dentro de nosotros.

Esto no es el resultado de nuestro esfuerzo, sino del Espíritu Santo. Lo que es, es una actitud que permite al Espíritu Santo animarnos a perseverar. Si nosotros tenemos una vida que permite la entrada del Espíritu, entonces seremos odiados muy seguido, seremos insultados y denunciados, porque recordaremos a los demas de lo insuficiente que es su vida espíritual. Jesús siempre dijo la verdad con convicción y compasión, pero siempre hablo con la verdad. Fue querido por muchos porque Él les presento una posibilidad; y fue odiado por otros, porque les recordo de sus insuficiencias.

Jesús entonces ofrece las afliccónes. Estas afliccónes no son tanto maldiciónes, sino advertencias para quienes no tienen El Espiritu y no crean una disposición abierta a Él. Ellos parasíempre quedaran basíos, porque nosotros, quienes no fuimos hechos para este mundo, nunca podremos sentir satisfacción por las cosas de este mundo. Solamente él Aliento, cual fue respirado dentro de nosotros desde el principio, es el que nos puede llenar, al solo poseer una cosa. Una "actitud de ser."

SEVENTH SUNDAY IN TEMPUS PER ANNUM

(LEVITICUS 19:1-2, 17-18; PSALM 103; I CORINTHIANS 3:16-23; MATTHEW 5:38-48)

"Let your yes, be yes, and your no, be no."

In the early Christian church, they came to a crossroads: a place where the world in which they lived, intersected with the "way" that Jesus paved through his life, death and resurrection. At this crossroads, the Christian had to make a decision. This decision would not only impact *his* life, but the lives of his family and friends as well. The direction he took would mean turning his back on the other. And much like the movie from the nineteen eighties, where a young guitarist met the Devil at the crossroads, so too will we. Make no mistake, we are *in* the world. We do not live in some bubble far from the reality which is life, but we don't have to be *of* the world. In John's gospel, the word in Greek, *kosmos*, "world", is used frequently and almost always to denote the evil force that oppresses Christianity.

We are also at a crossroads. There is no room in the Church for the lukewarm Catholic. There is no room in the Church for those who accept only the teachings that do not limit their freedom or lifestyle. This isn't coming from me! Listen to St. Paul:

> *"Let no one delude himself. If any one of you thinks he is wise in a worldly way, he had better become a fool. In that way he will really be wise, for the wisdom of this world is absurdity with God."*

And yet there is the second chance. Paul warns us in another place, however, that their word was not "yes" and "no", but "yes." Yes with everything I do for my Lord. Yes, even when it is uncomfortable, I trust. Yes, even when those within the church fail me, I hope. Yes, even when I want to do what I want to do, I obey. Yes, even when I will have to sacrifice, I love. Jesus says again and again in the Gospel,

"You have heard it said . . . but I say to you . . ." In other words, knowing *about* Christ and knowing *about* his Word is not nearly as important as living Christ and his Word. What are we willing to do to **be Catholic** and get those who **were** Catholic back to church?

I want to ask you for your pledge today. We are called to be good stewards of the gifts that have been entrusted to us. That is not only monetary stewards, but stewards of all the gifts. For too long, our faith has not been a priority, or perhaps even ranked in the top ten. The way Catholics become *inactive Catholics* is that at the crossroads, they waver. Slowly they stop being so devout; slowly they compromise certain things, until nothing is certain anymore; everything is relative, so that even God or worship of God are no longer obligatory. At this point, we have made ourselves into a god. But much like the pagan gods of history, we really have no power over the most important things: life and death; health and peace . . . at least not without Him.

I want to ask you for your pledge today. That we be united in our Catholic Faith, the way the Church teaches the faith; the way Christ entrusted that faith to us. To pledge our conviction to these truths which we hold as sacred and revealed by Christ . . . . even those with which we struggle. It's not wrong to struggle with our faith; it's wrong to change our faith to conform to our lifestyle.

I ask you for your pledge today. That Mass will be a priority; that the religious education of our youth be a priority; that we will sacrifice for what we believe to be true!

I ask you to pledge today your sacrifice to invest in the future of this parish and the buildings that form our worship space, school, and activity centers. We are growing! We are young, and the future is full of opportunity. We must ensure that we have the facilities to support that growth, and continue the legacy entrusted to us; the stewards, many years ago.

Finally, I ask you to pledge your time and devotion to your Parish. To be an active member of our community, which is growing, and offer the gifts that have been entrusted to you, for the good of our assembly. Please be generous, as God is pleased with a generous heart. And know the dividends, which are safe from decay or thieves, will be numerous.

We are at a crossroads. Jesus says, I am "***the***" way, not "***a***" way. As Moses says: *"Be holy, for I, the Lord your God am holy."* Now is an acceptable time. What will we do with our gift? The gift of faith.

EIGHTH SUNDAY IN TEMPUS PER ANNUM

(ISAIAH 49:14-15; PSALM 62; I CORINTHIANS 4:1-5; MATTHEW 6:24-34)

Faith with Works

Jesus says that we cannot serve both God and *mammon*. Then he begins to discuss worries and anxieties. Finally he discusses clothes. It brought to mind for me my cruel sisters. We used to get ready to go out. You know, you hate your siblings growing up, but once you're older and a bit more mature (whatever that means) you can go out together and have a good time. We would go to clubs or parties and generally enjoy one another's company. But I recall that often, we would get ready to go out, and inevitably, regardless of how hard I tried, my sisters would look at me with an expression of disbelief and say, "You're going out . . . wearing that?" I thought it was a struggle when my mother always wanted to make sure I was wearing clean underwear, just in case I was in an accident. That's for another homily. They would then commence in trying to re-dress me in a way that was acceptable.

Whether we're talking about clothing to "go out," or houses, or security. All those things we worry about in life. Of all of those things, how many of them do we actually have control over? If we really think about it. Life and death? Health and security? How many?

So Jesus says, "You cannot serve both God and *mammon*." We need to put this in context. It is a question of faith and works. That is the argument we often encounter, most especially in the other Christian communities. Faith and works. Often, the non-Catholics will argue that all you need is faith. You cannot work your way to heaven. This is true! To say that we can save ourselves by what we say and do is an ancient heresy called *Pelagianism*[26]. We cannot "work" ourselves into heaven. There are non-Christian religions which allow for one to "work" their way into heaven. The Catholic Church does not teach that. We do not believe that we can "work" our way into heaven; however, we do *need* works . . . there's no doubt about it.

C.S. Lewis would say that there is a balance between faith and works. "You must have both faith and works. Because when you stress one over the other, it's like trying to use a pair of scissors by cutting with only one blade."[27] We cannot hold one over the other. He continues: "To have faith without works, is like praying that your mother-in-law gets well again, but you're unwilling to drive her to the hospital to help her to do so." So in a sense you're just "wishing her well" but not willing to do what is well within your power to take action. Thus enters, "the *mammon*."

Mammon, is a Hebrew word. What it means is, all my treasures, my goods, anything that I have invested in, I entrust to someone else. That *is* my *mammon*. That which I entrust to someone else. In a sense, it's like a bank of today. At the time that Jesus is preaching about this, however, what he's speaking of is no longer that kind of *mammon*.

So if we're trusting in this thing, which cannot buy us health; cannot buy us life; cannot buy us salvation, and we're not trusting in God, that doesn't make any sense!

The word that is used by Christ in the Gospel is *mamon*. The word changed from something I entrust to someone else, into something *I trust in*. See the difference there? Having a treasure that I would like *to entrust to someone*, is much different than having a treasure

---

26 Pelagianism was the theological system which hel that a man took the initial and fundamental steps towards salvation by his own efforts apart from the assistance of Divine Grace (*Oxford Dictionary of the Christian Church*).

27 C. S Lewis, *Mere Christianity*, (San Francisco, CA, Harper Collins, 1996), 148.

I trust in. Do not our own greenbacks read, "In God we Trust"? So this change in the word is neither accidental nor arbitrary. Jesus is clearly playing on the word to make the point that you cannot trust *in* this *thing* more than you trust *in God*. Not only is it idolatry, but it doesn't make sense. When we trust in a thing, of course we're gonna have worry and anxiety. Because it really has no power to affect a change.

We've been through a few years where the economy has been tough at best. People have lost hundreds, even thousands of dollars. This has happened not only in the stock market, but in these scams or bad investments made by seemingly trustworthy people. Some lost retirements, life savings . . . all to these crooks.

The other day I got a call in the office here at the parish. The person on the line said that I won a Lincoln Navigator! I thought, "That is awesome. I can get the car and sell it, and pay for an elevator for the church!" So then they began to ask personal information; account information, and all this stuff. I asked them if they would speak with my friend and get the information from him . . . . he is the District Attorney. There was a "click" on the line. It was almost immediate. They are still scamming, even in a terrible economy.

The reason they can do this, is that money is very fluid. Even the one who keeps the money in a mattress (I do not, just so you know) is not secure. At best they get a bad night's sleep and at worse, they get robbed or some kind of natural disaster claims their nest egg. We cannot put our faith in something so vulnerable or volatile.

Is there anything that's one hundred percent secure? I mean, what *is* foolproof? What is consistent? Our God. Our God who says through the prophet Isaiah today: *"Even though a mother forget her infant, I will not forget you."* We cannot even imagine it. A mother forget her infant? *I will not leave you.* This is coming toward the end of the book of the prophet Isaiah. They've been exiled. Now they're coming back and the fulfillment is finally here. They've felt like God's deserted them forever. And God is saying to them, "I never deserted you . . . even though *you* deserted me."

To place our faith in something that is consistently good and wants only the very best for us . . . I mean, who wouldn't do that? Yes, we can't see Him; smell him; taste him; touch him; hear him . . . or can we? The senses aren't everything. People wear masks we can see, but that's not who they are. They tell us lies that we can hear, but it is not reality. They can perfume themselves to attract a mate, and even make the foods that will lead to the man's heart. But God . . . God will not lie. If he doesn't like the way things are, He will change them. He is, who is, and needs no mask.

I don't know about your experience with things, but I have found that the more I worry about money and things; what I don't have . . . the less I have. The less I worry about finances and what I don't have . . . there's always plenty. Everything is taken care of. In a similar vein, almost selfishly: the more things I give away, the more things I get! On the contrary then, the more I cling to things and hoard things, the less I have, and the *more* I worry.

So how do we keep the balance? How do we use both blades of the scissors? By ensuring that our faith is lived out in our works. That's it! That our faith is infused through every aspect of our life! When people can see us wherever we are: in the office, in the mall, in the market or the park, they will know what we believe. It is not enough to say we believe; *sola fidei* is not enough. Even James in his letter would say, *"Show me your faith and I will show you my works."*

Lent is coming along very shortly and it is a wonderful time to ask: "What is in my life that I need to let go of? What have I been clinging to and hoarding that I just need to let relinquish? And what have I needed in my life for a long time, that I have not yet obtained or incorporated into my life?" Maybe because I was afraid of change, or afraid of going beyond the boundaries of my "comfort zone"? How do I live out my faith? How can I transform this *mammon* that *I trust in*, into a treasure that *I entrust to* someone else? Someone who loves me more than I love myself. Loves me more than I could ask for or imagine? *Rest in God alone my soul.*

Ash Wednesday
(SEE APPENDIX I)

Temptation in the Desert, sketched at General Cepeda MX.

First Sunday of Lent
(Genesis 2: 7-9, 3:1-7; Psalm 51; Romans 5: 12-19; Matthew 4:1-11)

Isn't it time that we walked <u>with</u> Him?

Years ago a warm and cuddly character was introduced to America via billboards, TV and radio in order to prevent something from destroying the land. He wanted to get our attention to sort of establish an agreement with us, and he had a memorable line for it: "Remember, only you can prevent forest fires." If we established a covenant with "Smokey," then we would preserve our lands for future generations and protect the animals that live there. We had to make a deal, and in the long run, the deal would be most beneficial to us.

If I asked you to tell me what common thread runs through the entire Bible, what would you answer? I hope that we would all answer with "*Covenant*." God establishes a covenant with his people. A covenant, in the common sense of the word usually refers to a formal, solemn, and binding agreement between two parties for the performance of some action. This is very interesting, because if God is all powerful, then what could he possibly get out of such an agreement? The answer is that God doesn't *need* anything, but what he wants to do is show his creation his utter and complete love.

On a very personal note, this for me, was one of the things that drove me into the faith and the ministry even further. The God that I was getting to know was not an evil and vindictive God who chooses only a few to be saved. He is, in fact, one who offers hope beyond hope to every person of this earth. He wants all of his creatures to enter into a binding covenant that guarantees benefits beyond measure for those who would accept it. To ratify this covenant, to make it stick, he would not just walk to the table with a contract for people to sign. This contract would require much, much more.

The word covenant in Hebrew is *Berit*. The word *Berit* literally means "binding" or "shackle" or "handcuff." When we enter into a covenant we are *shackling* our self to the other person. We are "binding" ourself in a way that goes beyond the paper and signatures. This covenant, is signed in blood.

We might look at this covenant as lopsided, and rightly so, after all, it is our *Creator*. However, the Lord lets us know in a very real way what are the risks He has already taken. For from the beginning, the plan was to give us his Son. And the Son, as the guarantor of the covenant, shows us with his very life, that his blood is something that will be surrendered for us . . . who can offer nothing that comes close in comparison.

Read Matthew's rendition of the temptation in the desert. Now I get it: it's the devil and Jesus *mono e mono* and we know in the story (spoiler alert if you haven't read it) Jesus wins in the end. But here's my question: What would've been wrong with turning stones into bread? Bread is good. The angels are gonna feed him in a few minutes anyway. What would that have hurt? If I had that power, I would've said, "Sit down in that chair right there and let me show you how it's done!"[28] I know none of YOU would have done that (wink) but I would have. Nothin' wrong there, right? However, it is in this short moment, during a seemingly endless duration of temptation, that Jesus shines. And not only does he shine, but he shows that sacrifice means much more than bloodletting. To swallow one's pride; to think of the other before the self; perhaps that is the greatest sacrifice; the greatest loss.

Jesus didn't turn the stones into bread, although we're well aware that he was capable, because it would have been a miracle done solely for himself! And Jesus never performed any miracles for himself. The very height of humility allowed him to conquer a fallen angel who Christ endured in his humanity. The whole thing is truly a mystery which we do not understand; however, we know that our God allows his very Son to be tempted so that each of us could understand a very

---

28 Charlie Daniels, *The Devil Went Down to Georgia.*

powerful truth: that although we will be tempted, we need not fear the test. Jesus in his *humanity*, overcame the *supernatural* tempter.

When we look at the first reading, we realize that the major moments in our lives from the beginning were *all* marked by covenants. In the book of Genesis, who is the "son" of God? Adam. He is also tempted in his humanity. With that temptation and the fall, the first covenant with God is broken. This covenant, like all others, would also involve blood, for the very rib of Adam is used in the creation of his Eve. Here also, we get a glimpse of what happens when we break our part of the covenant. God is merciful, but he is also just.

St. Paul's letter to the Romans supplies the glue that binds the two. As the first son of God, Adam, sinned; and that sin brought death as a result of the original covenant. Jesus now brings with him a new covenant sealed in his own blood, and death is no more. As Eve brought the instrument of sin, the forbidden fruit, and presented it to Adam, so Mary is the "new Eve" who, presenting the fruit of her womb to the world, renews our relationship with God and makes salvation possible once again.

So in this lopsided covenant, what is it that we sacrificed or surrendered in order to make salvation possible again? What is it that we sacrificed or surrendered in order to make reparation for our sin? The answer is simple: nothing. Nothing. We cannot by our failings or betrayals, take anything from God's glory and power. We cannot, by our repentance or triumphs over temptation, add anything to God's glory and power. But . . . because He loves so much; because He wishes that we are united with Him; He is patient with our failings and desires our repentance. You see, the gift has already been given, we need only receive it with gratitude. Our part of the covenant now, is to show our reception and gratitude by holding up our end of the bargain. We are "bound" in this *Berit*, to God. Isn't it about time that we *walked* with Him, instead of having ***Him*** carry ***us***?

SECOND SUNDAY OF LENT

(GENESIS 12:1-4; PSALM 33; II TIMOTHY 1:8-10; MATTHEW 17:1-9)

To know Him is to Love Him

The readings today speak of relationship. Think about it. We can know a lot *about* something, but not ***know*** it. We can know a lot *about* a person, and not really *know* them. Those of you who are married; imagine knowing everything about your spouse. You know their quirks, habits, looks, idiosyncrasies, and can know all that stuff and still not "know" them; not be in relationship with them. Relationship goes far beyond what we can ***know*** "about" a person.

Jesus is transfigured in the Gospel. But I think this was not necessarily anything that happened to Jesus, in so much as it was something that happened to the apostles. They saw him as he really ***was***. They had spent all this time with him and still did not "*know*" him. They knew all about him but did not *know* him. It was not a relationship with divinity, because they could not understand sacrifice. They saw the "Godness" and wanted to stay there forever. But Jesus seems to be saying, "to understand my divinity, you must understand suffering." And once down from the mountain, after it appeared they understood, Jesus would have to start instruction all over again!

Look at Abram. God speaks to him and says: "You know this land you're on . . . all the things you hold precious; the stability you've known for so long? You know what I'm talking about?" Abram responds, "Yes Lord." God says: "I want you to leave it!" In another way he's saying, get outside of the box and move out of your comfort zone and really enter into something special with me. As long as you're here and secure and stable, all you'll ever know is a God who is in the heavens." So he leaves. But don't think for a minute he didn't second guess himself. That maybe he even mourned the loss; that

Sarai got on his back or nagged saying, "Are you sure he said that?" But . . . he left.

See, we can be "cradle Catholics" or converts. We can know the beatitudes, the commandments, the precepts of the Church, we will have read all the Vatican documents and know the Bible, chapter and verse; but those things do not mean we know God. Those things don't make a relationship. They are tools for establishing the relationship, but they are not a relationship. Anybody can memorize those things and know them without even believing in God. Jesus is on the mountain with the Law (Moses) and the Prophets (Elijah), but they are not pointing to themselves . . . they are pointing to HIM! He *is* the point. All those things lead to him or they lead to nothing.

Sometimes it seems, we're doing so well, and we're growing in the faith and our relationship with God, but what happens is all of a sudden, we realize it, and stop! We think, "Man, things are so good, what is God going to ask of me, or what is He going to take away." And so we withdraw. And "because we will not allow God to be God, we halt any progress in a real relationship."[29] If we come to understand that any relationship requires sacrifice, and expect that sacrifice, then we can follow Jesus down from the mountain, having seen him transfigured, and embrace whatever that relationship demands.

I went to my doctor recently and he told me that my blood pressure was too high. He asked about my diet and medications and exercise and saw nothing to raise a flag in any of those categories. He asked if I had stress in my life, and I looked at him as if one couldn't tell by the gray hairs that had appeared in the last year. He asked if I did anything to relax and I told him of all the things I did that were relaxing for me. Finally he suggested, "You need to get a fish tank." "I have one and it is very relaxing, is not dependent on the weather and takes very little maintenance." So I decided to follow that prescription. My nephews were getting rid of their tank and

---

29 Peter, Van Breeman, S.J., *The God who won't Let Go*, (Notre Dame, IN, Ave Maria Press, 2001), 14.

the accessories, so the cost for me would be minimal. I put the tank together, filled it with water and finally got some fish and placed them into their new world. But as I watched them, it seemed like they were swimming so hard . . . I wondered if they could swim! This was not relaxing at all, but stressful! They never stopped moving and barely ate. Finally one morning I walked into the room and there they were . . . dead. What could've happened in such a short time? I took the fish back to the pet store and brought a sample of the water. I asked, "So what do you think they died from?" The lady replied, "They probably died of stress."

Hmmm. Even fish have stress. The difference is, their environment is made for them, and they have no choice. We have a choice. Suffering is going to happen, but the *way we respond* to that suffering, shapes the way we live our life.

I think I'm just going to get some plastic fish that I can put into the tank. It'll be less stress for all of us!

THIRD SUNDAY OF LENT
(EXODUS 17:3-7; PSALM 95;
ROMANS 5:1-2, 5-8; JOHN 4:5-42)

You *save her* . . . you *let her go.*

"Sometimes the master sin can be detected by discovering what defect makes us most angry when we are accused of it."[30] Some of us, however, over time, can become blind to such weakness as sin . . . we voluntarily accept blindness, instead of the pain that sometimes comes with the truth. On the other hand, there are those who are struggling in a life of sin. And because of the way we treat them, they have no chance of salvation. This is not because God has indicated they are damned, but that *we* have.

The readings over the last three weeks at Mass, have been about sight and enlightenment. John takes us on a journey, and through it, we encounter a woman at the well; a blind man; and one who is raised from the dead. The woman at the well is one of these, who perhaps, has become numb to the effects of sin. But to understand where she's coming from, we first need to understand a little bit about the Samaritans, and why they have such a bad rap in the first place.

You see, when the Babylonian exile occurred, they were very particular in who they chose to be exiled. The kings were not so naïve as to leave behind, those who would cause rebellion, or support those who were rebels. Therefore, the king gave very specific instructions that the learned, the rich, the politicians, the strong . . . they were the ones who were to be taken into exile. And so they were; with their scribes and priests, etc; but without a Temple. Those who were left behind, were the poor; the uneducated; those who *would* never start a rebellion, because they *could* not start a rebellion.

---

30 Fulton J. Sheen, *Lift Up Your Heart*, (New York, NY, McGraw-Hill Book Co., 1950), 135.

Those who were exiled had no temple, therefore, they organized themselves around the Law, so that it became more of a "religion of the book;" whereas, those who were left behind had a desecrated Temple, but no priests or politicians or defenders. As a result, those in exile grew closer to the Law. But without a Law, or Temple, those who were left behind began to mix with the pagans in the land. They began to take up *their* worship and *their* laws; began to marry *their* men and women and do business together.

When the time in exile had concluded, and the Israelites were not only permitted, but encouraged to return to Jerusalem, you can imagine their surprise, if not their outrage, at what had occurred while they were suffering in exile. So often, the prophets used the term, "fornication" or "adultery" to speak of the people who worshiped idols instead of God. Those who had remained behind were the fornicators *par exellence*! There was no way the people of the law could tolerate such a denial of God, so they (the exiles) now *exiled* those who had remained. They were not worthy of the "Promised Land," and therefore, they drove them out to the land of Samaria. And there, they remained; continuing to live as they had for the last generation. And there, they would be known as the dreaded "Samaritans" . . . until Jesus came along.

There's the background; the scene is set. Enter, the Messiah. Recall there are places in scripture where the Samaritans would not welcome Jesus, because he was heading toward Jerusalem (cf. Luke 9:54 ff.). The Samaritans are set up! There is no way they can continue to be Samaritans and still be part of the "chosen people." They were Samaritans . . . they have no chance. So Jesus will encounter this women, who thinks herself already damned . . . at least according to "the Law" and those who became a "people of the Law."

What becomes so clear in Matthew's Gospel, is how someone who is humble, and open, can, in effect, offer salvation even to one who appears damned. This is not for the timid, or the faint of heart. Jesus begins by asking her for a drink. You can imagine the scene. She knew he was a Jew; and she knew, he knew, she was a Samaritan and a woman. In the ancient world, a man could not speak to a woman in public, whom he was not related to in some way. See the audacity of Jesus? He was not politically correct, but he was not callous either. He did not waver in his proclamation of the truth, but he always spoke in love. Because of his love and his risk, he walks with this woman through her illumination and, perhaps, salvation.

Jesus brought many back from the dead. We read about such miracles, and beg him through prayer, to do it in *our day and age.* It is at those times that he responds as he did with his own apostles, when the people were hungry: *"You give them something to eat."* When he raises Lazarus from the dead: *"You unbind him."* And when we encounter those who, in our eyes, might be sinners beyond saving, "You save them . . . you bring them back to life." St. Paul says to the Romans: *"Though it is barely possible that for a good man someone may have the courage to die. It is precisely in this that God proves his love for us: that while we were still sinners, Christ died for us."*

The voice of the Lord is constantly speaking to us. *"If today you hear his voice, harden not your hearts."* His message is clear. *"The water that I give [shall] provide eternal life."* Isn't it time that we shared that water with those who need it most?

FOURTH SUNDAY OF LENT

(I SAMUEL 16:1, 6-7, 10-13; PSALM 23; EPHESIANS 5:8-14; JOHN 9:1-41)

Blindness: the ability to <u>see</u>

As the scholars of the law awaited the Messiah, they had three qualifications that would hearken his arrival. He would have to raise someone from the dead; would have to be able to exorcise demons, and finally, he would have to be able to cure someone born blind. In this Gospel today, then, we can understand why the leaders are becoming so uncomfortable. Jesus has done all three of these.

This story of curing blindness, however, much like the Gospel from last week with the Samaritan woman, is about enlightenment. We move from a blurry understanding of Jesus to full knowledge. The woman at the well went from addressing Jesus as "you, a Jew" to "sir" to "I see you are a prophet" to eventually, "the *Messiah*." This blind man makes a similar journey as he calls him "this man called Jesus" to "Sir" to "a prophet" and finally to the "Son of Man." But this journey isn't all about knowing who Jesus *is*.

There are two types of blindness. There are those who are born blind, and because of this, their brains never develop the ability to visualize as we do. They have no point of reference, because they have never seen. They can't conceptualize "blue" or a "tree," because their brain has no frame of reference. Those who became blind after birth do have a frame of reference, because they once were able to see. Jesus goes on to speak to the Pharisees and elders. He is trying to get through to them that "those born blind have an excuse . . . because they do not know . . . but those who once could see and become blind have no excuse, because they once knew."

Their sin goes beyond even *this*; however, because they are persecuting Jesus for healing on the Sabbath and saying that this man was a product of sin. Jesus has sight that looks beyond the ailments; the idiosyncrasies, and sees the soul and the intent of the man born blind. He sees a man who is not a result of sin in his parents, but someone who is struggling for a new chance at life.

I worked for a bakery in high school. And there was this girl there, who was just plain lovely. But every time I wanted to speak to her, my mouth would dry up, and I would speak as though my tongue was frozen to the roof of my mouth. I would rehearse what I was going to say to her, and was determined each day I entered the bakery that "today would be the day." But by the end of the day I would "wimp out" again. On the other hand, she would often discuss with me the issues in her life; one of which was her boyfriend and their problems (so I had the inside track).

One day she told me that they had finally ended the relationship. She went on and on about how he really didn't care for her, he just wanted a trophy, so to speak. And the words of Paul entered my mind: *"This is an acceptable time!"* I had to leave, so I said to her that I wanted to talk more about this, but how about we meet outside of work. She agreed, and then I suggested that we have dinner and she smiled and said okay. I was in!

I decided that this was a once in a lifetime opportunity, so I wasn't taking anything for granted. This would have to be a night she would remember. Now, usually my parents discouraged such extreme things, but surprisingly, they were trying to help out. I decided that the perfect evening would be to have dinner outside on the pond we had in my small town . . . but how would that happen.

I went to a farmer down the lane and got four tractor inner tubes. I fixed subflooring to the top of the tubes, and there was the raft. I had a small light table on top with all the plates and silver. I had my mom pick up the Chinese food and put it in the fondue with the *Sterno* on for our arrival. I went to pick her up and blindfolded her (I believe she was a little concerned by this), and brought her to the pond.

Upon our arrival, I lit the tiki torches on the corners of the makeshift raft and took her to the boat. The moment she stepped on the edge, the boat tipped a bit and the wine glasses went into the water. Man! No sparkling grape juice tonight, just an empty bottle in an ice bucket. I warned her to watch her step. She finally got seated and we sat on this raft in the pond on a beautifully clear night. I took off the blindfold and she laughed (a good laugh though).

Unfortunately, the Sterno had gone out, and the food got cold, so there we are eating general Tso's Chicken . . . . cold. We had no drinks, so we sucked on ice cubes, and then I looked over at the cheese cake I had prepared for dessert. I thought it looked kind of dark and wondered if the bakery had burned it. Only then did I come to realize that it wasn't burned. But that the top was covered with mosquitoes, which had lighted, and then pasted themselves to the top of it. I'm embarrassed to admit it, but I was actually thinking, "Do you think she would notice?" I was trying to think what I could cover the top with, but then just sighed, and as she looked the other way, knocked the cake into the pond.

Look, I said, "This is a disaster. I don't know what I was thinking. I just wanted to . . ." but she started tearing up a bit . . . and then a small sob escaped. Now I was really feeling terrible. She looked up at me and smiled amidst the tears and said, "Nobody . . . . (pause) nobody has ever done anything like this for me . . . ever. This was wonderful. Thank you so much." That was it! Everything went terribly wrong, even to the spectators who would have seen the scene unfold. But to her, she saw what was behind all the work and effort and really, what it was that was most important. She *saw* the best.

The reading from the book of Samuel says: *Not as man sees does God see, because man sees the appearance, but the Lord looks into the heart.* Jesus says, *"I came into this world to divide it, to make the sightless see and the seeing blind."* Are we one of those who have become blind over time? Or have we just chosen not to walk in the light and see life, as it really is? Miracles are still possible . . . if we want them.

FIFTH SUNDAY OF LENT
(EZEKIAL 37: 12-14; PSALM 130; ROMANS 8:8-11; JOHN 11: 1-45)

You, unbind him.

"Unbind him." Jesus commands the people in the gospel story to unbind Lazarus. In the Gospel of Matthew, he gives the Apostles the authority to bind and loose. He commands even the evil one, in the Gospel of Mark, *"Leave him be,"* and *"release him."* So what can possibly bind us, and how can we be released?

It is evil that binds us. And so often, it is not evil that pursues us, but we, who pursue evil. Fulton Sheen would say: "Left to ourselves, without God, one day our passions might desert us, but we would never desert our passions."[31] It's true. So how is it that evil binds us?

The first way I believe this occurs, is by promising us control of our lives. Let's face it, we are really not in control of anything that is important in this life. Life and death, health and disease, we have no control. But if we *could* control these things, would we not do what was necessary to obtain that control? But even if we were not all that keen on obtaining control, perhaps we were just curious. The ancients spoke of *curiositas* (a curiosity in things that were dangerous). We must be careful to avoid such things which allow evil, not only to endure, but to prosper. Things like false religions: *Santa ria, Santa Muerte,* worship of saints and angels, or idols. But the Devil is so evil, at times he can use something that even seems good or helpful to seduce us.

People will consult psychics or fortune tellers. They will swear they are speaking with a deceased person, and they want to know they

---

31 Bishop Fulton J. Sheen, *Lift Up Your Hearts,* (New York: McGraw-Hill Book Company, Inc., 1950), 200.

are okay. "But father, it was my grandfather. He told me things only my grandfather would know." If your grandfather is in heaven, then he would never go against the law of God . . . he couldn't (read Deuteronomy). If he is in hell, he would not be able to contact you at all. Then the inevitable question would surface, "Then who is it?" Remember, they are fallen angels and have been around longer than grandpa . . . they know more about you than he does. And once we open the door to evil, it is difficult to shut it again. This is how people get bound by demonic forces.

The easiest way is to avoid them. If a person is already bound, then they must find an apostle to unbind them. This occurs through exorcism or deliverance. Jesus gives the apostles the authority to exorcise demons, and they passed on this authority. Something that feeds this evil, and the evil around us at times, is guilt.

Guilt is another thing that can bind us. There is a good guilt . . . when we've done something wrong and we are sorry for it, but there is also bad guilt. When we feel guilty for something we cannot take back, but have made amends for, or something we were not responsible for, or could not change, that is a bad guilt.[32] This can often be more powerful than demonic possession, because it leads to despair. Lent is a good time to let go of the bad guilt, so that we can be free . . . unbound by such evil that leads us away from God.

Finally, we can be bound by a person or situation. Sometimes, we face tremendous difficulties and people who make us feel less than human by most standards. "To believe we are no better than anyone, but no worse than anyone either; to believe that we are the best one of 'us' that God could have created, and to never let anyone define us either by their compliments or their criticisms, because we hold within us the Divine"[33] . . . all beauty . . . all goodness . . . all light, which no one can take from us. And to remember, Jesus raised someone from the dead, but he left it up to us . . . to unbind him.

---

32 Peter, Van Breeman, S.J., *The God who won't Let Go*, (Notre Dame, IN, Ave Maria Press, 2001), 54.

33 Ibid., 39.

"Unbind her." Sketched during retreat at
St. Vincent Archabbey, Latrobe PA.

Cinquinto Domingo
de la Curesma
(Ezequiel 37: 12-14; Salmo 130; Romanos 8:8-11; Juan 11: 1-45)

Usted, *desatenlo.*

"Desatenlo." Jesus exigio al la gente en el evangelio, "desatenlo." En el evangelio de san Mateo, les da a los apostles la autoridad para atar y desatar. El exige a todos, incluso al malo en el evangelio de san marcos, *"dejalo"* y *"Libralo."* Entonces, que puede atarnos, y como podemos estar libre?

Primero, El Mal nos ata. Muchas veces, no es el malo que nos persige, pero somos nosotros que persigimos el malo. Sin Dios, quizas un dia nuestros pecados nos dejaron, pero sin Dios, nunca abandonariamos nuestros pecados. Es verdad! Así que como es possible para el malo que nos ate? La primera manera, yo creo, es por las promesas de Diablo. Las promesas son tomar control de nuestras vidas.

En verdad, nosotros no podamos controlar nada que is muy importante en este vida: vida y muerte; salud y enfermidades, no tenemos control. Pero, si *podemos* controlar estas cosas, hariamos lo necessario para obtener ese control. Aunque no queramos controlar las cosas mas importantes, quizas somos curiosos. Los ancianos dijeron sobre "curiositas" una palabra en latino, significa una curiosidad en las cosas eran peligrosos. Debemos tener cuidado para evitar estas cosas que permiten el mal: por ejemplo, espiritualistas, santa ria, santa muerte, alabanza de los santos, angeles, o idolos. Pero, el Diablo es tan malo, que a veces el usa algo que aperece bueno o algo que nos ayuda.

La gente consultaran con psicicos. Piensen que estan hablando con una persona difunta, y quierien saber que la persona esta bien. "Pero Padre" ellos dicen, "yo dije a mi abuelito." "El me dijo las cosas que solemente mi abuelo sabe." Si tu abuelo este en el cielo, entonces, el no puede romper un mandamiento de Dios. Si el esta en el infierno, no puede ser contactado. Así . . . que quienes es? Un demonio. Recuerdate, ellos son angeles malos, y han existido por mas tiempo que tu abuelito. Ellos saben mas sobre ti, que el. Y quando abrimos la Puerta del mal, es muy dificil para cerrarla.

Esto, es la manera por cual la gente se atan a demonios. La manera mas facile que podamos protegernos es evitarlos demonios. Si una persona esta atada, entonces necessitan buscar un apostle para desatarlo. Esto occure atraves del exorcismo. Jesus les da los apostles la autoridad de expulsar a los demonios, y ellos pasaron esta autoridad. Alguna cosa que alimenta este malo y el malo alrededor de nosotros a veces es cupable.

Hay la culpa Buena. Quando hemos hecho alguna cosa en una manera mala, y sentimos pena es culpa Buena. Pero, quando sentimos la culpa por alguna cosa que no podamos reparar o por alguna cosa que nosotros no tenemos responsibilidad o no podamos cambiar, esto es culpa mala. A veces, esto puede ser mas poderoso que un demonio, por que nos conduce a la desesperacion. La Cuaresma es una buen momento para dejar la culpa mala, para que podamos ser libre . . . . Desatado del mal que nos conduce lejos de Dios.

Finalmente, una persona o situacion puede atarnos. A veces, experimentemos difficultades grandes y gente que nos hace sentir menos que humana. Creer nosotros no somos major que otros, pero tampoco somos peor que otros. Creer que nosotros somos el major que Dios creo, y nunca permitir que cualquier persona nos defina, por sus complementarios o criticas, porque tenemos en nuestras almas el Divino . . . todo la belleza; todo la bondad; toda la luz . . . que ninguna persona nos puede quitar. Y recorder, que Jesus resucito a una persona de entre los muertos . . . pero es nuestro trabajo desatarlo.

Palm Sunday

(PROCESSION WITH PALMS: GOSPEL FROM MATTHEW 21:1-11)

MASS PROPER

(ISAIAH 50:4-7; PSALM 22; PHILIPPIANS 2:6-11; MATTHEW 26:14-27, 66)

There is no resurrection without a Passion

The passion of Christ. In Latin, the word means suffering. What is our passion? For what do we sacrifice? The passion of Christ was for his father and his people. For whom is our passion?

There are some people here, who use their phones or send messages if they receive them during the Mass. There are some people here, who prefer to speak to a person or be with a person rather than speak to God. Others will bring their children to be baptized or receive first Communion, but not for Sunday Mass. Perhaps they come to church only to celebrate the major feasts. But, devotion to God is not about the party or "holiday" we celebrate on our own. For one such as these, the baptism or communion are nothing more than a right of passage or something that is performed, "just in case."

Sometimes, people will request, if not demand, to receive these gifts from the priest, when they want to, how they want to, and even where they want to. However, at the end of this world, they will seek God . . . then they will seek God . . . and God . . . will not remember who they are.

If we have no passion, our devotion is empty. If we have not passion, we will abuse the Sacraments. And if we do not experience our passion, then how can we possibly hope for resurrection?

Domingo de las Ramas

(PROCESIÓN CON RAMAS:
EVANGELIO DE MATEO 21:1-11)

LA MISA

(ISAÍAS 50:4-7; SALMO 22;
FILIPENSES 2:6-11; MATEO 26: 14-27, 66)

Hay no resurrecion sin un pasión

La passion de Cristo. En Latino, la palabra significa sufriemiento. ¿Cual es nuestra pasión? Para que nos sacrificamos? La pasión de Cristo fue por su padre y su pueblo. Para quien nuestra pasión?

Hay algunas personas aquí, que hablarian en su cellular, o envian un mensaj si lo recibieron durante la misa. Hay algunas personas aquí, que prefieren hablar con la persona a ser lado, que hablar a Dios. Algunos solo traieran a sus ninos para hacer bautizados, o recibir comunión, pero no vienen ala misa. Quizas venian ala Iglesia solo para poder celebrar sus quinceañera. Pero la devoción a Dios no les preocupa comparado a la fiesta.

La primera comunión, o la confirmación son nada mas que un paso. A veces algunas personas le mentiran al sacerdote, para que ellos puedan recibir un sacramento en su modo, o su manera, o su fecha. Aunque a final de todo, le hacen burla a Dios . . . y Dios no lo olvidera.

Si nosotros no tenemos pasión, nuestra devocion es vacia.

Si nosostros no tenemos pasión, entonces abusareman de los sacramentos.

¿Si nosotros no tenemos nuestra pasión, entonces como podremos esperar nuestra resurrección?

Solemn Easter Triduum

Holy Thursday
(SEE APPENDIX I)

Good Friday
(SEE APPENDIX I)

Part of a tryptic sketched in Mexico City, "Breathe"

Holy Saturday (Vigil)
(SEE APPENDIX I)

Easter Sunday
(SEE APPENDIX I)

SECOND SUNDAY OF EASTER (DIVINE MERCY)

(ACTS 2:42-47; PSALM 118;
I PETER 1:3-9; JOHN 20:19-31)

Easter means new life

There is a humorous story that goes something like this:

> It was a hot Saturday morning. Because there was no air conditioning, the doors and windows were all open in the church to bring in a bit of air. Some worshipers, out of courtesy, gathered for the funeral service of an old man who had no family. They could also hear an auctioneer's voice from the next building, almost as clearly as they could hear their own minister.

> The service came to an end. "Lord, may thy servant depart in peace," said the minister. Through the window came the words, "going once, going twice, gone!"[34]

We are pilgrims. We are on a journey. The ancients knew what this meant, because they were nomads. They were constantly putting up their tents, making camp, and then moving their herds to the next feeding ground. What this required, was a thinning out of their possessions. They were going to have to carry whatever they kept, so it was not only a purging of the things they really did not need, but also a temperate attitude which excluded certain things.

> *All who believed were together and had all things in common; they would sell their property and possessions and divide them among all according to each one's need. Every day they devoted themselves to meeting together in the temple area and to breaking bread in their homes.*

---

34 Internet Forward

The apostles and their followers will come to leave everything, and follow this new religion. We are not asked to give up everything . . . but we are asked to give up those things which keep us from God. We celebrate Divine Mercy Sunday: that our Lord is so willing to pardon our offenses; so willing to forget the evil we have done, if *we* can only let go of those offenses.

Easter means new life . . . but we cannot live in the "new life" if we refuse to leave behind the old one.

DOMINGO DE DIVINO MISERICORDIOSO

(HECHOS 2:42-47; SALMO 118; I PEDRO 1:3-9; JUAN 20:19-31)

La Pascua significa una vida nueva.

Fue un sabado, por la manana. Por que hay no aire-condicionado, las puertas y las ventanas estaban abiertas en la Iglesia. Algunos Catolicos congregaron en la Iglesia para un funeral de un anciano que no tenia una familia. Ellos pudieron escuchar una subasta a fuera de la Iglesia porque fue Ruidoso.

La misa terminaba y el sacerdote dijo, "Senor, el serviente descanse en paz." Y atraves de la ventana se escuchaban las palabras de la sabasta . . ."a la una, a las dos, vendido!"

Somos peregrinos. Estamos en una jornada. Los antepasados comprendian el significado porque fueran nomados. Muchas veces erigian las carpas y despues, conducian las manadas al proximo campo. Esto requeria que ellos dejaran algunas pertinencias. Necesitaban cargar todo lo que valorisaban, entonces necesitaban no solo dejar cosas pero tambien necesitaban escoger una casa sobre otra.

> *Y todos los que habían creído estaban juntos y tenían en común todas las cosas; y vendían sus posesiones y sus bienes, y lo repartían a todos, según la necesidad de cada uno. Y perseveraban unánimes cada día en el templo y, partiendo el pan en las casas, comían juntos con alegría y con sencillez de corazón.*

Los apostoles y sus discipulos dejaran todo, y seguiran esta religion nueva. El Senor no nos esta pidiendo que dejemos todo, pero el nos esta pidiendo dejar los cosas que nos separan de Dios. Hoy, celebramos el Domingo de la Divina misericordia. Nuestro Senor quiere pardoner nuestros pecados; El quiere olvidar el mal que hemos hecho, si estamos despuestos a abandoner las offensas.

La Pascua significa una vida nueva. Pero, nosotros no podamos vivir la vida nueva, si negamos a dejar la vida posada.

THIRD SUNDAY OF EASTER

(ACTS 2:14, 22-28; PSALM 16;
I PETER 1:17-21; LUKE 24:13-35)

To Love, with the heart of Faith

At times, it is more difficult to love God than it is to love a human. Some might disagree, because they know some humans who seem unlovable. I'm not speaking of the "lovability" of a person, but in general, for a human, it is easier at times to love a human. We need to *see* them; *smell* them; *hear* them; and *feel* their touch. On a tough day, we need to feel their arms embrace us; on a good day, we need to see their smile, reflecting our own. We need them to listen to us, and we need them to trust us with their thoughts and secrets and dreams. At times, it is easier to love a human than it is to love God.

For this reason, he sent his son. Is there any doubt? These disciples on the road to Emmaus are running; running away, because they are scared. Do you think they would be running scared if the person of Jesus was still with them? Isn't that what he promised? *"I will be with you until the end of the ages?"* Sure. So what happens when he appears? They are suspicious . . . maybe a bit paranoid. Perhaps it is a spy; perhaps it is a thief. And yet they are caught off guard, and further surprised, when he begins to preach to them . . . again they can hear his voice; but the scent is unfamiliar; the sound unfamiliar; the touch unfamiliar, until they taste . . . until he breaks the bread for them . . . then they understand.

We have the Sacraments in the Church as the physical presence of God, which we cannot always see, taste, touch, smell, hear. We have the incense, which we smell, reminding us of the presence of God; we have the words of Scripture, and the prayers which roll from the tongue; we have the touch of others, and the feeling of grace within us, through the Sacraments, and the taste of the Eucharist, which feeds us more than any earthly food.

We are given these gifts so that God might have a part in our lives. And if we can love a person, think of the one we love most; if we can offer God the love we would offer our greatest love; how much time would we spend talking to Him; being with Him? What would we be willing to sacrifice for Him? Imagine the presence in our lives; imagine the presence in our heart; imagine the difference it would make, not only to us . . . not only to the two on the road to Emmaus, but to the five thousand who would later be converted, and the five thousand we will encounter in our days ahead.

La Tercera Domingo de Pascua
(Hechos 2:14, 22-28; Salmo 16;
I Pedro 1:17-21; Lucas 24:13-35)

A veces, es mas dificil amar a Dios, que amar a un ser humano. Algunas personas no estaran de acuerdo, por que ellos conocen una persona que es muy dificil amar. Yo estoy hablando en general, es mas facil amar a un ser humano, porque nosotros podemos verlo; podemos olerlo; podemos escucharlo; y podemos sentirlo. En un dia dificil, necesitamos sentir sus brazos alrededor de nosotros; en un buen dia, necesitamos ver su sonrisa. Los necesitamos escuchar y necesitamos confiar nuestros pensamientos, y secretos, y suenos en ellos. A veces es mas facil amar una humana, que amar a Dios.

Por eso razon, envio a su Hijo. Estos discipulos, en rumbo a Emmaus estan corriendo; estan corriendo lejos de Jerusalem porque sentieron miedo. Creen, que si Jesus estuvo presente, habrian non temor? Pero, Jesus prometio, *"Yo estoy con ustedes, todos los dias hasta el fin del mundo."* Sin duda! Entonces, que ocurio quando Jesus aparacio? Se sienten disconfiado. Quizas, el es un espia; quizas un bandido; y todavía, se sentieron inseguros, y estuvieron surprendidos quando Jesus les praedico . . . otra ves, escuchan su voz; pero el olor es diferente; el sonido es diferente; el toque es diferente; hasta, su sabor . . . hasta el partio el pan para ellos . . . entonces, comprenden.

Nosotros tenemos los Sacramentos en la Iglesia; la presencia corporal de Dios, que nosotros no podamos ver ni escuchar, ni tocar, ni oler. Tenemos el incienso, que podemos oler; tenemos las palabras de la escritura, y las oraciones que decimos; tenemos el toque de los demas, y a veces sentimos la gracia atraves de los sacramentos; y tenemos el sabor de la Eucaristia, que nos da alimenta mas que otra comida.

Nosotros tenemos estos dones, para que Dios puede compartir en nuestras vidas. Y si nosotros podemos amar al otro, piensen por un momento cuanto le amamos. Consideran la persona que amamos mas que alguno. Y ahora, ama Dios igual que tu amas esta persona. Cuantas horas compartiamos con el otro? Que sacrificamos por el? Imaginen la precencia en nuestras vidas; imaginen la presencia en nuestros corezones? Imaginen la diferencia en nosotros mismos; y el efecto en otros. Imaginen la diferencia, no solo para los hombres en la calle, pero los cinco mil que mas tarde serian convertidos y lo cinco mil que toda via no conocemos.

Fourth Sunday of Easter

(Acts 2:14, 36-41; Psalm 23;
1 Peter 2:20-25; John 10:1-10)

Living as Sheep of the Good Shepherd

Shepherds and sheep; fences and gates; that's what the Lord has for us this Sunday. I mean let's face it, Psalm 23 has been quoted beyond the walls of churches for centuries. The shepherds hold dominion over the sheep, in obedience to the first command Adam received in the garden. This dominion is a "deal," when you pare it down to what in reality is experienced. *Dominion*, from the Latin *dominus*, which means lord, describes the rold of the lord as the caretaker of the kingdom. The lord protects the serfs and vassals and others within the kingdom from the outside, while on the inside providing them with food and shelter and clothing. The job of the subjects then, is to serve the lord and support the kingdom. There's the deal . . . the *covenant* if you will.

My parents take care of my nephews a few times a week. On one occasion, my dad brought up two rotary phones from the basement of the house, and hooked them up so the boys could play on them (If you don't know what a rotary phone is, look it up in your history book on technology in the 20th century). After a little playtime, my nephew, Logan, approached my dad with the rotary phone in his arms and a confounded look. My dad asked what was wrong, and Logan replied, looking at the phone, "But Papa . . . how did they text?" Smart kid! If you don't know what texting is, ask someone born in the 21st century!

My mother has a place for everything in the living room. I have eleven nieces and nephews. If you can imagine all of those kids coming through, she would have to keep some order. So when it was time to put the toys away, they knew where everything was to be placed. Toward the end though, I observed my younger nephew

Kyle, standing in the middle of the room with the rotary phone in his arms. I asked him what was wrong and he replied, "There's no *place* for this."

"There's no place for this." For some, this phrase is a mantra. We find ourselves confounded with the experiences we live through daily and we ask that question. Whatever we face in life, there is no place for this. I would beg to differ. There is a place for this . . . and that place is here! So often, we deny that part of us that is Godly. We try to find a place where our "stuff" goes, but, as hard as we try, we come up desperately empty. Because there is not a place, this side of time and space, where we can deposit all that stuff, we come up empty! But there is a place for it. Our church has many people who are Catholic, but do not live Catholic. Perhaps because they don't know the teachings of the Church, or misunderstand those teachings. Peter says to the people, *"Save yourselves from this generation which has gone astray."*

What if I stood up here one weekend and said this: "You must fast an hour before Mass on Sunday, every Sunday . . . unless you get hungry; then you don't have to fast." "You cannot use artificial contraceptives, it is against God's intent . . . unless you do not want to have children." "You must go to confession to receive absolution for your sins . . . . unless you're embarrassed or afraid or don't have time, then you can just confess on your own in the privacy of your home." "You must get married in the church, so that your marriage is sacramental . . . unless you want to get married somewhere else." "You must come to Mass on Sunday, or it is a mortal sin . . . unless you have other plans, or it's inconvenient for you, then you don't have to go." Can you imagine? We would have a church full of people, perhaps, who feel good about themselves, and the sacrifices they are *not* making and the sins they are retaining. Where is the sacrifice for our side of the bargain?

Listen to the first letter of St. Peter: " *If you put up with suffering for doing what is right, this is acceptable in God's eyes. It was for this that you were called, since Christ suffered for you in just this way and left you an example, to have you follow in his footsteps."* Jesus does *not* say, *"Whoever does not enter the sheepfold through the gate, but climbs in some other way, is a thief and a marauder . . .* unless your way is easier than mine." He does *not* say at another place, *"Take up your cross and follow me . . .* unless it's too heavy." He essentially says, "If you won't do what I ask (at the very least) then you cannot be my follower . . . so don't pretend."

I'm not speaking of *struggling* with the faith and the teachings of the Church. I'm speaking of *giving up* and just attending without any investment on our part. We are in a covenant as members of the Body of Christ. Covenant comes from the Hebrew word for binding or shackle. But it's time that we start walking **with** God, instead of having him carry our corpse behind him.

There is a place in the heart of God where we can place all our anxieties and struggles; tragedies and triumphs, but there is a responsibility that we must accept as well. To live according to *His* design, not our own; to renew our commitment to this covenant, and accept the cross. It doesn't mean that we run towards it, or chase after it; it doesn't mean we look for suffering, in order to be a servant. It means that we honor the covenant God made with us, which he sealed with the blood of his Son. That we walk with him, who as the good shepherd, calls us by name.

Fifth Sunday of Easter
(Acts 6:1-7; Psalm 33; I Peter 2:4-9; John 14:1-12)

Hope never disappoints

> *Do not let your hearts be troubled. You have faith in God, have faith also in me. In my Father's house there are many dwelling places; otherwise, how could I have told you that I am going to prepare a place for you? . . . Thomas said to him, "Lord we do not know where you are going. How can we know the way?"*

How can we know the way? We do not know where you are going. Why are these guys so scared, when they're with Jesus? The word "love" is used in John's gospel far greater than any other. To speak of love in our day and age can sometimes be confusing, but for the people who were living around John and his ministry at the time this letter was being written, there was no question what love meant.

Let's go back to the nineties. I don't mean the 1990's or even the 1890's, but I mean *the* 90's! The original first century 90's. During the reign of all of the emperors of Rome from the time of Christ, the Christian would be seen as a gadfly; and killed as such. The writer of the fourth Gospel is living in the time of Domitian, who many would see as a reincarnation of Nero. Those caught celebrating the Liturgy (most often in catacombs or graveyards, due to the aversion of Romans to these places) would be killed; or worse yet, have their family killed in their presence, while they were permitted to live. At the time this gospel is being written, many Christians had been crucified, tortured or sacrificed in the coliseum. And so those who continued to live their faith, even amidst this terrible persecution, did so out of a sacrificial love. But even as strong as they were; with a true lived understanding of that *agape* which characterizes John's gospel, they still needed hope.

You can imagine them all sitting huddled together in a cave or a tomb somewhere, having just finished the Mass, and then they ask John: "Tell us what he said again. Tell us that, in the midst of all this pain, one day we will have our reward." And sure enough, the writer of the fourth Gospel would begin, *"Do not let your hearts be troubled."* He wanted them to understand that we were not made for this world, but for the next. He wanted them to understand, that the end of all things, or their death, would not be the end, but a "way" to the "life."

Not all Christians suffered in this manner. There were many who did what they were told by the authorities. They offered incense to idols and worshipped Caesar as a god, even though they didn't believe in that. They were spared, because they didn't actively live their Christian faith. I'm not speaking of them when I speak of this suffering in a sacrificial love. They didn't suffer, at least not in the way some did. They were *uncomfortable*, no doubt about it, but suffering? Not when you do what you're told.

I differentiate between the two, because at times when we discuss suffering, we're not really talking about suffering at all; we're talking about discomfort. When my nephews are in the woods, and they can't get their 4G, or they don't have enough bars on their phone, they claim they are suffering. To me that sounds like discomfort. We might complain about the hard church pews or the long homilies and say we're suffering. And although there might be some truth to that, I would dare to say, that's more discomfort. The people of the 90's were losing their lives, their homes and their livelihoods, because of their loving devotion to their God.

The author of the Letter of St. Peter, is trying to give hope to the people of his congregation, who are also suffering persecution. *That you who have placed your faith in the stone, which is rejected by society, will find yourselves in the house of the Lord, the cornerstone of which is Christ.*

There is a story that comes to us from Cardinal Dolan, back when he was Msgr. Dolan. In his book, *Priests for the Third Millennium*, he writes about a seminarian who was dying from cancer. He seemed so hopeful. When a priest went to visit him and asked him how he could be so positive, knowing that he might die never being ordained a priest he said he had hope. The priest inquired further, "What is hope?" The seminarian responded: "Hope is the gift that God gives us, that keeps us going; when we believe that Jesus is asleep."[35] This is a great message. A message for those of us who suffer because of our faith or any number of other reasons. There is hope in suffering, for a Lover of us who has prepared a place for us. We do not chase after suffering, but it will inevitably find us.

There is no need for hope in discomfort, or the little annoyances of life, but for suffering; hope does not disappoint; and a kingdom awaits.

---

35   Timothy Cardinal Dolan, *Priests for the Third Millenium*, (Huntington, IN, Our Sunday Visitor, 2000), 30.

SIXTH SUNDAY OF EASTER

(ACTS 8:5-8, 14-17; PSALM 66; I PETER 3:15-18; JOHN 14:15-21)

I love equality . . . but I love God more

"I love equality." This was the bumper sticker I saw on the way to cover another church for Masses the other day. It had a rainbow in the background and underneath the symbols for six different religions. There was everything from the "Star of David" to the Wicca symbol. "I love equality." I don't know about you, but my understanding of equal is "same." This means that the sticker would literally mean, "I love sameness" or essentially, I love everyone being treated the same, regardless of who they are.

This sticker had such a profound effect on me because of the wording and what was with it. You see, this person obviously was not a believer in God. How can I make this assertion by a short glance at a bumper sticker? Because they had the "equality" phrase coupled with the symbols for all religions. What that means is that they are all the same or equal, or that none is the truth but they all are the truth. Only a person who believes in nothing, can make such an assertion that "they are all equally the truth." This is a terrible contradiction, and I'm sure they weren't aware of this when they placed the sticker on their car, but think about it.

What is it that makes us equal? Not our intelligence, because there are people smarter than I am. Not our strength, for there are people much stronger than I. Not our speed or our abilities at a certain craft; there are people who are much faster, and have more gifts or less than we do. It must not be our political affiliation or our organizations, because they are as varied as the people who possess them. What is it then that makes us equal? A soul. We each have a soul. And despite the fact that we are created unlike any other ever, we are equal in the eyes of God. We have equal value in the eyes of God. Therefore, the only way we can be equal, is if we have a soul. But . . . if we have no God, then there are no souls. If there are no souls, then there is no equality. And if there is no equality, then "survival of the fittest" is the rule of the day. For the one who does not believe in God, there can be no reason *for* equality, because equality is a lie. But for the one who does believe, equality is not "a" way to live, it is the only way to live!

Now that we have established that you, as a believer, cannot have a bumper sticker that lists the world religions as equal, but as a believer, must treat people as equal in the eyes of God, what does this mean for our life? It means that we live by another set of rules. If there is an objective truth, and if you believe in God there *is* objective truth, then we are designed in a fashion that dictates we follow this divine plan. Jesus will warn us about how difficult this can be:

> *If you love me you will keep my commandments. And I will ask the Father and he will give you another Paraclete . . . to be with you always: the Spirit of truth, whom the world cannot accept, since it neither sees him nor recognizes him; but you can recognize him because he remains with you and will be within you.*

Peter tells us that we need to venerate Christ in our hearts. It is a lifestyle we speak of, but sometimes we tempt the waters . . . we get dangerously close to what might be our demise. Leaving our Lord is not something that usually happens in an instant, or in a day, but happens over time.

I went on retreat one week in late April. It was so nice to sit by the fire in the evenings, and just relax and pray, and even doze on occasion. At the retreat house, they had these little bucket candles of citronella to keep the insects away. These candles represented the absolute irony, because the purpose of citronella is to drive the bugs away, and yet I saw so many which were drawn to the flames, and who knows, even the scent. Perhaps these were the less expensive candles. As I sat, I observed one of these infamous marmorated stinkbugs, which we loathe here in Pennsylvania. He hovered his heavy body around this candle. He would get so close to the flame and then veer off to the left or right. Again, he would hover there, and then dive toward the flame, and, it would appear, his demise, but then he would bank left or right and avoid his incineration once again. I found myself sitting there and gasping as he would get close. I know; I know . . . it's like I was invested in this critter now. And I watched for about five minutes (I know I'll never get those minutes back!), but he got closer and closer until finally, he dove directly into the flame.

The next morning, long after the candles had been extinguished, I saw his body, along with many of his brothers and sisters, forever fossilized in a waxy grave. This was an important lesson for me, which I would like to share with you today. See, they couldn't just experience the light, or feel the gentle heat of the candle. That wasn't enough. They flew by closer and closer, and came out a little hotter, or with the glare still in their compound eyes . . . but they survived. So they took another swoop! It's never enough. They got closer and closer until they were finally consumed.

We're trying to follow the way we were designed, but we get off track. We tempt fate, so to speak. And so things that might draw us away from God, because they are so attractive, soon possess us to the point where we forget to whom we belong. "I love equality" too. But I love God more.

Feast of the Ascension of our Lord
(SEE APPENDIX I)

SEVENTH SUNDAY OF EASTER

(ACTS 1:12-14; PSALM 27;
I PETER 4:13-16; JOHN 17:1-11A)

Whose glory do I show?

John's Gospel can appear confusing if some words aren't explained (and even if some words are explained!). Jesus uses the word "glorify" and "glory" again and again. This word is much like the *Shekinah* of the Old Testament. It means "making seen the presence of God." When Jesus glorifies the Father, he is making Him seen. And when the apostles glorify Jesus, they are making him manifest (seen) to the world through them.

A way we glorify God . . . make God present in the world, is through our everyday actions. But, although our intentions are often good, are our motives pure? Do we work for our neighbor, only to expect something in return? Do we lend money, only to remind those we lended money to every other day or week? Do we perform acts of kindness with the expectation of being thanked or praised? What are our motives? It's a good question to keep us glorifying *God* as opposed to merely gaining for ourselves.

> There was a village in southern Africa. The days were red hot and the nights were freezing, but they had no way to warm themselves. They had to eat, but had no way to heat their food, so they ate their meats and vegetables raw. They had no way to forge weapons and tools, for they had nothing with which to melt metal.

> One day a man came to the village and brought with him fire. He gave the fire to the villagers, but also taught them how to make their own fire, with two sticks rubbed together, a flint, and various other means. He encouraged those who had fire to share it with their neighbors, and before too long, the whole village

had hot food, heated homes and were able to make tools and weapons.

One day, the man who brought the fire moved on to another village to teach them also. For awhile the villagers didn't even notice, because they were so caught up in the great things that fire could do. After a few years someone asked who had first brought the fire in their midst . . . and they couldn't remember.[36]

It's a normal part of life to go through change. Part of that change is having people come through your life and then leave. I know you have had many people enter your lives with a "fire." You may not remember them now; that's normal. You will move on and may forget who those individuals are who brought you that warmth, and illumination. That's normal. But never forget the fire. ***That's when we glorify God***. Our cooperation with the Holy Spirit; our working together; ***that*** keeps the fire alive and burning. Forget the one who brought it, but don't forget the fire . . . the fire is the important thing.

---

36 Internet Forward.

Sieto Domingo de Pascua
(Hechos 1:12-14; Salmo 27;
I Pedro 4:13-16; Juan 17:1-11a)

El Fuego

Había un pueblo en Sur África. Durante los días hacía bastante calor y las noches se sentian heladas. Ellos tenían alimentos, pero no tenían con que arling su comida, en consequencia tenían que comer la carne y las verduras crudas. No tenían manera de forjar armas ni herramientas, porque no tenían con que fundir el fierro.

Un día un hombre llegó al pueblo y trajo consigo el fuego. Le dio fuego a las personas del pueblo, pero también les enseño comó hacer su propio fuego, con dos palos rozados juntos, una piedra, y varios otros medios. El animó a quienes tenían fuego a compartirlo con sus vecinos, y en muy poco tiempo, el pueblo entero tenía comida caliente, hogares con calefacción, y fueron capaces de hacer armas y herramientas.

Un día el hombre que trajo el fuego se fue a otro pueblo para también poder enseñarles alli. Por un tiempo, las personas del pueblo no se dieron cuenta, porque estaban tan asombrados con todo lo que el fuego podia hacer. Después de pocos anos, alguien pregunto quien habia sido el primero en traer el fuego . . . y no pudieron arling.
Pasar por cambios es parte normal en el curso de la vida.

El cardinal Neuman decia: "Vivir es cambiar; vivir perfectamente es haber cambiado a menudo." Parte de ese cambio es formado por la gente que entra a su vida y despues se van. Se que han tenido varias personas quienes han entrado a su vida con ese "fuego." Quizas no los recuerden hoy: esto es normal. Su vida continuará y quizas un día olvidaran esas personas quienes les brindaron calor e iluminación. Eso es normal. Pero nunca olviden el fuego. Nuestra coperación con el Espíritu Santo; nuestro trabajo juntos; eso es lo que mantiene el fuego encendido y ardiendo. Olvida a quien trajo el fuego, pero mantiene el fuego . . . el fuego es lo mas importante.

PENTECOST SUNDAY[37]

(ACTS 2:1-11; PSALM 104; I CORINTHIANS 12:3B-7, 12-13; JOHN 15:26-27; 16:12-15)

Utinam tales esse sani perseveremus quales nos
futures profitemur infirmi.[38]
~*Pliny the Younger, Epistulae, VII, 26*

Thank you for allowing me to share in this celebration. I have never confirmed any classes of children in my almost ten years as a priest. And although I requested several times for a Bishop to be able to offer this Sacrament to you, I can't lie . . . I'm so happy that I am able to confer the Sacrament on you today.

For some of you, this Confirmation will be a stepping stone. It is something we do at the end of eighth grade like a graduation of sorts. For others it will mean a party and presents, or a nice dinner to celebrate. While for others, this will be something that they really did *not* want to do, but have done for fear of hell, or the punishment of their parents, whichever might be worse! And for some of you; you have been looking forward to this for years; perhaps many years, and although you know all "about" the Sacrament, do not have a clue how it will play out in your life, in the years ahead. Today, I address each and all of these groups with the same message. "There will come a time when you believe that everything is finished . . . that will be the beginning."[39]

---

37 Our Bishop having passed away suddenly, I was thrust in the position of "Confirmer", much to my joyful delight! Here is the homily, reflecting on Pentecost and the meaning for these ninth graders who would be confirmed.

38 "If we would only become when well, the men we promised to become when we were sick."

39 Louis L'Amore, *Lonely on the Mountain*, (New York: Bantam books, 1984).

So, first things first. How do we know there is a God? Because if there isn't one, then this is all just a sham and we might as well all go home. I've done this exercise with some of you before, but I think it's important to understand that to be a witness to the faith doesn't mean we understand it completely, but that we can at least demonstrate *WHY* we believe. The early Christians probably knew much less than you do about the faith, and yet they offered their lives for it. I would suggest that they offered their lives, not because they knew everything, but because they had a "why" for their belief.

How do we know there is a God? Think about it. Some of the most brilliant people in the world are self proclaimed atheists. They believe the world and all we know began with a big bang. That is probably the theory you were taught (it is a theory you know). So we have this big bang and all of a sudden, over millions of years this explosion yields order. Wouldn't that be nice? Perhaps your room would be clean more often than not! A law, not a theory, is that everything in the universe tends to disorder . . . not order. So that doesn't seem to jibe, but for the sake of argument, let's say that this explosion or "bang" did yield some kind of order. It still begs the question, "Who lit the fuse?" That is the question right? We all know a firecracker doesn't go off unless the fuse is lit, so this "bang" just have had something outside of the bang to light the fuse. How does that work?

Well it so happens that even the most staunch atheistic scientists acknowledge this quandary. And as they do with most phenomena, they name it. They have called this "lighter of the fuse" the "Singularity." And yes, they signify it with a capital "S." Many of these writers from Dawkins to Gould seem to acknowledge some possibility beyond what we know of the universe.

> Unless half his scientific colleagues were total fools . . . a presumption that Gould rightly dismissed as nonsense, whoever half it is applied to . . . there could be no other responsible way

of making sense of the varied responses to reality on the part of the intelligent, informed people that he knew.[40]

So we've established there is a god (note the small "g," or the capital "S"). Now, is it a good God? Now is where we might move from a small "g" to a capital one. If this god is good, then far from simply being a force, it has a personality. A person is never an object and therefore deserves a capital. Some would argue that we know it is a good God, because he creates. Creation is an act of goodness, but the devil's advocates in the room might argue that with so much evil in the world, it can't be a good God. Perhaps it is a god who creates only to destroy. Although this argument is tempting, it begs the question, what is the focus of evil? And what would evil demand that its creatures focus on. The answer is easy . . . the self. Evil is turned in on the self, and therefore would demand that creation would follow suit. There could be no possibility of rebellion or . . . choice. Do we have choice? Absolutely. We can choose to believe or not believe; love or not love; and therefore, we have free will. An evil god would never create and allow for free will, and therefore, we have a good God, who would rather have the risk of us not believing, or not loving, than have puppets with no ability to love.

So we have a God. And this God is good. But is it a loving God? There is an old adage, "Nemo dat quam non habet." He cannot give what he does not have. I cannot give you money if I have none. I cannot teach you how to sew if I do not know how. Therefore, since we come from God and everything we have is from God, then He must love, because we have the ability to love, no? How many of you love someone? (few hands raised). What! You loveless bunch, how many of you love someone? (More hands this time). Do your parents know you feel this way?! Sure, we love, and therefore, we must have free will; and therefore, we must have received that ability from God. And the God who created all of this; and created you, unlike any

---

40 Stephen Jay Gould, "Impeaching a Self-Appointed Judge." in Alister McGrath and Joanna Collicutt McGrath, *The Dawkins Delusion?: Atheist Fundamentalism and the Denial of the Divine*, (Downers Grove, IL, Intervarsity Press, 2007), 11.

other, can put himself into our human state. And a God who can do that, can put his essence into a piece of bread and a cup of wine . . . that's childsplay to him. And this one who created you, also wants to be in relationship with you.

Someone who is seemingly unreachable . . . do you think He would want you to be able to have a relationship with him? No? Then why did he give you free will? If he didn't want our love, he would surely want us to live according to his design, and therefore, would not offer us free will. So, he wants a relationship with us, and desires to engage with us; and desires that all be saved. So he has spoken, always, to his people. Through the Law and the prophets; through Jesus, and finally through the Holy Spirit, which is what we celebrate today. And as he sent the Spirit; the Spirit did not come empty-handed, but brought gifts. A gift, remember, is not something that we are "due" but something given freely. When we buy a gift, we usually think of getting the person something they can use, or will use. The same is true with God, so he gave us gifts. What are these gifts? Knowledge, Understanding, Right Judgement, Wisdom, Courage, Wonder and Awe, Reverence.

When I was younger I wanted to be Superman. In fact, my mother had made me a red cape out of material and one night, I made a deal with God. I said, "God, if I sleep the whole night with this cape over me, then in the morning, make me Superman." I woke up in the middle of the night, probably because I was cold, and there on the floor was my cape. I had not made it through the whole night, and that is why I am not Superman to this day!

I decided since Superman was out of the question, I would be Batman, because he was, after all, a human with no really special powers, but an ingenuity and courage that I wished to have. As I got older, I began to compile a list of skills and tools I would need in order to fulfill this dream. Some of those skills, whether fighting skills, chemistry skills, driving or scuba diving, I have obtained over time and study, whereas the others I have not yet mastered. In our confirmation, the Lord is providing us with the skills to be a hero, and not just in the faith by any means . . . but in life!

This means an opportunity for change. Putting on the new self . . . a "do over" if you will. That for so long perhaps we were being good, or not being good; being loving, or not being loving; being generous, or being selfish. Our motive was not for goodness, but out of a fear of Hell. "There comes a time when you begin to do what you do, not for fear of hell, but out of Love for God." And that makes all the difference in the world!

This is the story of the apostles, who hung out with Jesus, probably because he was famous; that he promised this "kingdom thing"; that he had magical powers and that, really . . . people loved him. They followed him because they didn't want to go to *Sheol*; they followed him because they wanted some power over their lives; they followed him because he forgave everyone. But . . . after he died . . . after he was gone . . . why didn't they leave too? They are holed up in a room, worried that they will die. They are at the end of their ropes; the power is gone, the fame is gone; the magic is gone. And then . . .

A low rumble begins. It is night. Night when Judas left; night when evil triumphs . . . it was night. They are in darkness for fear that if a light is seen, their hiding place will be exposed. The rumbling continues, almost like a sandstorm; much like the storm on the sea, or the earthquake at the cross; and Peter lights a small taper and moves toward the door as the rumbling increases. And then in a moment, Whooosh! The door flies open and a fiery wind enters the room; and "The darkness does not overcome it." Immediately, the fear is gone and there is courage; the doubt is replaced by understanding and knowledge; the insecurity with wisdom and right judgment; and they stand in awe with reverence for the God of the living and the dead. This is Pentecost . . . this is confirmation.

You see, the *Lord hears the cry of the oppressed; and he is not deaf to the wail of the orphan. He knows no favorites,* so he offers to all of us, in equal extravagance, his gifts. *He does not forget our prayer nor does he deny what we need.*

As the psalmist says: "*He is close to the broken-hearted and those who are crushed in spirit.*" Have you ever been broken hearted? I hope not, but you will be one day. Has your spirit ever been crushed? I hope not, but it will be one day. This is for you! This is for you! It is not something you are being asked to produce, this is for you! This is a gift . . . but we must receive the gift . . . the gifts.

I remember a time when I was like this Pharisee in the Gospels. I had decided before going to college that I might become a priest one day (go figure!). So I would try to stay clear of all those things that are not necessarily good for a student, let alone anyone. So drugs and alcohol and some of the behaviors that follow would be verboten to me. The danger, however, when you try to keep yourself on the straight and narrow, is that you might begin to isolate others. I began to set myself up as the judge. I would observe some others participating in the activities I had placed beneath me, and so they also were beneath me. And as I condemned people, perhaps for the only thing they were doing wrong, I began to become more and more isolated. I was an island. And what followed was lonliness and depression. But I could not escape from this prison I erected around myself.

I remember at times praying for death (yes I still prayed). And one of those evenings, I received a call from a friend on campus who was sick and wanted me to walk her to the medical center on campus. Shippensburg campus was dark back then, so reluctantly, I agreed and we made our way to the health center. As she was in seeing the doctor on call, I picked up what was the closest magazine I could find. In this magazine, was a page designated "quotable quotes" and as I perused the page, all of a sudden something caught my eye. I read the quote twice . . . and then again. I was struck at how time seemed to stop. It was as though a haze was lifting and for the first time in a long time . . . I could see! I looked around to see if anyone was watching and I tore that page from the magazine. Up until a few years ago, it was framed in my office, because it changed my life. I had been praying for a miracle, and that miracle was here. The quote read, "There will come a time when you believe everything is finished . . . that will be the beginning." And for me, it was.

That, was when *my* confirmation took place! Then . . . at that moment . . . I received the gifts that had been offered six years before.

I can only imagine how different that time would have been, had I welcomed the Spirit when I needed it most, as opposed to when I was in the upper room awaiting death.

So I ask you today . . . what do you want? What do you want? We have established there is a God. We've established this God who created you when He didn't have to, desires to give you what you need. This God who wants to embrace you when your heart is broken; lift you up when your spirit is crushed. This is not some mythology or ancient religion that is powerless to affect our life. This is a force that cannot be controlled by us any more than life or death or health. But one that is freely offered to us if we but receive it.

My dear dear children. This is the gift that no one can ever take from you; This is the day in which the Lord has made a special appointment to be with you; the day when you receive what you need to be a hero . . . a heroic witness to the power of the supernatural in the world. What do you want for your life? Is this a stepping stone? A mini-graduation? A party and some presents? Because there will come a time when you believe that everything is finished . . . perhaps *this* is that time . . . let it be the beginning.

TRINITY SUNDAY

(EXODUS 34:4B-6, 8-9; DANIEL 3:52-56; II CORINTHIANS 13:11-13; JOHN 3:16-18)

One turn deserves another . . .

"John 3:16." It's a bumper sticker, a sound byte, a quotable quote. We like those. Short and to the point. The promise of salvation and a God who loves. But what is the responsibility that goes with that citation. You see, there's not only one verse in John chapter three; and there are other chapters that help to illumine what he wants us to know.

The Gospel stresses that Jesus did not come into the world to condemn, but make no mistake, he will judge. If we continue that Gospel, he says: *"Just as Moses lifted up the serpent in the desert, so the Son of Man will be lifted up."* Now, recall that Moses mounted the serpent on the pole, because the stiff-necked people sinned against God, and moreover, rebelled against God. This was not an accidental sin or offense, but down right rebellion. When the people looked on the serpent, mounted on the pole, they were healed. And as we *"look upon him whom we have pierced"* we too are healed. Because both the serpent, and the savior represent our rebellion.

St. Paul will say, *"He who knew no sin, became sin . . ."* And only when we acknowledge that sinfulness can we be healed. The verses from the Second reading today, finish the letter to the Corinthians. The message is much the same: look at your rebellion and make a change. Well, what does this have to do with Trinity Sunday?

We believe that our God is three persons, equal in majesty and splendor. But within this Trinity of Love, is a generosity of being. We are invited into relationship with a Trinitarian God that not only loves us into being, but guides us with a Spirit of knowledge and wisdom and courage and judgement and understanding and piety

137

and, wonder and awe. And yet with all these gifts, when we rebel and wander like honery sheep, we have a Good Shepherd who is not only willing to bring us back, but pay the ransome for our rebellion.

The sad reality is that even with a Trinitarian parent the rearing is not without its challenges. Ask any of the prophets. But the opportunity for the fulfillment of the promise is there. Jesus will state later in John's Gospel: *"The Father does not wish that I should lose any of those that he gave me, but that I should raise them up on the last day."* He can't lose what was never there.

We are given the opportunity again and again. The statement of John 3:16 is true to form, and as St. Paul says: *"God will always be faithful, for he cannot deny himself."* He will not lose any of them that he was given . . . but many will walk away. The first step is a turning of the self . . . a metanoia. A turning toward the symbol of our sin, and then a turning away from the sin, to the Savior. And then anything we do after, will always be "In the name of the Father, and of the Son, and of the Holy Spirit.

FEAST OF CORPUS CHRISTI

(DEUTERONOMY 8:2-3, 14-16; PSALM 147;
1 CORINTHIANS 10:16-17; JOHN 6:51-58)

I believe . . .

Why am I here? What am I to do? How will, what I do make a difference? Those are life's questions, no? These are what the journey is all about. But I want to take it to a different level. In fact, I want to make it immediately important, and hopefully immediately answerable. Why am I . . . here? Well, not me. I'm here because the Bishop sent me. But why am I here in a church as opposed to any other place? What am I to do? Yeah, right. In this life and the life to come, sure I know what I'm supposed to do . . . but because I am HERE, what am I supposed to do? And how will what I do make a difference? That IS the question.

Why am I here? Because if I miss Mass I might go to Hell. Well . . . that's true, but a reason to be here? Because my parents made me come . . . . GOOD! Nothing wrong with that. They make you go to school too, and left to yourselves, you might not go on your own. But why am I here? Nothing else to do on Sunday . . . sense of guilt if I don't? Want to see my friends? Perhaps it would be better to flash back about 1900 years ago.

They were huddled in a crypt, the dank smell of death around them. Probably the faint odor of spent olive oil as the few torches waxed and waned, casting shadows on the stone walls of a cave where no one expected to find the living. Many of us would now understand the words of the angel to Mary of Magdala, "Why do you seek the living among the dead?" And there, they shuddered as they heard a sound, for fear this might be the last one . . . the last what? The last Mass. They would risk it all . . . land, children, lives, for what? For the Eucharist! The Body and Blood of Christ.

There was no question why they were there; the reason was obvious. The Eucharist. For them it was not a matter of being entertained or comfortable; on the contrary, they were scared. It was not a matter of going to Hell if they did not attend, for they had every reason not to. For them, even amidst the threat of persecution, the Mass was not an inconvenience, or something they did, on the way to something else. It was the source of life for them. Why ARE we here? This is why. Jesus said: *"Unless you eat my flesh and drink my blood you have no life within you."*

What am I to do? BELIEVE IT! Some might question it; some might say it is a symbol; some might say it's just spiritual, and if they know the truth, they are liars, if they do not, then they are ignorant. But if we know the truth, and live as if we don't; or don't know the truth and act as though we do, then we are the most pitiable of men. They would not have risked everything in the catacombs for a piece of bread . . . for a symbol. I will not die for a picture of my niece or nephew; but would I die for the person? Absolutely!

We must believe because Jesus said it is so. If a God can create all of nature, and mankind as we know it, to put His very essence in a piece of bread is nothing! It is true. Because people will not erect great cathedrals and basilicas to a symbol; they will not write great hymns and psalms to a mythology, and they will **not** suffer and die for a God who cannot save! They will not. This is not a part of our faith, but the foundation of our faith. Without it . . . what else is there?

Fr. Ted tells a story of his priestly assignment in Shamokin, Pennsylvania. He said one evening that a parishioner approached the house with her grandson. Her grandson was not Catholic, and she wanted to take him into the church and point out all of the different aspects of the Catholic church. As she walked him through the church and showed him all the statues and pictures, the altar, and the baptismal font, suddenly the boy paused and asked: "What's that red candle for?" He was pointing to the sanctuary lamp that indicates Jesus is present. She replied, "That's to draw attention to Jesus. He is in that gold box called a tabernacle." "Jesus is in there?!" he replied.

"Yes. He's in there all the time." The boy looked up with admiration and said: "Boy, your church is so lucky!"[41]

How will what I do make a difference? If we believe what we say we believe, then we will necessarily live our life differently. We must. So we will not pray to be seen, but not be afraid to be seen praying. We will not dress for others to see, when we come to Mass, but so that others will see what is most important; we will fast, knowing that the most important thing in the world is about to make His home in my body. We will carry ourselves differently; we will love differently; we will look at others differently and in that way, help them to see beyond what appears to be a piece of bread in this world; to what those who have gone before us now see in reality . . . the *Corpus Christi* . . . the resurrected Body of Christ!

Our church is lucky? No. We don't believe in luck. Our church is ***blessed***!

---

41 Keating, Fr. Ted. Comments made during his forty hours devotions, Tuesday, September 17th 2013.

La Fiesta del Cuerpo y Sangre de Cristo

(Deuteronomio 8:2-3, 14-16; Salmo 147; I Corintios 10:16-17; Juan 6:51-58)

Yo creo

Todos estamos en busca de "lo real." A nadie le gusta las imitaciones. " Es hecho en casa?" Estas usando "madera real?" "Esto es autentico?" "Lo viste en vivo en concierto?" Aun con nuestros deportes, cuando nos enteramos que alguien esta usando drogas para mejorar su funcionamiento, o nos enteramos que un cantante solo esta sincronizando sus labios, nos sentimos engañados o robados. Nadie, si les preguntarían si quisieran la imitación o lo verdadero, escogerían la imitación. Deseamos lo real y verdadero y bueno, no un impostor barato; no algo fabricado y hecho para parecer real.

En el decimoquinto siglo, nuestra iglesia paso por una división destrazosa. Un sacerdote agustino llamado Martin Luther vio que habían abusos en la iglesia. Algunos de estos, él menciono, tenían que ver con indulgencias que fueron vendidas en ese tiempo a varios sacerdotes y obispos. El no estaba de acuerdo con la parte que el idioma latín tenia que ver en la misa y quería que la gente usara el idioma común. El pensaba que la Eucaristía era tan importante, y que debe ser ofrecida con mas frecuencia y bajo los especies (la hostia y el cáliz). Lo que quizás le sorprenderá es que él no quiso separarse de la iglesia Católica; y que nunca quiso una reformacion.

Martin Luther fue el ultimo monje en dejar su monasterio, y cuando se marcho, todavía tenia su habito y tenia la tonsura afeitada en su cabeza. El tenia alguno de las escrituras mas bonitas sobre los Santos y la Virgen María, y si leen sus escrituras, no habrá duda que el creyó en la Virgen María y en la Verdadera Presencia en la Eucaristía. Entonces que paso? La iglesia Luterana surgió y tuvo el dominio; los calvinistas hicieron una asamblea en Ginebra y después tomaron sus modificaciones de la fe católica y desde ese entonces tenemos iglesias llamadas no por santos, sino por fundadores o "estilos de religión." Ahora, en ese tiempo el norte y oeste de Europa se estaban separando, muchos se agregaron a la separación, no para hacer un esfuerzo para encontrar la verdad, sino para poder tomar mas esposas y de esa tradición otras asambleas comenzaron a salir. Y mientras todo esto sucedía . . . Martin Luther estaba dando vueltas en su tumba!

Los Judíos murmuraban de Jesús porque el dijo, "Yo soy el pan de vida que ha bajado del cielo," entonces como es que sabemos? Solo en Lebanon hay sienes de iglesias, muchas se encuentran en una calle. Entonces que tenemos nosotros que no tengan ellos? NOSOTROS tenemos la Eucaristía . . . el centro de nuestra fe. "Pensé que el centro de nuestra fe es Jesús?"

EXACTAMENTE. Solo en la misa, Jesús transforma el pan y vino en el "Pan de vida y el cáliz de la salvación eterna." La comunidad Luterana no tiene esto; la comunidad Metodista no tiene esto; la comunidad Anglica no tiene esto; la iglesia unida en Cristo no tiene esto; los evangélicos no tienen esto, y el misterio es que ELLOS NO LO NEGARAN!

Ellos tienen "comunión" a quien cualquiera puede ir, por que es una representación de Cristo. Un símbolo. Hasta algunas comunidades mas cercanas a nosotros dicen que ellos tienen la presencia de Cristo en el "pan", y dicen que Cristo esta presente a un lado del pan y cuando el servicio termina, el pan se reserva únicamente pan. Nosotros no decimos que Cristo existe "con" el pan, nosotros decimos que el pan es transformado en el cuerpo de Cristo y el vino en su sangre.

Nuestra fe es diferente, por que la creencia en la Eucaristía no es un "aspecto" de esto, sino lo mas esencial. Creer en la presencia real de Cristo en la Eucaristía es la fundación de nuestra fe. Si El no nos entrego su cuerpo y sangre, entonces lo que el dice en el Evangelio debe de, en el mejor de los casos, frustrarnos y en el peor de los casos, nos espantaría: "Yo soy el pan vivo que ha bajado del cielo; el que coma de este pan vivirá para siempre: y el pan que yo les daré es mi carne para que el mundo tenga vida."

No quedamos satisfechos con las imitaciones en nuestras vidas. NOSOTROS queremos lo que es real y autentico, lo que cambia vidas, no alguna imitación barata. Solamente hay un lugar a donde ir para recibir a Nuestro Señor en la Eucaristía. Solo hay una celebración donde podemos recibir el cuerpo glorioso de Cristo en nuestro cuerpo. Como sabemos? Por que el nos dijo, y después le dijo al primer papa, Pedro y a los primeros obispos. Los apóstoles: "Te he entregado las llaves del Reino del cielo. Lo que tu ates aquí, quedara atado; lo que tu desates aquí quedara desatado." Y dijo: "Hagan esto en memoria mía."

NINTH SUNDAY IN TEMPUS PER ANNUM

(DEUTERONOMY 11:18, 26-28; PSALM 31; ROMANS 3:21-25, 28; MATTHEW 7:21-27)

Will we Settle, or Soar?

There is a story of a man who was on a diet. He knew he was supposed to eat better, because his doctor told him that. He knew he needed to lose weight, because his clothes were tight. (It's not me, just so you know.) But he was driving down the street and just wanted a fresh donut. He could smell them as he approached that Cumberland street intersection, and so he made a deal with God. He said, "Lord, if you want me to have a fresh donut, then as I pull through the next intersection, there will be an open parking spot for me in front of the store. If there is not, then I will know you wanted me to just drive on by." As he pulled around the intersection, there, in front of the store was an open place. The man muttered his gratitude: "Thank you Lord, that I only had to go around the block eight times before a place opened up."[42]

One who builds his house on sand, eats up his time by continually putting in more supports; retaining walls and grasses in the hope that it might become more structurally sound. In the end, though, it really *is* like trying to "stack sand." Someone either wastes a tremendous amount of time or a tremendous amount of resources. But why do we do it? Because we have lost our inner peace? Because we are restless? When did we lose our inner peace? We didn't lose it . . . we surrendered it. We traded in the rock, for the sand, not realizing that sand is really only weak rock that tumbled through the mountain rivulets into the ocean; to be moved by whichever current was strongest at the time.

---

42 Internet Forward

Many of us have no opinions anymore. Sheen would say:

> Mass opinion is created by the few magazines which are most
> widely sold . . . Mechanized opinion, imitation of our cheap
> 'celebrities' dependence on "they say" or "they are wearing" for
> our guidance dwarf the modern man's individuality."[43]

Is this not true? So we try for the greatest and biggest, in our
super-size society, in order to fill the void we have created, where once
our peace of mind rested. We try to keep up, and in keeping up we
devalue our person.

> "Pliny once said, 'Not being able to make our values beautiful,
> we make them huge.' So our country comes to be known, not
> for its values, but for its architectural wonders and wealth, lest we
> forget that Egypt build her greatest pyramids on the eve of her
> decline."[44]

What is the solution then against this monster? How can we combat
a loud force that is not satisfied with denying God, but seeks to
destroy Him? By building our house on solid rock. Reclaiming
the inner peace which tells us that we have all we need within our
covenant with God. He says it in the beginning:

> *I set before you here, this day, a blessing and a curse: a blessing for*
> *obeying the commandments of the LORD, your God, which I*
> *enjoin on you today; a curse if you do not obey the commandments*
> *of the LORD, your God, but turn aside from the way I ordain*
> *for you today, to follow other gods, whom you have not known.*
> *(Deut. 11:26-28)*

A curse is not something that God casts on us. The Lord says: "I set
before you . . ." It is a choice. A choice to build on sand . . . or stone.
The choice is the God we know . . . or the ones we have not known

---

43 Fulton J. Sheen, *Lift Up Your Heart*, (New York, NY, McGraw-Hill Book
    Co., 1950), 204.
44 Ibid., 205.

(because they are illusions!) Only when we build our house on this foundation, do we even have a chance of surviving. So it's not all up to God. He offers the foundation, but it is up to us to build. Our willpower is not enough, because we are flawed. We must anchor the structure on rock, but then build the structure. It is up to us, working hand in hand with the divine architect.

In the end the choice is ours. It's the difference between building our house on sand, or anchoring it in stone; the difference between depending on our willpower, or counting on the one from whom we have received everything; between going several times around the block just to get a donut, or taking a different path; going in a different direction; away from what holds us grounded, and building towards the sky.

Noveno Domingo del Tiempo Ordinario

(Deuteronomia 11:18, 26-28; Salmo 31; Romanos 3:21-25, 28; Mateo 7:21-27)

He aquí yo pongo hoy delante de ustedes la bendición
y la maldición.

Hay una historia de un hombre que estaba siguiendo una dieta. Él sabía que debería alimentarse con comida saludable, porque se lo había ordenado su doctor. Sabía que tenía que bajar de peso, porque sentía su ropa un poco ajustada. Pero un día estaba conduciendo por la calle y quería un pastelillo. Él puede oler los pastelillos mientras llegaba al cruce de la calle de Cumberland. Así que hizo un trato con Dios. Él dijo, "Señor, si quieres que yo disfrute de un pastelillo fresco, entonces debe haber un estacionamiento libre para mi enfrente de la tienda." Así que, mientras el conducía cerca de la tienda, allí, enfrente de la tienda, había un estacionamiento libre. Él hombre murmuraba su agradecimiento: "Gracias Señor, estuve que dar la vuelta ochos veces antes de que hubiera un espacio libre."

Quien construye su casa sobre la arena, pierde su tiempo en poner más soporte en el hogar; manteniendo paredes firmes y pastos verdes, con la esperanza de que un día la casa pueda ser más segura. A pesar de esto, al final, verdaderamente es como intentar de apilar arena. En el major de los casos, es una pédida de tiempo, en el peor de los casos, es imposible. ¿Pero, por qué lo hacemos? Porque hemos perdido nuestra paz interior. ¿Cúando fue que perdimos nuestra paz interior? Nunca la perdimos . . . la renunciamos. Renunciamos a la roca, al elegir la arena, sin darnos cuenta que la arena es roca debil, que cayó de las montañas al mar para ser por cualquier corriente en ese momento.

Muchos de nosotros, ya no tenemos opiniones. El Obisbo Sheen diría:

La gran opinión es creada por las pocas revistas que son ampliamente vendidas . . . las opinions mecanizadas, la imitación de nuestras celebridades de mal gusto y la dependencia que sientimos al desear saber lo que "ellos dicen" o lo que "ellos visten" porque nuestra orientación es disminuida por la individualidad del hombre." [45]

¿Acaso no es donde una vez habitaba nuestra paz interior? Intentamos conseguir lo más grande de todo en nuestro mundo para de llenar ese basío que hemos creado donde una vez habitaba nuestra paz interior. Tratamos de mantenernos al tanto, y mientras hacemos esto, nos devaluamos a nosotros mismos.

"Pliny dijo una vez, 'Al no poder hacer nuestros valores hermosos, los hacemos inmensos.' Así se llega a conocer nuestro país, no por sus valores, sino por sus edificios y sus riquezas, y no olvidemos que Egipto construyo sus gran piramides en la vispera de su derrota."

¿ Qué es la solución contra este monstro? ¿Cómo podemos arling a un mundo que no esta satisfecho con negar a Dios, sino tambien busca destruirlo? Construir nuestra casa sobre la roca. Reclamar la paz interior cual nos dice que tenemos todo lo que necesitamos dentro de nosotros. Él dice en el principio, "He aquí yo pongo hoy delante de ustedes la bendición y la maldición. La bendición, si obedecen los mandamientos des Señor, su Dios, que yo les promulgo hoy; la maldición, si no obedecen los mandamientos del Señor, su Dios, y se apartan del camino que les señalo hoy, arling en pos de otros dioses que ustedes no conocen."

Una maldición no es algo que Dios impone. El libro dice "He aquí yo pongo ante ustedes . . ." Es una opción. La opción para construir sobre la arena . . . o sobra la roca. La opción es entre el Dios que conocemos . . . a los que no hemos conocido (porque ellos son iluciones). Sólo cuando construimos la casa en esta fundación, es que tenemos la oportunidad de sobrevivir. Así que no todo depende de

---

45 Ibid., 204.

Dios. Él ofrece la base, pero de nosotros depende si construimos sobre esa base. Nuesta voluntad no es suficiente porque tenemos defectos. Debemos atar la estructura sobre la roca, y entonces nosotros construimos el edificio. Nosotros necesitamos a trabajar al lado del Arquitecto divino.

Al final la decision es nuestra. Es la diferencia entre la construcción de nuestra casa sobre la arena, o atarla a la roca; la diferencia entre depender en nuestra voluntad o depender de Quien hemos recibido todo; entre manejando varias veces alrededor de la cuadra para comprar un pastelillo, o tomar un camino diferente; lejos de lo que nos ata y no mantiene construyendo, un camino hacia el cielo.

TENTH SUNDAY IN TEMPUS PER ANNUM

(HOSEA 6:3-6; PSALM 50; ROMANS 4:18-25; MATTHEW 9:9-13)

The greatest gifts are presence

Hope is not naïve. Hope is to give up everything for a dream, even if others can't see that dream. Hope is to see the eagle in the egg and the butterfly in the caterpillar.[46] One can only truly love if they have hope. Because without hope, we cannot see the best, and so we might begin to confine people to what we know of them, and forget that we are all born of God's longing.

Hope is what the book of Hosea is all about. It doesn't mean things will always go our way, but that if we cooperate with God, things will always go the best for us. Hosea is a great book for us, because it illustrates most completely God's mercy . . . God's love.

Paul speaks of Abraham as one who has hope. He was promised a son, and yet was getting "up there" in years. Anyone else would've given up at that point and began to second guess what they were told by God, but not Abraham. He waited, and he was rewarded for his patience. We can only have hope, however, if we can trust. Remember Hosea.

Last Thursday, I celebrated my eighth anniversary as a priest. It was pretty uneventful, considering it really is like a wedding anniversary for me. Make no mistake, my ordination day was one that will remain at the top of my list for the years to come. The day I felt most like a priest, however, was not that day in June, 2004; but the year after. It was my one year anniversary. I had made plans to have a Mass with my family and friends in the afternoon at my home parish of St.

---

46 Rev. Anthony DeMello, *Conferences*.

Anthony of Padua in Lancaster. We were to have Mass and then go to a nice restaurant afterwards. The plans were all set, but as I sat in the rectory, preparing for the afternoon, the phone rang. The rule in the house was that whoever answered the phone, dealt with whomever was calling.

The call came from the hospital. It seemed one of my high school kids was in the psychiatric unit at the medical center, and her parents wanted me to go in and see her. The nurse was careful to tell me that the parents requested my visit, not the girl. I made the call to my parents, and told them that I had to take care of this, and, if they wished to do so, they could still go out for dinner (of course I would not be paying for said dinner!). I gathered my things and headed out the door to the hospital.

I have to admit (although I'm embarrassed to do so) that I was a bit resentful. My first anniversary with all these plans in place, and now this. I thought about how hard I had worked throughout the year, and all that had been accomplished. I became more resentful as I grew closer to the hospital and my encounter with this patient.

I entered the wing on the second floor, and the nurse asked me to sign-in while inquiring who I was here to see. She remarked, "Father, she's not talking to anyone. She doesn't want to see anyone." "Well, she's gonna see me!" I responded a bit curtly. I entered the room, and her blond head rested on her hands. She looked up briefly enough to let out a "humph!" and then lowered her head once again. Not knowing how long I would be there, or whether I would have to wait to see her, I brought my breviary along. This is the prayer book that priests and religious use daily as their prayer for the Church. It did not appear that she was going to speak, and I considered that I had cancelled plans and drove all the way out here, so I decided that at least I would pray with her, even if she did not participate.

In the breviary, there is a section for Night Prayer, the prayer we pray at the very end of the day. Friday evening of this sequence has Psalm 88 as the centerpiece. Now most of the Psalms will end on a high note. Sure, many times they will drag us through the basement of Hell, but the end makes it all worthwhile. Psalm 88 is different. Psalm 88 kinda leaves you in the basement. The last line goes something like: "You have taken away all my friends; my only friend is darkness." If you weren't depressed when you started praying this one, you certainly were at the end. But something within me pressed the words to that Psalm from my mouth. As I prayed this Psalm, the girl looked up, and this time, her head did not drop back. I noticed in the periphery, a few tearlets dropping from her eyes. And then the prayer was finished.

She looked at me and said: "That's . . . in there?" In other words, someone from the Bible felt like that? Felt like I feel? Then the words rolled very quickly from her tongue. She found a companion on the journey from this lonely psalmist, who many hundreds of years ago, felt as she did right now. She spoke for a few hours, and then I really did have to leave. That day began a relationship that lasts to this day. She is everyday a part of my prayer.

I returned to the parish. All the lights were off. Everything was locked up. I walked into the little daily Mass chapel by myself, and celebrated Mass for my first anniversary . . . alone. I have never felt more like a priest than that day. And I shudder to think that I might have missed that gift!

That God sees the best in me, even when I do not show him the best: that is hope. And when I can look at crisis and find opportunity, and even a gift; then I have that hope. And it is such hope, that made Hosea the man he was; it is such hope that lead Jesus to choose a tax-collector for an apostle; and it is such hope that can offer us a second chance; when we would not offer ourselves a second chance. St. Paul said it best: *Hope does not disappoint*. And the fruit of hope is Love.

ELEVENTH SUNDAY IN TEMPUS PER ANNUM

(EXODUS 19:2-6; PSALM 100; ROMANS 5:6-11; MATTHEW 9:36-10:8)

Son of Man, In-Humanity

Jesus, in his humanity, must have had days when he was just tired. Days when the paralytics, the demon-possessed, the lepers and the lame were just too much for him. I imagine as well, that there were times when he had a bit too much of the apostles. It was during these times, that I think he would send them out on mission. That would give him time to refresh, and give them time to get to know each other.

I don't believe that this seemingly selfish reason is the *only* reason Jesus sent them out; I mean there was much work to be done. But the work that had to be done was not only external; within the field of the faithful, but also internal among the apostles themselves. Lest we forget that one will betray him, one will deny him, two will argue about who is the greatest in the kingdom, one will doubt him and the others will have their own issues. Jesus was not the H.R. rep for this troop, but at times *de facto*, he had to deal with personnel issues. So if his motive was not getting rid of them for a few days, what was the purpose of training these "harvesters?"

The Israelites had come a long way since the Exodus, when God made the new covenant with them saying: *"If you hearken to my voice and keep my covenant, you shall be my special possession, dearer to me than all other people, though all the earth is mine. You shall be to me a kingdom of priests, a holy nation."* Now many years later, the "holy nation," this *Am Segulah,* is falling into the same traps as the "not so chosen" people. Paul speaks of this to the Romans: *"For if when we were God's enemies, we were reconciled to him by the death of his Son, it is all the more certain, that we who have been reconciled, will be saved by his life."* God's enemies?! Wow. That's a strong word. This is the broken world that Christ was sent to save, and he comes to realize that the world is so broken, that he's gonna need some help. What's more, he will need custodians to remain, once he ascends to the father. These custodians will have to rely on each other; and work together to build up the kingdom. They will also have to wield power with humility; the humility that Christ displayed in his care of the sheep.

Even in his humility, however, Jesus must have been intimidating to many. We've heard of the episode when Jesus approaches Peter after the miracle of the catch of fish, and hard-headed, emboldened, earthy, Peter, falls to his knees, not even looking at Jesus. So what Jesus does is train these emissaries (the word comes from the same root as missionary) so they can be sent to the people in order to extend his love and forgiveness and healing, through a less intimidating, less famous channel.

The other method to this mission, is trying to empower these Apostles to learn to love each other, and depend on each other, so that they can survive together in the years to come. Jesus probably lined them up, and then found the two of each group that couldn't *stand* each other; and then paired them up for a few days to work it out!

In our diocese, we have a program for seminarians. During a summer, they will go out on a farm, just a few of them, and there, they will pray and work and cook and clean together. It is an exercise in living together with those you don't always like; working together with those who might not work as you do; praying together with some who have a different prayer style or charism. And at the end of the summer, these men are changed. Having experienced this hot, uncomfortable summer on mission, it was not ***they*** who went forward to heal and expel demons and offer forgiveness, but it was they who were healed; gave up their demons, and were forgiven.

In this lesson today, Christ gives us the model of how to live as part of a Christian community, and how to evangelize in the kingdom. The harvest is abundant, but the laborers are few, because most laborers are unwilling to make such sacrifices. The apostles put the human face on Jesus, and by adopting the way of Jesus and showing others Jesus wherever they went, they made Jesus incarnate again.

There was once a man who didn't believe in God, and he didn't hesitate to let others know how he felt about religion and religious holidays, like Christmas. His wife, however, did believe, and she raised their children to also have faith in God and Jesus, despite his disparaging comments.

One snowy Christmas Eve, his wife was taking their children to a Christmas Eve service in the farm community in which they lived. She asked him to come, but he refused. "That story is nonsense!" he said. "Why would God lower Himself to come to Earth as a man? That's ridiculous!" So she and the children left, and he stayed home.

A while later, the winds grew stronger and the snow turned into a blizzard. As the man looked out the window, all he saw was a blinding snowstorm. He sat down to relax before the fire for the evening. Then he heard a loud thump. Something had hit the window. Then another thump. He looked out, but couldn't see more than a few feet. When the snow let up a little, he ventured outside to see what could have been beating on his window. In the field near his house, he saw a flock of wild geese. Apparently they had been flying south for the winter, when they got caught in the snowstorm and couldn't go on. They were lost and stranded on his farm, with no food or shelter. They just flapped their wings and flew around the field in low circles, blindly and aimlessly. A couple of them had flown into his window, it seemed.

The man felt sorry for the geese and wanted to help them. The barn would be a great place for them to stay, he thought. It's warm and safe; surely they could spend the night and wait out the storm. So he walked over to the barn and opened the doors wide, then watched and waited, hoping they would notice the open barn and go inside. But the geese just fluttered around aimlessly, and didn't seem to notice the barn or realize what it could mean for them. The man tried to get their attention, but that just seemed to scare them, and they moved further away. He went into the house and came with some bread, broke it up, and made a breadcrumbs trail leading to the barn. They still didn't catch on. Now he was getting frustrated. He got behind them and tried to "shoo" them toward the barn, but they only got more scared, and scattered in every direction except toward the barn.

Nothing he did could get them to go into the barn, where they would be warm and safe. "Why don't they follow me?" he exclaimed. "Can't they see this is the only place where they can survive the storm?" He thought for a moment and realized that they just wouldn't follow a human. "If only I were a goose, then I could save them," he said out loud. Then he had an idea. He went into barn, got one of his own geese, and carried it in his arms, as he circled around behind the flock of wild geese. He then released it. His goose flew through the flock and straight into the barn-and one by one the other geese followed it to safety.

He stood silently for a moment, as the words he had spoken a few minutes earlier replayed in his mind: "If only I were a goose, then I could save them!" Then he thought about what he had said to his wife earlier. "Why would God want to be like us? That's ridiculous!" Suddenly it all made sense. That is what God had done. We were like the geese-blind, lost, perishing. God had His Son become like us, so He could show us the way and save us. That was the meaning of the Incarnation, he realized. As the winds and blinding snow died down, his soul became quiet, and pondered this wonderful thought.

Suddenly, he understood what the Incarnation was all about, why Christ had come. Years of doubt and disbelief vanished like the passing storm. He fell to his knees in the snow, and prayed his first prayer: "Thank You, God, for coming in human form to get me out of the storm!"[47]

We are the feet and hands and voice of Jesus to those in the storm. We are the incarnated Christ for those **who need to see, to believe**. We can still heal and expel and forgive and the irony is that when **we** do those things, we become the one who is saved!

---

47 Internet Forward

TWELFTH SUNDAY IN TEMPUS PER ANNUM

(JEREMIAH 20:10-13; PSALM 69; ROMANS 5:12-15; MATTHEW 10:26-33)

Chastity[48]

"But the Lord is with me like a mighty champion." So he says: *"Nothing is concealed that will not be revealed, nor secret that will not be known."* What do we fear? WE fear the unknown. Christ says to us that *there is nothing that will be unknown* . . . therefore, there must be nothing to fear. Unless we doubt. So often, we experience God in a way that we haven't before, or think we get a sign, but then begin to second guess. Perhaps what we need is not more signs, but sight. The ability to see the signs around us, sometimes in the most subtle ways.

From about third grade on, I pretty much thought I was supposed to be a priest. I used to get up early in the morning and celebrate Mass for my stuffed animals. I even preached, and they made not a single move . . . they sat most attentively for sometimes thirty minutes! I have since trimmed down the content a bit, but I look on those days as some of the best days. By the time I got to high school, my interests changed a bit. I started dating, and was interested in the sciences. And yet, despite all of that, my vocation was still in the back of my mind.

I decided at sixteen to make a pilgrimage. I didn't even really know what one was at that point, and yet, I felt it was what I needed to do. I drove to Harrisburg to the cathedral of St. Patrick, and spent an hour there. I prayed: "Lord, if you want me to be a priest, then you gotta give me a sign. What is it that you want of me?" And I

---

48 This story is very special to Fr. Mark Weiss of the Diocese of Harrisburg. He hates when I tell it!

waited . . . and waited . . . and waited. Finally an hour was up, and I figured he had His chance and didn't take it. I had waited for the sign and there was none, so I decided to leave. I could now rest easily. I walked out the doors and the first thing that caught my eye was a billboard. The billboard read: "Need a sign? Dial 1-800 . . . ." I looked up to the heavens and said: "Gimme another sign."

Even when I did eventually decide to enter the seminary, the seeds of doubt were still present. It was only a month before I was to enter, and I was on a trip with my family. We came up through West Virginia, and stopped at an Inn. I always had told my mom that I would fall in love with a southern girl . . . there was just something about that drawl that melted me. The hostess was the most charming southern girl I had met, and it was all I could do to follow her to our seats. After awhile we started chatting, and I melted when she spoke. But the thought that kept entering my mind was: "This is not a good idea, seeing as how you will be in the seminary in less than a month." Listening to this voice, I politely excused myself. As I walked away, she called after me and said: *"At least tale me yore name."* I couldn't believe it. I hadn't even told her my name. I responded: "My name's Mike, what's yours." And in the sweetest southern drawl she could muster she said, "ma' name's CHASTITY. Again, I looked up and this time declared: "YOU win!"

The gift we need is not more and more signs or miracles. The gift we need is sight. The Lord has now offered me another gift. And I would be lying if I said I wasn't scared. I ask for your patience and your prayers. But know this. In everything I do and breathe and live, I believe what my God says. And I believe it would be unfair of Him to ask something of me that He hasn't given me the tools to accomplish with His help. And so I don't pray with the psalmist who today speaks: *"Lord in your great love answer me."* I have my answer, to the question, "what is it that you want of me?" and His answer is this: "Look at your fears and embrace them; because through these fears, is the path, to Me."

THIRTEENTH SUNDAY IN TEMPUS PER ANNUM

FEAST OF SAINTS PETER AND PAUL

(ACTS 12: 1-11; PSALM 2; TIMOTHY 4:6-8; 17-18; MATTHEW 16:13-19)

Where is God's perfection in us?

Let me tell you a story.

In Brooklyn, New York, Chush is a school that caters to learning-disabled children. At a Chush fund-raising dinner, the father of a Chush child delivered a speech that would never be forgotten by all who attended. After extolling the school and its dedicated staff, he cried out, "Where is the perfection in my son Shaya? Everything God does is done with perfection. But my child cannot understand things as other children do. My child cannot remember facts and figures as other children do. Where is God's perfection?"

The audience was shocked by the question, pained by the father's anguish and stilled by the piercing query. "I believe," the father answered, "that when God brings a child like this into the world, the perfection that He seeks is in the way people react to this child."

He then told the following story about his son Shaya. One afternoon, Shaya and his father walked past a park where some boys Shaya knew were playing baseball. Shaya asked, "Do you think they'll let me play?" Shaya's father knew that his son was not at all athletic, and that most boys would not want him on their team. But Shaya's father also understood that if his son was chosen to play, it would give him a comfortable sense of belonging. Shaya's father approached one of the boys in the field and asked if Shaya could play. The boy looked around for guidance from his team-mates. Getting none, he took matters into his own hands and said, "We are losing by six runs and the game is in the eighth inning. I guess he can be on our team and we'll try to put him up to bat in the ninth inning."

Shaya's father was ecstatic as Shaya smiled broadly. Shaya was told to put on a glove and go out to play short center field. In the bottom of the eighth inning, Shaya's team scored a few runs but was still behind by three. In the bottom of the ninth inning, Shaya's team scored again and now with two outs and the bases loaded with the potential winning run on base, Shaya was scheduled to be up. Would the team actually let Shaya bat at this juncture and give away their chance to win the game?

Surprisingly, Shaya was given the bat. Everyone knew that it was all but impossible because Shaya didn't even know how to hold the bat properly, let alone hit with it. However, as Shaya stepped up to the plate, the pitcher moved a few steps in, to lob the ball softly so Shaya should at least be able to make contact. The first pitch came in and Shaya swung clumsily and missed. One of Shaya's team-mates came up to Shaya and showed him how to hold the bat and swing. Again, the pitcher took a few steps forward to toss the ball softly toward Shaya. As the pitch came in, Shaya and his team-mate swung the bat and together they hit a slow ground ball to the pitcher.

The pitcher picked up the soft grounder and could easily have thrown the ball to the first baseman. Shaya would have been out and that would have ended the game. Instead, the pitcher took the ball and threw it on a high arc to right field, far beyond reach of the first baseman. Everyone started yelling, "Shaya, run to first. Run to first!" Never in his life had Shaya "run to first." He scampered down the baseline wide-eyed and startled. By the time he reached first base, the right fielder had the ball. He could have thrown the ball to the second baseman who would tag out Shaya, who was still running. But the right fielder understood what the pitcher's intentions were, so he threw the ball high and far over the third baseman's head.

Everyone yelled, "Run to second, run to second." Shaya ran towards second base as the runners ahead of him deliriously circled the bases towards home. As Shaya reached second base, the opposing short-stop ran to him, turned him in the direction of third base and shouted, "Run to third." As Shaya rounded third, the boys from both teams ran behind him screaming, "Shaya run home!" Shaya ran home, stepped on home plate and all eighteen boys lifted him on their shoulders and made him the hero, as he had just hit a "grand slam" and won the game for his team.

"That day," said the father softly with tears now rolling down his face, "those eighteen boys reached their level of God's perfection."[49]

We celebrate today the feast of two great saints in the Church: Peter and Paul. I would suggest, however, that they are not great so much as a result of what they did, but because of the way people reacted to them. Paul would be the first to tell us of his weaknesses and failings. Peter, hot-tempered, and the only disciple Jesus ever referred to as Satan, would also deny him three times. Paul was a persecutor of the Church he would one day defend, and yet both are saints.

We all fit nicely into that category where, like Paul we do the things we hate, and don't do the things we wish we would. But our sanctification goes beyond any attempts *we* make towards perfection. I believe that when God brings a child like **US** into the world, the perfection he seeks is in the way people react to *this* child. So . . . how **DO** people react to you?

---

49 Internet Forward

DÉCIMOTERCER DOMINGO EN TEMPUS PER ANNUM
LA FIESTA DE SAN PEDRO Y SAN PABLO
(HECHOS 12:1-11; SALMO 2; TIMOTEO 4:6-8, 17-18; MATEO 16:13-19)

¿Dónde está la perfección de dios en nosotros?

Dejarme contarte una historia.

En Brooklyn, Nueva York, Chush es una escuela que abastece a los niños aprender-lisiados. En una cena de la movilización de fondos de Chush, el padre de un niño de Chush entregó un discurso que nunca ser olvidado por todos que atendieron. Después de extolling a la escuela y a su personal dedicado, él gritó, " ¿Dónde está la perfección en mi hijo Shaya? Todo dios hace se hace con la perfección. Pero mi niño no puede entender cosas como hacen otros niños. Mi niño no puede compredar y jugar como otros niños. ¿Dónde está la perfección de dios?" La pregunta dio una sacudida eléctrica, fue dolida por la angustia del padre y calmada a la audiencia por la pregunta piercing.

"Creo, "el padre contestado," eso cuando dios trae a niño como esto en el mundo, la perfección que él busca está de la manera que la gente reacciona a este child."

Él entonces contó la historia siguiente sobre su hijo Shaya: Una tarde Shaya y su padre caminaron más allá de un parque en donde algunos muchachos que Shaya conocía jugaban béisbol. Shaya pidió, " ¿Los piensas me dejarás jugar? " El padre de Shaya sabía que su hijo no era atlético y que la mayoría de los muchachos no lo querrían en su equipo. Pero el padre de Shaya entendía que si eligieran a su hijo para jugar te daría un sentimiento de pertenencia cómodo. El padre de Shaya se acercó a uno de los muchachos en el campo y preguntó si Shaya podría jugar. El muchacho miraba alrededor para la dirección de sus compañeros de equipo. Consiguiendo a ningunos, él tomó materias en sus propias manos y dijo, el " Somos perdidosos por seis funcionamientos y el juego está en el octavo turno. Conjeturo que él puede estar en nuestro equipo e intentaremos apuesto te hasta palo en el noveno inning." El padre de Shaya era extático pues sonrió Shaya amplio.

Shaya fue dicho para poner un guante y para salir jugar el jardín central corto. En la parte inferior del octavo turno, el equipo de Shaya anotó algunos funcionamientos pero todavía estaba detrás para golpear. En la parte inferior del arlin turno, el equipo de Shaya anotó otra vez y ahora con dos salidas y las bases cargadas con el run ganador potencial en base, Shaya fue programado para estar para arriba. ¿El equipo dejar realmente el palo de Shaya en esta coyuntura y dar lejos su oportunidad de ganar el juego?

Asombrosamente, Shaya fue dado el palo. Cada uno sabía que era todo sino imposible porque Shaya incluso no sabía sostener el palo correctamente, aún menos golpe con él. Sin embargo, como Shaya intensificado a la placa, la jarra movió algunos pasos para volear la bola desde muy alto en suavemente así que Shaya debe por lo menos poder hacer el contacto. La primera echada vino adentro y Shaya hizo pivotar torpe y faltó. Uno de los compañeros de equipo de Shaya subió a Shaya y juntos sostuvieron el palo e hicieron frente a la jarra que esperaba la echada siguiente. La jarra tomó otra vez algunas medidas adelante para sacudir la bola suavemente hacia Shaya. Como vino la echadaen, Shaya y su compañero de equipo hicieron pivotar el palo y juntos golpearon una bola de tierra lenta a la jarra. La jarra cogió la bola baja suave y habría podido lanzar fácilmentebola a las primeras bases. Shaya habría estado hacia fuera y ése habría terminado el juego. En lugar, la jarra tomó la bola y la lanzó en un alto arco al campo correcto, mucho más allá del alcance de las primeras bases. Cada uno comenzó a gritar, "Shaya, funcionar a primero. ¡Funcionar a primero! " Nunca en su vida hizo Shaya funcionar a primero. Él scampered abajo de la línea de fondo con los ojos abiertos y asustó. Para el momento en que él alcanzara la primera base, el centro campo adecuado tenía la bola. Él habría podido lanzar la bola a las segundas bases que marcarían hacia fuera Shaya con etiqueta, que todavía funcionaba. Pero el centro campo adecuado entendía cuáles eran las intenciones de la jarra, así que él lanzó el colmo de la bola y lejos sobre la cabeza de las terceras bases. Cada uno gritado, " Funcionar a, funcionar a second." Shaya funcionó hacia la segunda base mientras que los corredores delante de él delirante circundaron las bases hacia hogar. Pues Shaya alcanzó la segunda base, el campo corto de oposición funcionó a él, dado vuelta te en la dirección de la tercera base y gritado, " Funcionar a third." Pues Shaya redondeó tercero, los muchachos de ambos equipos funcionaron detrás de él que gritaba, " ¡Hogar del funcionamiento de Shaya! " Shaya funcionó a casa, caminó en la placa casera y los 18 muchachos lo levantaron en sus y te hicieron a héroe, pues él acababa de golpear un " slam" magnífico; y el juego para su equipo.

Ese día, " dijo a padre suavemente con los rasgones ahora que rodaban abajo su cara, " esos 18 muchachos alcanzaron su nivel de perfection." De Dios; Celebramos hoy el banquete de dos grandes santos en la iglesia: Peter y Paul. Sugeriría, sin embargo, que ella no es grande tanto como resultado de lo que ella hizo, pero debido a manera la gente reaccionó a él. Paul sería el primer a decirnos de sus debilidades y failings. Peter, de mal genio y el único discípulo Jesús Satan nunca llamado también te negarían tres veces.

Paul era un perseguidor de la iglesia que él un día defendería pero ambos son santos. Cabemos todo agradable en esa categoría donde, como Paul hacemos las cosas que odiamos y que no hacemos las cosas deseamos que. Pero nuestra santificación va más allá de cualesquiera nos hace hacia la perfección.

Creo que cuando dios trae a niño como los *ustedes* en el mundo, la perfección que él busca está de la manera la gente reacciona a *este* niño. ¿ . . . Cómo HACER la gente reacciona tan a *nosotros*?

FOURTEENTH SUNDAY IN TEMPUS PER ANNUM

(ZECHARIAH 9:9-10; PSALM 145; ROMANS 8:9, 11-13; MATTHEW 11:25-30)

My y-o-k-e is Easy; My burden Light

". . . Take my yoke upon you and learn from me. For my yoke is easy and my burden is light." A yoke is a harness placed over the shoulders of an ox or ass, in order for it to carry a load. In ancient times, these were specifically carved for every animal so that it fit perfectly, and therefore, allowed the animal to carry the largest load possible. If the yoke from one was given to another it wouldn't fit right, and therefore, would be less effective.

"Take my yoke upon you and learn from me, for my yoke is easy," BECAUSE my burden is light. What does that mean? This has a few possible interpretations, but I'm gonna give you my two, because they both apply to us. 1) He says take *MY yoke* . . . listen to the prophet Zechariah, one of the minor prophets: *"Our savior, meek; riding on an ass.* The savior is essentially the yoke of the ass . . . he's the yoke the animal supports, and so, where are *we* in the story? (ha ha). His yoke during his life here was the same as ours.

Listen to Matthew: *"All things have been handed over to me by my Father . . ."* in other words, He is my yoke and all he gives me is my burden. If we take *his* yoke upon us, we can fulfill those same words.

The other interpretation comes from the statement *"MY yoke."* In other words, the yoke I created for you . . . perfectly for you, so that you might bear any burdens that are laid upon you. And you will find rest . . . instead of restlessness. *"Come to me all you who labor and are burdened and I will refresh you"* . . . if you come to me. He is saying, *"If* you come to me and accept my yoke. Why are you trying to pull a heavier load with a yoke you have created?" Remember this Acronym.

YOKE. This Y-O-K-E we carry consists of "Your Own Kooky Expectations." (and I looked up *kooky*, so don't bother). This is *our* Yoke so we spend life struggling and worrying over a yoke that wasn't even made for us to carry. Psychologists say 80% of the things we worry about never happen. And worry never adds days or years to our life . . . but takes them away. Have you ever heard of a bird with an ulcer? Why do they sing? Reptiles have some of the most potent stomach acid in the world—they don't need Maalox or Tums . . . WE DO! Have you ever seen dogs or cats with ulcers or anxiety? You better believe it. Why? Because they've been hanging around with us for so long, they're becoming as anxious as we are. Your Own Kooky Expectations! That's our YOKE.

Now . . . Take **MY** Yoke. What's the difference? **Y**ahweh's **O**verpowering **K**ind **E**mbrace. A yoke in the old days did that. It embraced the shoulders and neck, so the animal could carry much more than otherwise. We are working against the grain, and we need to Wake UP! Stop fighting it so much and just try it! Thirty day guarantee; if your life's not better, then send it back. But try it and you'll find rest. Let go of the kooky expectations we place on ourselves, knowing that there is never enough time to do all the things we WANT to do; but there is always enough time to do what God wants of us. Let go of the expectations and labels others have placed on you . . . the yokes others have given to you, and perhaps you to yourself . . . and approach God . . . open to that which He has prepared for you. The yoke that is easy . . . the burden which is light . . . because it was fashioned for you from the very beginning, by a Father who loves you more than you love yourself.

CATORCENO DOMINGO EN TEMPUS PER ANNUM

(ZACARÍAS 9:9-10; SALMO 145; ROMANOS 8:9; 11-13; MATEO 11:25-30)

Mi yugo es fácil y mi carga es luz

". . . Tomar mi yugo sobre ti y aprender de mí. Para mi yugo es fácil y mi carga es luz." Un yugo es un arnés colocado sobre los hambros de un buey o de un asno para que lleve una carga. En épocas antiguas, éstos fueron talládos específicamente para cada animal de modo que cupiera perfectamente y por lo tanto permitiera que el animal llevara la carga más grande posible. Si el yugo a partir del uno fuera dado a otro no cabría a la derecha y por lo tanto no sería lo más menos eficaz.

Tomar mi yugo sobre ti y aprender de mí, porque mi yugo es fácil, PORQUE por carga está la luz. ¿Qué hace ese medio? Esto tiene dos interpretaciones posibles pero voy a darlas ambas porque ambas se aplican a nosotros. 1) él dice toma MI yugo . . . escucha el profeta Zechariah, uno de los profetas de menor importancia: "Nuestro Salvador, manso; el montar en un asno. ¿El Salvador es esencialmente el yugo del asno . . . que él está el yugo las ayudas del animal y tan donde es nosotros en la historia? (ha ha). Su yugo durante su vida aquí era igual que los nuestros.

Escuchar San Mateo: "Todas las cosas han sido entregadas a mí por mi padre . . ." es decir mi yugo y toda lo que él me da es mi carga. Si tomamos su yugo sobre nosotros, podemos satisfacer esas mismas palabras. 2) la otra interpretación viene de la declaración "MI yugo." Es decir el yugo que creé para ti . . . perfectamente para ti, de modo que puede ser que lleves cualquier carga que se ponga sobre ti. Y encontrarás resto . . . en vez de desasosiego. "Vienes a mí todo que trabaje y se cargue y te restauraré . . . si vienes a mí. Si vienes a mí y aceptas mi yugo. ¿Por qué estás intentando tirar de una carga más pesada con un yugo que has creado? Recordar estas siglas.

YUGO. Este YUGO que llevamos consiste en "tus propias expectativas Kooky." (y parecía para arriba Kooky así que no hago incomodidad). Éste es nuestro yugo así que pasamos vida que luchan y que se preocupan sobre un yugo que incluso no fue hecho para que nos llevemos. Los psicólogos dicen que alrededor nunca suceden los 80% de las cosas que nos preocupamos. Y la preocupación nunca agrega días o años a nuestra vida . . . pero los toma lejos. Tienes nunca oído hablar un pájaro con una úlcera. ¿Por qué cantan? ¡Los reptiles tienen algo del ácido de estómago más potente en mundo-ellos no necesitan Maalox o los Tums . . . HACEMOS! ¿Has visto nunca perros o gatos con las úlceras o la ansiedad? Lo crees. ¿Por qué? Porque han estado colgando alrededor con nosotros durante tanto tiempo, están llegando a ser tan ansiosos como somos. ¡Tus propias expectativas Kooky! Ése es nuestro YUGO. Ahora . . . tomar MI yugo. ¿Cuál es la diferencia?

Abrazo bueno que domina de Yahweh. Un yugo en los viejos días hizo eso. Abrazó los hombros y el cuello así que el animal podría llevar mucho más que de otra manera. ¡Estamos trabajando contra el grano y necesitamos despertar! ¡Parar el luchar de él tanto y apenas intentarlo! Garantía de 30 días; si tu vida no es mejor, entonces la devuelve. Pero intentarla y encontrarás resto. Dejado ir de las expectativas kooky que ponemos en nosotros mismos, sabiendo que nunca hay bastante tiempo de hacer todas las cosas QUEREMOS hacer, pero hay siempre bastante tiempo de hacer lo que quiere dios de nosotros. Dejado ir de las expectativas y etiqueta otras han colocado en ti . . . los yugos que otros te han dado, y quizás a se . . . y a dios del acercamiento . . . te abres en el a que él ha preparado para ti. El yugo que es fácil . . . la carga que es ligera . . . porque fue formada para ti desde el principio, por un padre que te ama más que se amas.

FIFTEENTH SUNDAY IN TEMPUS PER ANNUM
(ISAIAH 55:10-11; PSALM 65;
ROMANS 8:18-23; MATTHEW 13:1-23)

Arbores serit diligens agricola, quarum adspiciet
baccam ipse numquam.[50]
~*Cicero,* Tusculanarum Disputationum (I, 14)

Last week in the Gospel, Jesus was speaking of the yoke, and the community in which God's loving embrace is understood completely. So now he continues with agricultural metaphors, and it gives us food for reflection. Have you ever really thought about a seed? Here is this small thing that really does nothing. Leave it in a package or a drawer and open it up in ten years . . . it's still there. And yet the seed can grow thousands of times its own size. Wow! But in order to grow and bear fruit, the right conditions are necessary.

God provides the seed; He provides the starting product. Now these seeds are many and varied. Some will produce thirty or sixty fold, while others one hundred. But could you imagine a tomato saying, "I wish I were a plum." Or an apple saying, "I wish I were a pear." Although we do have "pear-apples" now. So God creates the seed, each different for their particular purpose. We contain the seed. God provides the soil, water and nourishment, *"the rain and the snow come down, and do not return there till they have watered the earth, making it fertile and fruitful."* But it is we who can change the consistency of the soil, and therefore, affect the growth.

This is the way God wanted it. Listen to Paul: *"Creation was made subject to futility . . . in the hope that creation itself would be set free from slavery to corruption . . . and share in the freedom of the children*

---

50 "The diligent farmer plants trees, of which he himself will never see the fruit."

of God." Dependence on God. So where is the seed we were given? (Does this sound like it's connected to the yoke?) And what kind of media do we have for the seed in which to grow?

1. **The Path**: Traveled by many. Farmers will use crop rotation in order to preserve the soil. Soil that is overused erodes quickly, and with nothing anchoring it, the seed will not grow. When we fear rejection and love loss, not trusting in God, we have allowed our seed to be taken from us.

2. **Rocky Ground**: Rocky ground provides opportunity, because it forces us to climb out. If we use the rocks as stepping stones and not stumbling blocks, we will be warmed by the **Son**. The Son which offers us life. But if we don't have stepping stones, and simply wallow in our stumble, we will remain unmoved, and one cannot survive such heat.

3. **Thorns**: A thorn is mentioned in Paul's letter to the Corinthians when he speaks of the thorn in his side. The thorns choke the sprout right at a very crucial time in its growth; however, the choking occurs much earlier than can be seen. The roots of these thorns are like a net that strangles the roots of all around it first. It cuts off the water and nourishment, so that by the time the thorns are strangling above the ground, it's too late. The roots of our faith are always under attack first. If we're not careful, by the time we see the sprout, it's too late. Only when exposed, can the plant be saved.

4. **Good soil**: supple, receptive and embraces the seed and plant. We are the good soil . . . (in Hebrew *Adamah* from which the name, Adam comes). Just as God breathed his Spirit into the soil and made man, so too does His Son give life to the plant. The God that Heaven could not contain is then contained within the soil.

Reading this Gospel begs the question, why did he put down the seed before he plowed? Well, we're used to our modern agriculture, but in the ancient world (and even now in some places) the seeds were scattered first, and then they were plowed under. The fault of the sower is not that he scattered the seed first, but that he put off plowing it under. Sometimes, it's not that we haven't done a good job at scattering seed . . . sometimes, it just that we have put off cultivating and nourishing that seed.

So we bring our easy path; our stones; our thorns to God, and He shows us how to cultivate and bear the fruit our own seed was given to produce. But lest we be frustrated and fear it might never grow, remember the sidewalk paved overtop the little green sprout and visit it twenty years later . . . the oak tree pushing its massive trunk through the pavement, as though it were so much rubble. Ask for the will of the one who planted the seed, and He will give your plant life . . . true life.

SIXTEENTH SUNDAY IN TEMPUS PER ANNUM

(WISDOM 12:13, 16-19; PSALM 86; ROMANS 8: 26-27; MATTHEW 13:24-43)

Weeds to Wheat

There is a story that comes to us from Henri Nouwen that I have here paraphrased.

> A monk is walking with his disciples along a small stream near the desert. As they pass, the monk notices a scorpion in the water struggling to get a foothold on dry land. The monk reached down into the water and rescued the drowning creature. Upon releasing it on dry land, the scorpion quickly twitched its body and stung its savior on the hand. One of the disciples came forward and offered to kill the wretched thing. The monk replied, "Why would you kill what I have saved. It is the nature of the scorpion to sting; and the nature of man to save."[51]

And you taught your people, by these deeds, that those who are just must be kind; and you gave your children good ground for hope that you would permit repentance for their sins. Those who are just must be kind . . . you would permit repentance for their sins. We all screw up! That's the nature of living in a world of sin . . . not all of us, however, will change. Some will screw up again and again and again. I'm not alone in this right? . . . oh . . . well, I am alone in this then, but that's okay! It is the scorpion's nature to sting, and it is man's nature to save.

There are two advocates for hope in this situation. The first comes from the psalmist: *Lord you are good and forgiving*, and secondly from the Letter of St. Paul: *"The Spirit comes to the aid of our weakness."* So

---

51 Henri Nouwen, *Seeds of Hope*, Ed. Robert Durback (New York, NY: Doubleday Books, 1997), 180.

we are in a sinful world, and it will appear at times that the deck is stacked against us . . . but then we remember that our God is a God of second chance. That even though *WE* sting, he still saves. But . . . we must **want** to be saved.

If that's true, and we must **want to be saved** and if **we want to be saved**, God **will** save us, what about the weeds and the wheat? Why do we have to struggle so much when the weeds could be eliminated so easily?

There is humorous story which might help to illustrate.

> A woman was at work when she received a phone call that her small daughter was very sick with a fever. She left her work, and stopped by the pharmacy to get some medication. She got back to her car and found that she had locked her keys in the car. She didn't know what to do, so she called home, and told the baby sitter what had happened. The baby sitter told her that the fever was getting worse.
>
> She said, "You might find a coat hanger and use that to open the door." The woman looked around and found an old rusty coat hanger that had been left on the ground, possibly by someone else who at some time had locked their keys in their car. She looked at the hanger and said, "I don't know how to use this." She bowed her head, and asked God to send her help. Within five minutes, a beat up old motorcycle pulled up, with a dirty, greasy, bearded man, who was wearing an old biker skull rag on his head. The woman thought, "This is what you sent to help me?" But, she was desperate, so she was also very thankful.
>
> The man got off of his cycle and asked if he could help. She said, "Yes, my daughter is very sick. I stopped to get her some medication, and I locked my keys in my car. I must get home to her. Please, can you use this hanger to unlock my car?
>
> He said, "Sure." He walked over to the car, and in less than a minute, the car was opened. She hugged the man and through

her tears she said, "Thank You So Much! You are a very nice man." The man replied, "Lady, I am not a nice man. I just got out of prison today. I was in prison for car theft, and have only been out for about an hour."

The woman hugged the man again, and with sobbing tears cried out loud, "Oh, Thank you God! You even sent me a Professional!"[52]

The weeds and the wheat are allowed to grow together. And I imagine, what Jesus said about pulling up the weeds and damaging the wheat is probably true, however, I would like to *posit* another reason. Perhaps given time and the opportunity, the man who could change water into wine, might also even be able to transform weeds, into wheat!

---

52 Internet Forward

SEVENTEENTH SUNDAY IN TEMPUS PER ANNUM

(I KINGS 3: 5, 7-12; PSALM 119; ROMANS 8: 28-30; MATTHEW 13: 34-52)

What is the pearl beyond great price?

The Lord said to Solomon: "Because you have asked for this . . . not for a long life for yourself, nor for riches, nor for the death of your enemies, I do as you requested." For *"those he justifies, He also glorifies."*

A man was wading in the creek. As he waded, he saw a sparkling pearl, the largest he had ever seen. He took the pearl, and placing it in his satchel, he continued his journey. A homeless man approached him looking for food. The man was quick to offer some help and reached into his bag. As he did, the homeless person noticed the large pearl. "I'll take that pearl instead. With that I could buy lots of food." The man, without hesitation, offered the homeless man the pearl. He took it greedily into his hands, and scurried off into the woods.

That night, he tossed and turned. He was constantly on the lookout for thieves, and was worried about losing the pearl. But as he sat up all night, guarding that thing, he began to wonder. In the morning, he found the old man who had given him the pearl, wading in the creek again. He approached him and offered him back the pearl. The man said: "Could the pearl not buy you food? What more can I do for you?" The man replied: "I want what you possess, that allows you to give such treasures so freely."[53]

This is the pearl beyond price. What is it? What is it that could allow such carefree living? It's not something we are able to put into

---

53 Internet Forward

words . . . it goes beyond that. For me, I need only look at my Great Aunt, and I know.

My Aunt Rainey celebrated her 93rd birthday this year. Ninety-three years young! I recall speaking with her last winter, and she said: "Honey (she called everyone honey, or sweetie) before I die, I want to read the whole Bible. Where should I start?" I said to start with the Gospels in the New Testament, and in the Old Testament with Genesis. I then added: "But you can skip Leviticus, because it's just regulations for the priests and such." She scurried off into the other room and then returned a moment later to say: "Honey . . . what other books can I skip? I *am* ninety-three you know." She has a simple faith that places God in the center. She would tell you, "I love going to Mass at Mary Queen, and when her children accompanied her, it is priceless.

This is a woman who would use a whole loaf of bread, making peanut-butter and jelly sandwiches for only a hand full of people at the picnic; afraid that we'd never have enough to eat. This is a woman whose favorite store was the *Dollar Tree*, where she would buy for others, never for herself. Who is a great grandmother, great aunt, and her children would say, Great Mother! Who held only God ahead of her family, and even then it was close. And when she's with you, she treats you as though she's been waiting ninety-three years to meet you. Even when her husband died, (Big Johnny) after her caring for him during his illness, she couldn't but smile even as she cried.

How? She gets it! She gets it. It is never about her . . . it is all about the *other*. The gift that we possess, the one only God can give, is the love in our hearts that we hold for others. What is our treasure that allows us to give so freely? I can't say in words, but I know it exists, because I've seen it. And I'll bet you know someone in whom you've seen it too. So the next time you see them, ask what it is . . . and when I see Aunt Rainey, I'll ask her for you.

"Aunt Rainey"

Decimoséptimo siete Domingo en Tempus per Annum

(1 Reyes 3:5, 7-12; Salmo 119; Romanos 8: 28-30; Mateo 13: 34-52)

La Tesura Grande

El Señor dijo a Salomón: "*Ya que has pedido esto y no te has pedido una larga vida, ni te has pedido riquezas, ni la muerte de tus enemigos, cumplo con tu petición por inteligencia para administrar justicia.*" porque "*los que él justifica, él glorifica también.*"

Hay un cuento de un hombre que vadeaba en un riachuelo. Mientras que él vadeaba, él vio una perla brillante, la más grande que él había visto nunca. Él tomó la perla y colocándola en su cartera, él continuó en su viaje. Un hombre sin hogar se acercó a él y le pedía comida. El hombre no tardó en ofrecer ayuda y metió la mano en su bolsa.

Mientras lo hacía el mendigo vio la perla grande. "Tomaría esa perla en vez de comida. Con ésa yo podría comprar mucha comida." El hombre, sin vacilación, le ofreció la perla al hombre sin hogar. Él la tomó codiciosamente en sus manos y salió disparado al bosque. Esa noche daba vueltas y estaba constantemente al acecho de los ladrones, y se preocupaba por perder la perla. Pero mientras se quedaba despierto toda la noche haciendo guardia, él comenzó a preguntarse. Por la mañana él encontró al viejo que le había dado la perla. Estaba vadeando el riachuelo de nuevo.

Se acercó a él y le ofreció a devolver la perla. El hombre dijo: ¿"La perla no podía comprarte comida? ¿Qué más puedo hacer para ti?" El hombre contestó: "Quiero lo que posees, lo que te permite regalar tesoros tan libremente.

Ésta es la perla invalorable. ¿Qué es? ¿Qué es lo que te permite vivir tan despreocupado?
No es algo que podemos expresar con palabras . . . va más allá de ése. Para mí, necesito solo mirar a mi tía abuela, y yo sé.

Mi ti ti Rainey cumplió noventa y tres años este año. ¡Una joven de noventa y tres años! Recuerdo hablar con ella el invierno pasado y ella me dijo: "Cariño (así ella llamaba a todos o les decía querido) antes de que yo muera, quiero leer la biblia entera. ¿Dónde debo comenzar?" Le dije de comenzar con los evangelios en el nuevo testamento y en el viejo testamento con génesis. Entonces añadí: "Puedes saltar Leviticus porque se trata solo de las reglas para los sacerdotes y tales." Ella salió disparado al otro cuarto y volvió en un momento más para decir: ¿"Cuáles otros libros puedo saltar? Tengo noventa y tres años sabes." Ella tiene una fe sencilla que se centra en Dios. Ella te diría, "me encanta ir a Misa a la reina María" y cuando sus niños la acompañaron era inestimable.

Ésta es una mujer que usaba toda una barra de pan entera para hacer bocadillos de mantequilla de maní y jalea para solo un grupito de nosotros en un picnic porque ella temía que no tendríamos bastante a comer. Ésta es una mujer cuyo almacén preferido era el "árbol del dólar", donde ella compraría para otros, pero nunca para ella. ¡Ella es la bisabuela, la tía abuela y sus hijos dirían, gran madre! Quién ponía solamente a Dios delante de su familia, e aún así estaba bien reñido. Y cuando ella está contigo te trata como si ella hubiera estado esperando noventa y tres años para conocerte. Cuando su marido murió después de haberlo cuidado durante su enfermedad, ella no podría evitar una sonrisa incluso mientras lloraba. ¿Cómo? ¡Ella lo entiende! Ella lo entiende.

Nunca se trata de ella . . . Se trata totalmente del otro. El regalo que poseemos, lo que solo Dios puede darnos es el amor en nuestro corazón que tenemos para otros. Cuál es nuestro tesoro que nos permite dar tan libremente. No puedo expresar con palabras, pero sé que existe porque lo he visto. Y apostaré que conoces a alguien en quién lo has visto también. Así que la próxima vez que lo ves, pregúntale cuál es . . . y cuando veo a tía Rainey, yo le pediré para ti.

Eighteenth Sunday in Tempus per Annum

(Isaiah 55:1-3; Psalm 145; Romans 8:35, 37-39; Matthew 14:13-21)

At least I . . .

What is our intention . . . our motivation, in what we do for God? Imagine, if we defended our role as a part of our family by saying, "I might not do anything to help out, or to support the family, but at least I live in the house with them." Or as a parent to those who might critique our parenting, "Well at least I feed the children." or "At least I give them a place to stay." Or to our employer, "Listen, at least I show up to work." Or to our doctors or trainers, "At least I go to the health club." At least, at least, at least! As opposed to saying, "At most I . . ."

Some will use this expression with regards to Mass. "Do you participate at Mass?" "Listen father, at least I come to church." Or, "Do you dress modestly for Mass?" "At least I come to church." "Do you come habitually late or leave Mass early every week?" "At least I come to church." We must be vigilant that when we talk about God, we do not include that phrase, "at least." Because when God showers His goodness upon us, it is always with extravagance. So if we speak of God and in the same breath utter, "At least I . . ." then we are no better than Cain, who did not give the first fruits to God, but the *least* of his harvest.

This is why in scripture, it stipulated which sacrifices to God were acceptable and which were not. Why we couldn't offer the lamb that had only three legs and chased its tail all day, but the top ewe. We could not give the corn or wheat that was afflicted with blight, but the absolute prime of the harvest. That attitude of the best for God, is unfortunately, not the one that prevails. We decide that if we have time for God, then we can spend time with him. We decide that we will go to Mass on Christmas and Easter, because these are the most important days of the year, but that the other Sundays are optional. Who taught us that? In reality, the Sundays of Christmas and Easter are equal to the rest of the Sundays of the year! I know, I know . . . well, at least I go twice a year. At least, at least, at least.

"What will separate us from the love of Christ? Trial, or distress, or persecution, or hunger, or nakedness, or danger, or the sword?" Asks St. Paul to the Romans. Of all of the excuses Paul has that might separate us from Christ, which one applies to our situation? He names seven here, which I'm sure had meaning to him, if not to the Romans. This "seven" consists of the perfect combination that might dissuade the early Christians from practicing. Which one applies to us? Trial? We don't go to Church because it is too trying for our life? Distress? We are concerned for the safety of our family and our health, so we will not make the journey to worship? The persecution I will face for going to a Catholic Mass on Sunday is unbearable? I am starving to death, and so cannot even begin to think about my spiritual life? I have nothing to wear, as opposed to wearing nothing to Mass (let the reader understand). I would be in imminent danger if I were caught celebrating the Eucharist? I might be martyred by letting it be known that I am a Christian? I mean really? Come on! For those in the first century of the church? Absolutely; especially in Rome. To us in a first world country? For most, I don't think so.

This story of the multiplication of the loaves and fishes, is one that spans all four Gospels. With every miracle of Jesus, the miracle itself is not nearly as important as the teaching that accompanies it. For this miracle, all they have is a few meager loaves and some fish to offer all these people. Our first impulse might be to criticize and say "this is the least they offered." Quite to the contrary, however, what was offered was the best. As poor and meager the offering was, it was offered as the best they had for themselves. So they offered up the best they had . . . it was gone . . . theirs no more. And Jesus took it, and blessed it, and with the blessing of the best fruits they could provide came a rich feast. The bread went from being meager, to becoming so precious that the crusts were collected so that none would be wasted.

Now there were many people there; and some of them probably had food. But they kept it to themselves. The reason might have been good, like keeping it for their family, so that they would not be hungry, but the apostles (or in another Gospel, the child) gave up their stash to God. They made the offering in trust that God would do far more greater things with their hunger, than they could do with their full belly. That's what he can do with *our* first fruits!

Our Lord can transform our first fruits, not only into something so precious that not a crust can be wasted, but into something that is so abundant, it is able to nurture and feed thousands of others: something we could not do ourselves. The question we must ask is regarding how we address our God in our prayer; in what we do for the church; about how we enter into worship. When we offer those things to God, are we saying, "*This* is the least I can offer to you?" Or do we offer our first fruits: our first and freshest hour of each day; that when I come to Mass, I ensure that I allot enough time to pray before the Mass begins, and offer thanks after it ends; that I pray consistently throughout the week, not just when I'm driving, or have some idle time with nothing to do. If we can offer our first fruits to God, then our "at least I" having been transformed into "at most I," will not only become more robust and precious, but also will have the power to feed many of those, who have not yet ascended from the *acedia* of the minimum.

DECIMOCTAVO DOMINGO DEL TIEMPO ORDINARIO AÑO "B"

(ÉXODO 16: 2-4, 12-15; SALMO 78; EFESIOS 4: 17, 20-24; JUAN 6:24-34)

Debes Querer Vivir

Alguna vez fue dicho: "Quines hablen de 'los tiempos pasados' no los vivieron." Creo que parte de esto puede ser cierto. Nosotros hablamos del pasado, y parece que nos olvidamos de las dificultades que tuvimos, y adornamos las aflicciones mientras vemos el presente como la peor situación posible. La reflexión puede traer mucho fruto, en saber de donde venimos. Lo milagroso de los milagros es el hecho de que suceden delicadamente atravéz de la naturaleza. Los milagros suceden a su tiempo. Piénsenlo, si alguien deja una costumbre, o se cura de una herida después de veinte y cuatro años, nosotros creemos que es apropiado. Las cosas buenas suceden a su tiempo. Sin embargo, si esa misma cosa sucedería en un día, nosotros lo llamaríamos un milagro.

Dios interviene en nuestras vidas todo el tiempo, El quita el tiempo que se toma para que ocurra algo (recuerden que un día es como mil años para Dios, y mil años como un día). Parece que los Israelitas están cayendo en una trampa en que seguido caemos nosotros. La trampa de creer que no fue Dios el responsable de nuestra salvación, pero que de algún modo nosotros mismos nos salvamos. En el momento que sucede esto, podemos creer en los milagros, hasta que entra el temor de la duda, y nos demuestra cuanto la ciencia puede explicar lo que paso, o cuanto tuvimos que ver con lo sucedido.

Pablo lo dice muy claramente: *"Revístanse del nuevo yo, creado a imagen de Dios, en la justicia y en la santidad de la verdad."* Mucha gente te puede decir el momento, la hora y fecha en que fueron salvados. Como católicos, decimos que "somos salvados" una y otra vez. Esto no es algo que podemos hacer solos, sino algo que Dios hace por nosotros. Es un regalo, si solo nosotros lo aceptaríamos. Los Israelitas estaban dispuestos a aceptar los regalos cuando todo les parecía bien en el mundo, pero tan pronto las cosas se hicieron difíciles; en cuanto parecía que ellos no estaban "en control", maldecían al Dios que los libero. Dios les da lo que necesitan y ellos lo alaban por este don, y sin embargo, denuevo en poco tiempo olvidan quien fue; comenzaron a sentir desprecio por los dones que ellos mismos recibieron en el principio.

Lo inauténtico de nosotros lucha sin cesar para resistir y rechazar la vida de Cristo.

> En mil novecientos sesenta y ocho, cuando Philip Blaiberg recibió un nuevo corazón durante la cirugía de transplante, y hasta Agosto de mil novecientos sesenta y nueve, cuando murió, su cuerpo entero, desde su cerebro hasta la célula mas importante lucho con una ferocidad asombrosa e inventiva para rechazar el nuevo corazón que, sin embargo era necesario para el.[54]

Nosotros hacemos lo mismo. La inautendidad dentro de nosotros cual no quiere ser gobernado por un Dios o una iglesia, o la religión, o tradición, o por cualquier cosa, es como el cuerpo que rechaza el mismo corazón que es necesario para sobrevivir.

Dice Jesús: *"El pan de Dios es el que viene del cielo y da vida al mundo."* La palabra que se utiliza para representar la vida es Zoe, que significa verdadera y plena vida. No es la clase de vida llamada "bio" que se utiliza para representar las creaturas, sino la palabra para representar el corazón, la mente, el alma, la fortaleza dentro de nosotros! Esto es el corazón que se mantiene inquieto hasta que descansa en El. No lo buscaban por lo milagros. Lo buscaban por que les ofrecía algo que jamás habían tenido. El creo en ellos un anhelo. Que por primera vez

---

54 Peter Van Breeman, *Called by Name*, (NJ: Denville, Dimension Books, 1976), 50.

en sus vidas, el cuerpo dejo de luchar contra el "corazón" lo suficiente que sentían esa vida . . . la vida real y verdadera.

Se nos ha entregado la oportunidad de ser hijos de Dios. Hemos sido bendecidos con esta vida para salir y hacer una diferencia. Y como quiera, algunos hemos tomado el pan, pero no hemos visto las señales. Algunos hemos intentado salvarnos a nosotros mismos por tanto tiempo, y no nos hemos acercado mas a convertirnos en santos. Ahora es el tiempo de cambiar. Miren a su alrededor en su vida. Ven a gente que es buena y fiel. No estoy hablando de gloria en vanidad, o en los que lo hacen por apariencia. Me refiero a los que son verdaderos fieles . . . los que uno desea ser por que son tan buenos. Que es lo que tienen? Y como seria si por un momento, vivimos como ellos? Realizando que en verdad no tenemos control de nuestra salvación. Me imagino que seria como una persona sosteniendo su aliento, cuando finalmente llega a la superficie del agua que pensaba estar millas encima de ellos. Eso es la vida. Dios mío que vida! Y es tuya. Pero debes querer vivir.

NINETEENTH SUNDAY IN TEMPUS PER ANNUM

(I KINGS 19:9, 11-13; PSALM 85; ROMANS 9:1-5; MATTHEW 14:23-33)

Lord, if that is you; ask me to . . .

For those of us who are "fair weather" fishermen, three o'clock in the morning is a bit early; or late depending on how you look at it. For most of us, we could get up just before dawn, take our time walking down to the *honey hole*, and get a pretty nice morning catch of some trout or sucker fish. But for the professional, this would never fly. They would go out towards dusk and drop the nets, only to be catching fish throughout the night. Their day would end at dawn, as they came in and washed their nets before heading home for a rest.

I believe a few things happened here. Remember, we're dealing with people, not characters in a movie. The apostles were probably begging Jesus all day to let them go fishing, and finally, wearied by their whining, he gave in like a reluctant parent to their stubborn first-born. This also allotted him the time for solitary prayer, which was always in demand. So that gets them out on the lake; the scene is set, and something remarkable happened.

For many of us, 3:00 a. m. is when we get up to go to the bathroom or let the dog out, only to return to our nap, until the alarm abruptly ends our slumber. But during the middle ages, the time of 3:00 a. m. became significant. In an era of superstition, and an acute awareness of the supernatural, times and dates and places held a sort of power. For them, 3:00 a. m. was very significant, because it was the exact opposite time that Jesus died on the cross. The cross was our moment of salvation. This middle hour was the hour of damnation, and came to be known as the "witching hour." In scripture, this is often the time when a storm comes upon the water. John's Gospel remarks that *Judas left the supper and it was dark*. Now that we have set up the scene, what happens?

As Jesus comes walking across the water, it is natural for the apostles to think it is a ghost. Remember, this *is* the "witching hour." Jesus, sounding like a frustrated parent, chides them slightly, telling them to *"get a hold of yourselves."* But . . . they are not convinced even by this. Jesus must prove who he is, before they will believe.

Now, if you were trying to ascertain whether this was Jesus or not, what would you ask him to do in order to prove it? How about calm the storm! There's a first step. How about performing some miracle, as he did over and over again? Sounds promising, right? Nope, Peter, the man who always seems to speak before the filter catches it, says: *"If it is you Lord,"* now this is a good start. He's asking for proof. But the next words out of his mouth don't follow. It seems like Peter's done it again. But wait . . . let's see what happens.

"If it is you Lord, tell me to come to you across the water." Wait, what? I thought we were going to ask him for a miracle to prove his identity. But Peter doesn't do that. He says, *if it is you Lord*, ask *ME* to do something. Now this is big. I mean he not only says, *"ask me to do something,"* but he says, "ask me to do something that is seemingly impossible." And it goes further. I know Peter was a fisherman, but I don't think he could swim. I believe this, because when he does walk across the water and begins to sink, he cries out for Jesus to save him. If he could swim, he would have treaded water. So get this: "If you are Jesus, not only ask ME to do something, but make it something that is impossible; make it something I fear the most. And if you can ask me to do *that*, then I know you are Jesus."

Why did it have to be that way? Many times, people will respond to the teachings of the Church and will remark that "my Jesus wouldn't expect that of me." And perhaps that's true. Your Jesus would not; but your Jesus is not God either. Peter on the other hand, knew the Master, and knew that if the one walking across the water did not ask something that Peter feared, or that was impossible, then it probably *was* a ghost. During this witching hour, it was not evil and weakness and egoism that triumphed, but the Christ . . . the true God. The one who asks much of us, many times to walk toward our fears. So now, perhaps you're reading this at 3:00 a. m. in the hopes of falling asleep (shame on you!). Fill in the blank. You see Jesus coming to you on the water and you say: "Lord if that is you . . . ask *ME* to _____.

Come out of him!" Sketched at Pangaea

Twentieth Sunday in Tempus per Annum

(Isaiah 56:1, 6-7; Psalm 67; Romans 11:13-15, 29-32; Matthew 15:21-28)

Because we needed someone who would understand

Of all the stories in all of the Gospels, I really love this one. We said that in Matthew's gospel, the humanity of Jesus really shines. That humanity isn't always the most attractive to us. In fact, some might read this passage and say to themselves, "Jesus seemed kinda mean to that person." This is a great example, not only of Jesus' rigidity with respect to his mission to go to the "chosen people" first, but also, that he was probably sarcastic at times, if not downright funny!

Jesus is in Tyre and Sidon. These areas, which he will pass through always on his way to somewhere else, were bastions of the pagan cults and religions. The Canaanites were known in the time of Abraham for their human sacrifices and only up until the time of the Josian reforms had ceased (at least in a public way) from sacrificing infants. (Perhaps we could learn something from the past about bans on infant sacrifice.)

So Jesus is passing through this area, and people have obviously heard of him, for even without Twitter or Facebook, word did travel pretty fast at times, depending on what the word was. This woman's daughter is tormented by a demon. This was more common than not, because they worship demons. If you mess with the fire, you're gonna get burned. Even in our day and age, people experiment with demons, unaware that they cannot control that which they summon. So not only is the woman's daughter infected, but the woman herself, and her culture is responsible for this oppression. Furthermore, this woman sees Jesus as no more than a shaman or a witchdoctor. She knows nothing of the Messiah, or his mission, or his message. She knows what she heard in pagan territory: that this shaman has great powers over evil. With this in mind now, does Jesus appear as mean when he's responding to this woman? I mean, at least the Israelites he's healing have an idea of who he is and what he's about. She just wants the cure.

So what wins this woman a miracle? Going toe-to-toe with the Messiah. She does not give up, and in fact, it is her response to his rebuke that gets her what she wants. Jesus says that he will not throw to dogs what is reserved for the children. The term "dog" is not so much cruel as it was descriptive. The pagans were called "dogs," because, like the feral dogs of the time, they took scraps from many different religions. Whatever was the flavor of the week, that became their religion. But the way the woman responds must have been so cleverly sarcastic that Jesus decided, "you win!" The Greek is very clear. She says: *"Even the little puppies get the scraps that fall from the master's table."* Jesus probably let out a belly laugh at that remark and obviously is very moved when he says to her: *"You have great faith! Your wish will come to pass."*

We are called to be like Jesus. That doesn't mean that we must be sarcastic (not everyone has that gift. I thank God I do!). What it means is that, when we are living our faith, we do not put on a mask that hides who we are. Our lived faith is not an accessory to who we are, but should *be* who we are. Our personality and idiosyncrasies will shine through. We are humans who are living in the world, as Jesus did. And we will have those who have wandered from the faith, or even dabbled in other religions in a search for truth, or out of convenience. We can evangelize and preach all we want, but more successful, is the one who does not hide behind a mask or act differently when someone is watching. The most successful person of faith is the one who meets those individuals where they are in their life; we do not waver in our conviction, but give them at the very least, a door they can walk through when they are ready.

We don't know any more about this woman in the Gospel. Maybe she got her miracle and went back to her pagan religions. And perhaps her daughter was oppressed again, if not possessed this time. And maybe, just maybe, because Jesus left that door ajar, through that first encounter, she came to the point where she walked away from the religion of the dogs; walked through the door, and towards salvation. "Jesus' feeling for the possessed [girl] is different from his feeling for the beloved disciple; but the love is one . . . feelings dwell in man, but man dwells in his love."[55] After all; that is why Jesus came, right? Because we needed someone who was human, who would understand.

He painted a sign advertising the twenty pups. And set about nailing it to a post on the edge of his yard. As he was driving the last nail into the post, he felt a tug on his overalls. He looked down into the eyes of a little boy. "Mister," he said, "I want to buy one of your puppies." "Well," said the farmer, as he rubbed the sweat off the back of his neck, "These puppies come from fine parents, and cost a good deal of money."

The boy dropped his head for a moment. Then reaching deep into his pocket, he pulled out a handful of change and held it up to the farmer. "I've got thirty-nine cents. Is that enough to take a look?" "Sure," said the farmer. And with that he let out a whistle, "Here, Dolly!" he called. Out from the doghouse and down the ramp ran Dolly, followed by four little balls of fur.

The little boy pressed his face against the chain link fence. His eyes danced with delight. As the dogs made their way to the fence, the little boy noticed something else stirring inside the doghouse. Slowly, another little ball appeared, this one noticeably smaller. Down the ramp it slid. Then in a somewhat awkward manner, the little pup began hobbling toward the others, doing its best to catch up . . . ."I want that one," the little boy said, pointing to the runt.

The farmer knelt down at the boy's side and said, "Son, you don't want that puppy. He will never be able to run and play with you like these other dogs would." With that, the little boy stepped

---

55 Martin Buber, *I and Thou*, (New York, NY., Simon & Schuster, 1970), 66.

back from the fence, reached down, and began rolling up one leg of his trousers. In doing so, he revealed a steel brace running down both sides of his leg, attaching itself to a specially made shoe.

Looking back up at the farmer, he said, "You see sir, I don't run too good myself, and he'll need someone who understands."[56]

---

56 Internet Forward

VIGÉSIMO DOMINGO DEL TIEMPO ORDINARIO AÑO "B"

(PROVERBIOS 9:1-6; SALMO 34; EFESIOS 5:15-20; JUAN 6:51-58)

¿Cual es la voluntad de Dios?

La gente dirá: "Mientras yo asísta a una iglesia, no importa a cual vaya." Algunas semanas antes, hablamos de otras mayores religiones del mundo, y porque nosotros no alabamos al mismo Dios. La semana pasada, nos enfocamos en la Eucaristía como la fundación de nuestra fe, y como somos distintos a otras tradiciones cristianas, porque nosotros tenemos el cuerpo y la sangre de Cristo. Cualquier otra cosa es solo una imitación. Dice Pablo a los Efesios:

> *"Tengan cuidado de portarse no como insensatos, sino como prudentes, aprovechando el momento presente, porque los tiempos son malos. No sean irreflexivos, antes bien, traten de entender cual es la voluntad de Dios."*

¿Cual es la voluntad de Dios? Solo nos hace falta leer el evangelio de hoy. *"Yo les aseguro: Sino comen la carne del Hijo de Dios y no beben su sangre, no podrán tener vida en ustedes. El que come mi carne y bebe mi sangre, tiene vida eterna y yo lo resucitare el ultimo día."* Muchos protestantes y cristianos no-católicos dicen que Jesús solo hablaba en símbolo. ¿O, en verdad?

"Si alguno es sencillo, que venga acá. Y a los faltos de juicio les dice: vengan a comer de mi pan y beber del vino que he preparado. Dejen su ignorancia y vivirán; avancen por el camino de la prudencia."

Juan 6:51-60 Muchos cristianos no-católicos no conocen estos versos, o desean no saberlos. Permítanme leer parte de esto en el idioma original en que fue escrito, Griego.

En Griego hay dos palabras que representan la "carne." La primera, soma, quiere decir carne muerta, como un cadáver. La palabra que se utiliza aquí, *"sarx"*, significa carne viva. El utiliza la palabra *"phagein"*, cual quiere decir comer, pero en la segunda frase cambia la palabra a *"trogon"*, que significa mascar o roer. El hace que la palabra tome mas significado físicamente. Esta es la única enseñanza doctrinal por la cual sus discípulos lo abandonaron. ¿Lo habrían dejado por un símbolo?

Jesús desea clarificarlo, y sin dejar duda que el hablaba literalmente. Si seguimos leyendo descubrimos . . ."*Desde ese entonces muchos de sus discípulos ya no lo seguían.*" ¿Cuantos de ustedes morirían por una foto de su hijo o un ser querido? Ninguno. ¿Pero daría usted la vida por su hijo? Absolutamente. Los primeros cristianos nunca hubieran dado su vida por un símbolo, pero por una persona, absolutamente.

Tenemos en la iglesia católica lo que no se puede encontrar en cualquier otro lugar. Hemos seguido el mandato de Cristo de comer su carne y beber su sangre. Hay muchos de nuestros hermanos y hermanas que, sin embargo, se han marchado. Quieren ser entretenidos, o quieren vivir su vida como les de la gana y aun así han dejado la vida real. Pero no están solos, *"muchos ya no lo seguían."*

Y sin embargo, aquí estamos. Almas pobres y llenas de lastima, poniendo nuestra fe en algo que parece imposible. ¿Y aun así, como se puede creer en todo lo que Jesús dijo, menos esto? No tiene sentido. Pero así como muchos lo abandonaron (incluyendo nuestros familiares y amigos) nosotros estamos en buena compañía, cuando permanecemos y con un acto de fe creemos en las palabras de Cristo. Por que entonces habían doce. Cuando tengas lo verdadero, cualquier otra cosa es solo una imitación barata. Y si acaso dudas de esto por un minuto, escucha las palabras del primer Papa: "¿A quien iremos Señor? Tienes palabras de vida eterna."

TWENTY-FIRST SUNDAY IN TEMPUS PER ANNUM

(ISAIAH 22:15, 19-23; PSALM 138; ROMANS 11: 33-36; MATTHEW 16:13-20)

Mundus vult decipi[57]

This week I went camping in a cabin with my nephews. They're teenagers now. We went to sleep, and in fact they went to bed a little earlier than we usually do when out in the woods. When I got into bed, I heard it for the first time. A fly, was stuck to the fly tape hanging from the ceiling. And he wasn't dead yet, so he was buzzing and carrying on and making a racket. And although my nephews eventually fell asleep as witnessed by their deep, slow breathing . . . I could not. I lay in my bed for about an hour and even tried putting in the earplugs we use for shooting, but now I was awake. So I stumbled out of bed, slid on my shoes and descended the steps as quietly as I could to the *great room* below.

I celebrated Mass, since it was already early in the morning, and made a holy hour. The windows were open, and the cool breeze vented through, and yet the only sound it carried with it was the light tapping of the rain. All the critters who usually filled the night with their clicks and chirps were silent, as if also in adoration of our Lord. It was so eerie, because most of the time the forest seems very much alive.

As I sat there in my holy hour, the Lord spoke to me, and was feeding me words for the homily for this weekend. And as the words came to me I replied: "Thank you so much . . . but I already have the homily planned for this weekend. But thank you anyway." I had already written my homily, and it worked very well with the readings. Then I dozed a bit, in and out of prayer, and once again the words

---

57 "The world wants to be deceived."

of the Lord came to me. The words of the Lord exhorting, "This is what I want you to say to the people." Again, I thanked God for the offer, but I already had it figured out. "Thank you Lord; I appreciate so much your inspiration and words, I have a good homily for this weekend; but thank you."

Again, I would pray, and doze off a little, and then pray some more. It came again . . . and kept coming to me. It's like one of those dreams you have where you are still in grade school, and there's a big test the next day, and you must wake up, so you never sleep that night out of anxiety. It kept waking me up and startling me, and so I began to write . . . and write and write. So the words I speak today, really are not my own, and quite frankly, I would rather preach the homily that I had written before. It worked well, and I worked hard on it . . . but who am I to deny the Lord?

I feel like the prophet Jeremiah at times. Throughout his life, he seemed so depressed and it was because he didn't want to say what the Lord wanted him to say . . . because people would not receive it well. He would much rather have delivered to them the warm—fuzzies. Yet, he says that the word of the Lord is like a fire within him. And he would try not to preach or prophesy, and the words would burn him up! So he has to give them! Isaiah is much in the same boat. The Lord speaks through him to the people of Jerusalem.

> *Thus says the Lord: up, go to that official, Shebna, master of the palace: "I will thrust you from your office and pull you down from your station. On that day I will summon my servant Eliakim, son of Hilkiah; I will clothe him with your robe and gird him with your sash, and give over to him your authority. He shall be a father to the inhabitants of Jerusalem . . ."*

Shebna wasn't being a true father to the people. As I wrote . . . and prayed over it, the readings came to light in a way that was much better than what I had originally composed, and probably could ever compose.

There was a comedian I saw a few years ago on TV named Ray Romano. And he spoke about growing up Catholic in New York, when he was younger. And he remarked how the families used to come to Mass on Sunday and when the Mass began, the men used to go to the back of the church, where they would eventually walk outside and smoke and gossip and talk, until time to take the collection. After they had performed that duty, they would go back outside and wait until the end of Mass.

Now I'm here to tell you today. Those men no more went to Mass than the "heathens" who stayed at home, whom they spoke about as they smoked their cigarettes outside of the church. They no more went to church! They came here, they dropped off their families, and perhaps even thought they had made their Sunday obligation.

I would say the same thing is true of those who come and worship . . . but then they go home and live as if they are not Catholic. We have to be very careful here. The Gospel for today proclaims Peter's confession: *"You are the Messiah, the Son of the living God."* If Jesus is the Son of God; if Jesus *IS* in fact God, then what he says *is* law. And in some respects what he does *not* say, is also law.

The second reading from the letter of St. Paul to the Romans says: *For who has known the mind of the Lord? Or who has been his counselor? Who has given him anything so as to deserve return?* The first response from many people to this passage would be to condemn the church leaders. For *"who can know the mind of the Lord?"* And yet in the Gospel, Jesus will also say: *"I will entrust to you the keys of the kingdom of heaven. Whatever you declare bound on earth shall be bound in heaven. And whatever you declare loosed on earth, will be loosed in heaven."*

Now, I imagine at times, the apostles dealt with some of the issues we deal with today. And the Apostles would go out and heal and teach and cure and then return to Jesus. They would probably start to question our Lord, "Master, there were people who were confused about abortion, or alternative lifestyles" or other issues they had back then. "Should we tell them that you are the 'Good Shepherd', kind and merciful, and that you accept all people and you love all people and that you would understand?" And Jesus would probably respond as it is written of him in John's Gospel, *"If the world hates you, it hated me first."* I'm just throwin' that out there. *"If the world hates you . . . it hated me first."* Because the world ain't gonna like what I gotta say about this!

But the apostles are learning too, and they will say, "No Lord, you will never go to Jerusalem and suffer," to which Jesus responds, *"Get behind me Satan."* James and John are arguing about who is greater, and Jesus pulls aside a little child to teach them. The apostles want to call down fire upon the Samaritans because they will not welcome Jesus, and Judas comments that the alabaster jar of spike nard could have been sold and the money offered to the poor. So, they're still learning too. They don't know it all. But they were faithful. And we know that even though they are "two-hearted" here, all of them will be martyrs, save for John. And even him they tried to martyr. All of them would end up dying for their faith. A person who dies for his faith is not someone who is wishy-washy . . . not someone who is two-hearted. Not someone who is "I'm okay, you're okay," or "Live and let live." It is someone who is convicted by their faith.

What happens sometimes, is that we get caught up in the spin and the buzz of all these issues. In the seminary, they tried to prepare us for the groups who would be in opposition to us. They prepared us for the Protestants, who they said we must watch in our study of scripture, and how to combat their arguments. They tried to ready us for the non-Christians, Muslims, Buddhists, Hindus, etc. who would argue against Jesus' messiahship. Finally, they tried to prepare us for the culture of secular humanism and how to react with philosophy, in order to confound their arguments. But there was a group from whose attack they never prepared us. Probably one of the hardest groups to deal with, and the one which is causing the most opposition at times . . . The Catholics!

We say, "I am catholic" but we don't live as though we are. We do not live our Catholic faith . . . we don't. We may come to Mass and we keep all the easier laws that are easy to keep, but we do not live the faith when it is difficult or uncomfortable. Now I can't deal with all the issues, we'll be here all day, but I want to touch on two major issues and give Christ's teaching definitively. That to be Catholic, we must believe in this way.

And I would say, first . . . a person cannot be *pro-choice* and Catholic. A person cannot, be pro-Choice and Catholic. They cannot. The two are diametrically opposed to each other. Because, what that is saying, is that I support a person's right to kill another who is innocent. That's what we're saying. Now we might argue: "We don't know for certain that life begins at conception. Can you prove that life begins at conception?" I would have to say, at this point, no, I cannot prove that life begins at conception. But I would ask: "Can you prove that it does not? Can you prove, with 100% certainty that life does NOT begin at conception?" Because, even if there is a percent of a percent of a percent of a chance that life *DOES* begin at conception, isn't it worth saving the life, rather than the alternative? Even if it is the miniscule chance that this IS a life, would we dare not err on the side of caution? Because, if it is a life, and we can determine that one day without a doubt, then we have saved it. But if it is not a life yet, then we have lost nothing? We've done nothing wrong by preserving it!

So if we are pro-choice, we cannot claim ignorance. There is no room for ignorance, at least not here where we are today. And let me offer this. As much flack as we get for this, (and we will get flack) if we have spent our lives trying to save these children, then I guarantee you that when we die and go to our judgment, these children, whether we were able to save them or not, will stand beside us as our advocates! They will plead our cause before the judgment seat of God, who says *"let the children come to me and do not hinder them" (Mark 10:14).*

We must be very cautious because of the *spin*. And whether you're conservative or liberal; progressive or traditional, it doesn't matter. Lock yourself in a room without those outside influences. Lock yourself in a room with our Lord, and ask the question totally objectively: "Can this ever be right?" So we cannot support the right to kill an innocent. We cannot. Anyone who says we can, either doesn't understand or they are just plain wrong!

Here's the problem though. When an issue like this comes up in the popular culture, and they choose to interview a religious authority, they will go to a place like Georgetown University. (A place that up to a few years ago was practicing experiments using embryonic stem cells; until they were told to stop.) This is who they interview. When it came out a few weeks ago that the Vatican and bishops are cracking down on religious women in the U.S., who did they interview? Those who were the subject of the crackdown . . . those communities who were dissenting. They interviewed the Joan Chittisters to find out the "official Church teaching." We must be so careful and cautious about the spin.

The same principle applies to civil unions or same-sex unions. I mean, St. Paul mentions this in a number of letters; Jesus speaks of the immorality in the Gospel. And what he does not say here is important. In his discussion of marriage, he could easily have said, "in the beginning it was not so. Male and female he made them . . . or male and male . . . or female and female. This is not a recent issue. This behavior had been long accepted in the Roman Empire. Jesus says in the gospel that *"lest you lead astray my little ones, it would be better that a donkey's millstone were hung about your neck and you thrown into the sea!"* This is the only place he says this. Can there be any question about the wrongness of abortion? Can there be any question about the wrongness of same-sex unions and trying to call it marriage?

The union of same-sex couples is not so much about benefits and insurance, etc., there are other ways to do that. They are attacking the institution of marriage, and in effect, the One who instituted it as a Sacrament, when He said in response to divorce: *"It was not so from the beginning. In the beginning he made them. In his image and likeness he made them; man and woman he created them."* It is about redefining something that Jesus has defined. If we believe Jesus is God, then God has defined this for us. We cannot allow them to redefine marriage . . . we can't!

203

I would go on to say then, that one cannot support same-sex unions and call themselves Catholic! And please understand me, <u>this is not about an individuals' alternative lifestyle</u>. I have encountered a large number of those who are struggling with this lifestyle and have all the love and respect they deserve as children of God. This is not about struggling. WE all struggle. We are all sinners. This is about saying something is right, when it is not! When it cannot be right. We have come to say, "I cannot live this lifestyle like I choose, so I will make it right, and then I can live it." And we will always be able to find those who will support us. So when this issue arises, (and it will again and again) they will go to the *dissenters* in order to quote "an authority of the Catholic Church." They will find those who say they are catholic, even priests and religious women, I'm afraid . . . but Jesus never would have said that. Again, it's not about the individuals, it is about taking something that is wrong . . . and making it right. We cannot do that. We must be convicted in what we say . . . we cannot be two-hearted. Or we are just as bad as the ones who came to church, only to smoke, out in the back lot, while Mass was occurring.

There are many of these issues that come up, and they are black and white. There's no gray in there, but what we must do is lock ourselves in a room with God and ask the question: "Lord would you support this?" I'm not saying it's easy . . . far from it. We're all sinners; we all struggle with sin . . . but we *need* to struggle. We need to struggle. We cannot give up. And we cannot give in to what is happening around us!.. and all the voices who will condone that type of behavior.

It's not enough that we come to Mass. I know some might say today, "Father you're preaching to the choir," and that may be true; but my hope is that the choir goes out and sings, if you know what I mean. But if I'm **not** preaching to the choir, please just think about it objectively. Cut off everything from the outside; all the media spin and everything else and think about it objectively with a good conscience and consult our Lord.

Today as we celebrate the Eucharist, we acknowledge a mystery. That common elements of bread and wine become the body and blood of Christ. We don't all understand the Eucharist; I don't understand it and I'm a priest! It's a mystery. But that doesn't mean I'm gonna give up on it! It doesn't mean I'm only going to believe the things I can understand or get. It's the truth! And if it's the truth, we need to believe it. WE can't create some kind of other truth.

We, though individuals, are called to be united in our Catholic Christian faith and not two-hearted. It was once said, that before a civilization is destroyed from without, they destroy themselves from within, and that is how we are crumbling as a Church. We crumble when we start to buy into the popular mentality: "I'm okay, you're okay. Live and let live." And we want everybody to feel okay, and we want everybody to belong; and we want everybody to be treated the same. WE cannot fall into such a trap. WE must be united. WE cannot be two-hearted about this. We must be faithful; and we must continue to struggle.

The apostles start out as two-hearted. By the end of their time, they would give their lives as martyrs for the Church. We pray that we might have the faith that they did. That we can struggle with these issues and more; that we keep our conscience pure, even when it is difficult; and that we preach the faith . . . the true faith . . . *in season and out of season.* Because when you get right down to it, that's what being Catholic, and Christian, is all about.

Vigésimo Primer Domingo del Tiempo Ordinario Año "B"

(Josué 24:1-2, 15-17, 18; Salmo 34; Efesios 5:21-32; Juan 6:60-69)

Es el espíritu que da vida, mientras la carne no da provecho."

Durante las ultimas semanas hemos platicado de la importancia de la Eucaristía en la iglesia. Que la Eucaristía para nosotros, no es simplemente parte de nuestra fe; sino la fundación de nuestra fe. ¿Que tenemos en nuestra iglesia algo que, no se puede encontrar en cualquier otra tradición de fe? Sabemos que *"muchos lo abandonaron porque dijeron que este dicho era muy difícil."* Nadie dijo que seria fácil, pero al final, nada provechoso, que en verdad sea de importancia, es fácil. Un buen matrimonio, por ejemplo, requiere muchísimo trabajo.

Escuché a un hombre cual fue corregido por otro hombre mayor en una recepción de bodas. El hombre dijo que el matrimonio cuesta trabajo . . . y se debe compartir cincuenta y cincuenta. El hombre mayor lo corrigió y dijo: "Estas equivocado. Un matrimonio debe ser cien diez por ciento y cien diez por ciento. Si los dos hacen ese esfuerzo, entonces tendrán un matrimonio maravilloso."

Pablo dice:

> *"Esposos, amen a su esposas, aun como Cristo amo a la iglesia, entregándose por ella para santificarla, lavándola con el agua de la palabra, que el pudiera presentar a si mismo la iglesia con resplandor, sin manchas ni arrugas, o cualquier otro defecto, para que ella sea pura y sin mancha."*

Imaginen eso! Recuerden, Jesús entrego su vida por la iglesia . . . ¿algunas preguntas? La verdad es, que cuando una pareja viene a mi con problemas, se me aparece que los dos simplemente "ya no están intentando." Que ellos se sienten cómodos, o que están cansados de dar y no recibir. De nuevo se presenta esta discusión de cincuenta y cincuenta. Para amar a su pareja como cristo ama a la iglesia se trata de mas que cincuenta y cincuenta. ¿Que tiene que ver esto con la Eucaristía? Todo.

He notado que algunos se acercan a recibir la comunión con goma de mascar en su boca. Otros tienen un dulce en su boca mientras están en misa. ¿Comprendo si estas enfermo o tienes dolor de garganta . . . pero cada semana? Puedo comprender si quieres que tu aliento huela bien, pero hay alguna cosas mas importantes. El ayuno es una manera que ofrecemos nuestro cien diez por ciento y decimos, "Dios, tu eres lo mas importante que recibo hoy, y por eso, dejare mi estomago vacío." Vacío de la azúcar que entra a nuestro cuerpo con la goma, el dulce o cualquier otra cosa.

Jesús dice: *"Es el espíritu que da vida, mientras la carne no da provecho."* En otras palabras, se están preocupando mas por las necesidades del cuerpo, en favor de hacer irreverencia al espíritu. Es tiempo de re-encender la reverencia por la Eucaristía dentro de nosotros. ¿Cuantos de ustedes, en su primera comunión, hubieran soñado con mascar goma? No . . . porque demostraban reverencia. Recibimos hoy el mismo Cristo que antes. Lo que ha cambiado, es que nos sentimos cómodos con nuestra pareja . . . ya no ofrecemos todo lo que tenemos.

Twenty-Second Sunday in Tempus per Annum

(Isaiah 22:15, 19-23; Psalm 138; Romans 11: 33-36; Matthew 16:13-20)

Good, pleasing and perfect

There is power in the sacrifice. Sacrifice has a double meaning in Latin. The *Sacra* and the *Facio* are significant. *Facio* means *make* or *do*, while *sacra* means *holy*. We get the word sacred and sacrament from this word. So a *sacrifice*, then, is not only a "holy doing" but it is a "making holy."

Jeremiah could teach us about sacrifice. Here's a guy who spends his life giving advice and warnings, not on his own behalf, but on behalf of God. No one wants to hear his advice and warnings, because it would mean change for them. And those who are in power and comfortable, rarely want to change.

Finally, the prophecies are fulfilled; people are killed or maimed; and there sits Jeremiah suffering with them. And I'm sure the words, "I told you so" kept rising in his mouth like a last meal to the seasick fisherman . . . but he didn't say it. I know *we* never feel that urge. Jeremiah was God's prophet and not his own. *That* is sacrifice. Even though he knew what was right, and made the right decisions, he would endure the punishment on the unrighteous. That doesn't seem quite fair . . . especially if you look at it from a world view. Why would he suffer, when he was doing what he was supposed to do? That's a valid question and has been addressed by everyone from Epicurus to Viktor Frankl and beyond.

As human persons with souls, we have free will. And whenever free will is involved, so is sin, and the possibility of sacrifice. Whenever more than one person is involved, then the actions or omissions in sin of one person will affect the other. And the same is true of sacrifice.

This is where the sacrifice comes in. We have the ability to take something that is bad, and make it holy. What?! I know . . . run with me for a minute here. We find meaning in the sacrifice. Sometimes that meaning comes from a prophet; at other times an unlikely prophet.

In his book, *Man's Search for Meaning*, Viktor Frankl speaks of his time in the death camp Auschwitz. As he's expounding on his discovery of *Logotherapy*, he relates a story about a boy and his mother.

> Once, the mother of a boy who had died at the age of eleven years was admitted to my hospital department after a suicide attempt. Dr. Kurt Kocourek invited her to join a therapeutic group, and it happened that I stepped into the room where he was conducting a psychodrama. She was telling her story. At the death of her boy she was left alone with another, older son, who was crippled, suffering from the effects of infantile paralysis. The poor boy had to be moved around in a wheelchair. His mother, however, rebelled against her fate. But when she tried to commit suicide together with him, it was the crippled son who prevented her from doing so. He liked living![58]

When we speak about *euthanasia* in the Church, we get a lot of flak from groups who say that it is a person's right to die. Obviously this mother thought the same. Probably a mix of her depression, and the thought of caring for this son who had no "quality of life." But he didn't want to die! So often we dismiss sacrifice and the effects it can have on the life of a person, who perhaps could never find meaning in it before. For Jesus, sacrifice is the meaning of his life. Not only the ultimate sacrifice that he will make at Calvary, but the daily sacrifice he offered of himself. Just as Jeremiah revealed the plan of God to the people who would ultimately be exiled for their disobedience, Jesus is the revelation of the Father, to those who are exiled from the kingdom of heaven.

---

58 Viktor E. Frankl, *Man's Search for Meaning: An Introduction to Logotherapy*, 3rd ed. (New York, NY, Simon and Schuster, 1984), 120.

The lesson of sacrifice is not an easy one. Peter obviously doesn't get it at this point, but will finally demonstrate his mastery as he is crucified in Rome. The one who leads away from the sacrifice or *making sacred*, is the epicurean demon who from the beginning would not serve. St. Paul leaves us with this exhortation: "*I beg you through the mercy of God to offer your bodies as a living sacrifice, holy and acceptable to God . . . be transformed by the renewal of your mind, so that you may judge what is God's will, what is good, pleasing and perfect.*" . . . what is *made holy*.

VIGÉSIMO SEGUNDO DOMINGO DEL TIEMPO ORDINARIO AÑO "B"

(DEUTERONOMIO 4:1-2, 6-8; SALMO 15; SANTIAGO 1:17-18, 21-22, 27; MARCOS 7:1-8, 14-15, 21-23)

¿Que significa ser discípulo?

"Este pueblo me honra con los labios, pero su corazón esta lejos de mi. Es inútil el culto que me rinden, porque enseñan doctrinas que no son sino preceptos humanos." ¿Esperen un momento, estara hablando en serio? ¿Jesús esta diciendo esto? ¿Esta hablando de lo que leemos en la primera lectura del libro de *Deuteronomio*? Moisés les dijo, *"Escuchen los mandatos y preceptos que les enseño, para que los pongas en practica y puedan vivir . . ."* ¿Cual pudiera ser el significado de lo que Cristo dijo?

Pablo lo explica diciendo: *"Su voluntad es traernos hacia el nacimiento con una palabra verdadera hablada para que podamos ser los primeros frutos de sus creaturas."* *"Por sus frutos los conocerán" (Mateo 7:16).* ¿Entonces a que viene todo esto? Nuestros labios pueden ofrecer oraciones; decir "te amo"; y nuestras mentes pueden saber todos los mandamientos. Pero saber y hablar de estas cosas no es lo que Dios desea. Lo que El desea es lo que esta por dentro . . . lo que El puso dentro de nosotros: que lo demostremos. Eso es lo que significa ser discípulo.

Mientras estaba en el seminario, fuimos visitados por ciertos dignatarios: cardinales, obispos, gobernadores, etc. Como seminarista, tuve mis días muy ocupados. Tenia que rezar, estudiar, ir a clases, rezar, asístir a reuniones y cenas, mas reuniones, actividades, aun mas reuniones, ir a practica de coro, etc. Un día estaba pensando en todo lo que tenia que hacer y apresurarme para hacerlo todo.

Vivía en el tercer piso, y este día decidí usar el elevador. ¡Este elevador era mas lento que la muerte! Presionabas el botón y esperabas siete horas hasta que por fin se cerraba la puerta. Entonces duraba otras siete horas para subir. Mientras, estoy parado esperando que la puertas cerraran . . . y después sucedió.

Usted sabe, quizás le ha sucedido a usted. Escuche voces en el pasíllo. Empecé a formular un plan, si la persona me veía antes de que la puerta cerrara entonces le permitiría entrar. Detendría la puerta porque ellos me podrían identificar. Pero . . . ¡si las puertas cerraban y no me podían ver, entonces seria libre! Y espere, y finalmente la puertas comenzaron a cerrar, pero las voces se acercaban mas y mas.

Las puertas comenzaron cerrar y entonces él dio vuelta a la esquina y vio mi cara . . . ¡era un cardinal, y fijo la mirada en mi! Entonces, en un esfuerzo para detener la puerta avente mi pie y cuando lo hice . . . todo lo que vi fue mi sandalia volando en el aire . . . y entonces las puertas se cerraron. Había pateado a uno de los oficiales mas altos de la iglesia . . . y solo era un seminarista.

Mientras comenzaba mi viaje hacia el tercer piso pensé, "¿Porque hiciste eso? ¿Porque no pudiste detener la puerta un minuto mas? No simplemente porque era un cardinal, sino por cualquier persona." Entonces reflexione aun mas: "¿Porque estoy en el seminario? No estoy aquí para rezar, aunque es muy necesario. No estoy aquí para estudiar, aunque es muy importante. No estoy aquí para asístir a reuniones y practicas y actividades, aunque todo esto sea esencial. Estoy aquí para ser mas como Cristo. Si no mes estoy convirtiendo mas como Cristo, entonces he falládo miserablemente. Decidí que iba a encontrar al cardinal y pedirle disculpas. No por patearlo, sino por falta de caridad.

Eventualmente llegue a mi cuarto y me prepare para el resto del día. Iba en camino a mi próxima clase (esta vez baje las escaleras) y me estaba acercando al elevador. Mientras me acercaba me di cuenta que había algo en la silla enfrente del elevador. Mientras me acercaba, me di cuenta que era mi sandalia. Cuando me acerque aun mas vi que había una nota pegada a mi sandalia. La recogí leí la nota que decía: "Gracias por intentar."

Este hombre no me conocía y pensó en el mejor escenario posible. Ese viaje en el elevador me permitió ver como estaba viviendo mi vida; en una manera que no era digna del reino. Había sentido el arrepentimiento verdadero por mi pecado, propuse firmemente cambiar esos modos. Y cuando hacemos este cambio, es Dios quien sonríe y nos toma de la mano, y nos guía a donde necesitamos estar.

Lo que Dios busca en nosotros es el discípulo. El discípulo es el que se da cuenta que cuando no actuamos en caridad . . . todo lo demás es para nada. Ahora, no somos perfectos. Pero siempre y cuando intentemos . . . siempre y cuando hagamos un esfuerzo de usar las santas practicas y los *"mandatos y preceptos"* para acercarnos a Dios en la caridad, entonces aunque fallemos, Dios sonríe y amablemente nos dice: "Gracias por intentar."

Twenty-Third Sunday in Tempus per Annum

(Ezekial 33:7-9; Psalm 95; Romans 13:8-10; Matthew 18:15-20)

Judge not, lest ye be judged.

Notice, I didn't put a scriptural citation after the quote above. I wonder why? For as many years as I have been alive (and I'm sure countless ones before that) this phrase has been used by those who want to live in a way that is unacceptable according to God's laws. "Don't judge me" or as a recent Miley Cyrus song put it, "Remember only God can judge us . . . Forget the haters 'cause somebody loves ya . . ."[59] It's really a commentary on how much those who are trying to live as Christians run up against a world that does not believe, or even beyond that, wants no one else to believe either. Those who "call it like it is"; those who say what is being done is unacceptable, are called *bigots* or "*haters*." It's the way we try to discredit the proclaimers of truth, and it is not new. Ask any of the prophets and they will tell you.

The prophet is told, *"You, son of man, I have appointed watchman for the house of Israel; when you hear me say anything, you shall warn them for me."* He goes on to say, *"If I tell the wicked man that he shall surely die, and you do not speak out to dissuade the wicked man from his way, he shall die for his guilt, but I will hold YOU responsible for his death."* (All caps my emphasis). It sounds like the Lord is telling Ezekial to "judge" what is *His* will and what is not, and to inform those what is, the will of God. Jesus says to his disciples,

---

59 Miley Cyrus, *"We Won't Stop,"* Williams, michael len / slaughter, pierre ramon / cyrus, miley / thomas, timothy / thomas, theron / davis, douglas / walters, ricky, 2013.

"If your brother should commit some wrong against you, go and point out his fault, but keep it between the two of you. If he listens, you have won your brother over. If he does not listen, however, summon another, so that every case may stand on the word of two or three witnesses."

Now I could be wrong, but it sounds like Jesus is saying, "Not only do I give you the authority to judge, but mandate that you do so."

So where do we get that, "Judge not lest ye be judged?" Let's look a little further back in the famous passage where Jesus talks about the speck in your brother's eye and the log in your own. Matthew, chapter seven begins with that phrase, Judge not . . . , however, then he goes on to talk about hypocrisy! In other words, the judges he is speaking of, are not "righteous judges." Jesus will later on call them the *"blind guides,"* who judge others for wrongs, they themselves are committing. There's no question that we are called to "judge" what is right and wrong. Jesus will go on to give the apostles the power to bind and loose, here on earth: the very source of our sacrament of Reconciliation. So, what are we to follow, if even those who condemn the Christian, quote Jesus' words? We are called **to judge**, but not **to condemn**!

Remember, as St. Paul says, *"Love is the fulfillment of the law."* So often we are quick to condemn; not *to judge*, but condemn. We have "damned the person," before we have given them any other option or guidance. So, love must be the root of judging; we judge, so that the one we love will do what will ultimately make them happy . . . will give them peace. We can fight this as creatures . . . we can decide we know better than God. C.S. Lewis says this:

Perhaps we feel inclined to disagree with him [God]. But there is a difficulty about disagreeing with God. He is the source from which all your reasoning power comes: you could not be right and He wrong, any more than a stream can rise higher than its own source. When you are arguing against Him you are arguing against the very power that makes you able to argue at all: it is like cutting off the branch you are sitting on.[60]

The second part of the judgment cannot be neglected. For when we judge, without forgiving, then we have actually condemned. Jesus, during his ministry, condemned only those who condemned others. He judged those Pharisees and scribes; the elders of the Jews who knew not *forgiveness*, but *condemnation*. "God rejoices in forgiving; for forgiveness is the completion of love."[61]

Jesus leaves us with this: *"If two of you join your voices on earth to pray for anything whatever, it shall be granted you by my Father in heaven."* Two who join their voices are reconciled. If they're not reconciled, they wouldn't join together nuthin'! The witnesses who judge are also the witnesses who forgive. And those acts, are acts of **love**. So "condemn not" and you shall not be condemned. But judge? Absolutely. And forgive? Always.

---

60 C.S. Lewis, *Mere Christianity*, (San Francisco, CA. Harper Collins Publishers, 2001) 48.

61 Fr. Peter van Breeman. *The God Who Won't Let Go*. (Notre Dame, IN: Ave Maria Press, 1991), 60.

Vigésimo Tercer Domingo del Tiempo Ordinario
Año "C"

(Sabiduría 9:13-18; Salmo 90; Filemón 9:10, 12-17; Lucas 14:25-33)

"Porque eres tibio, porque no eres ni caliente ni frío, te vomitaré de mi boca."

Cuando El Señor habla de renunciar a nuestra pocesiones, Él no nos da a entender que debemos renunciar a todos nuestros bienes. Él no quiere decirnos que no podemos tener dinero, ni que debemos separarnos de nuestras familias. Tampoco nos da a entender que debemos vivir en dolor y sufrimiento constante para poder ser discípulos buenos. Ninguna de estas cosas tiene sentido.

Lo que Él quiere decir es esto: cualquiera de estas cosas; sea una casa o algo que poseemos o el dinero o nuestra familia: cualquier cosa que los aleja de mí o impide que apoyes a mi iglesia; cualquiera de estas cosas que tiene una posición más alta en tu vida que Yo; esas son las cosas que debes renunciar. En otras palabras, si Dios no es lo más importante; o aún peor, si no le damos el tiempo que merece, entonces no estamos cargando con nuestra cruz; no lo estamos siguiendo, sino que vamos por el camino equivocado.

A veces, a causa de nuestros deseos por comodidades o la necesidad de tener seguridades; creamos una falta de voluntad en nostros mismos de ofrecer, cuando es nuestra obligación. Al final de nuestras vidas, El Señor nos preguntará *"¿Me has ofrecido todo lo que te he entregado?"* Y apesar nuestra contestación, ya sea el si o no, Él sabrá la verdad. Y habrá una recompensa por esa verdad . . . sea buena o mala.

Tenemos una comunidad maravillosa aquí en nuestra Iglesia, pero es una comunidad que esta dividida. Esta división no es una de raza, ni lugar de origen o idioma, sino que es una división entre quienes son miembros activos de la iglesia, y quienes no lo son. Es una división entre quienes entregan de si mismos, y quienes no lo hacen. Jesus reconoce a la viuda porque ella puso su única moneda en el cofre . . . porque era todo lo que tenía. Algunos de nosotros diríamos "no tengo nada que ofrecer a la iglesia." Y aún así, me imagino que si buscamos lo suficiente, podriamos encontrar al menos la moneda de la viuda.

Tengo claro que la economía no va muy bien ahora. Me he dado cuenta que muchos no tienen trabajo, y estan luchando para vivir. Pero tambien he observado la manera en que vive la gente. Sé que apesar de las dificultades, nosotros tenemos los fondos y recursos para conseguir las cosas que deseamos. Veo celulares en manos de sus hijos, que cuestan más de un mes de alimentos. He asístido a algunas fiestas de Quienceañeras, o bodas con cientas de personas. Aún para la celebración de Nuestra *Señora de Guadalupe*, la gente ofrece dinero para las mañanitas.

El punto que, yo quiero hacer es que no podemos sobrevivir como estamos ahora, como una parroquia dividida. Cuando hay pocas personas que ofrecen mucho y hacen más de lo que les corresponde, mientras los demás sólo se quedan mirando, o simplemente ofrecen a la iglesia el dinero que les sobra, la iglesia seguirá dividida. Jesús nos pide que, como un pueblo, carguemos nuestra cruz y lo sigamos, ¡Tenemos que despertar! Pregúntese si usted esta entregando a la iglesia todo lo que puede.

Cuando tenemos casí trecientas personas en la misa, y sólo cuarenta ayudan en el fesitval, no estamos ofreciendo lo mejor que podemos. Cuando hay trecientas personas en la misa, y sólo cuarenta ayudan en el picnic, o en actividades para recaudar fondos y en ventas de comida, es no es ofrecer lo mejor de nosotros. Y cuando tenemos el tiempo para hacer las cosas que deseamos hacer, pero no estamos activos en los ministerios de nuestra iglesia, eso no es ofrecerlo mejor de nosotros mismos. Nisiquiera estamos intentando.

Nuestro Señor dice en el libro del Apocalípsis: *"Porque eres tibio, porque no eres ni caliente ni frío, te vomitaré de mi boca."* No se engañen, es nuestra obligación regresar a Dios los dones que Él nos ha confiado. Él nos pide ser miembros activos de su comunidad y apoyarla tanto físicamente como financiaramente. Está es la hora. Porque cuando nos encontremos con Él en nuestro día final . . . en ese momento, todos los dones que nos ha entregado; nuestras poseciones, nuestro tiempo, y nuestros deseos . . . ni una de estas cosas tendrán valor.

Twenty-Fourth Sunday in Tempus per Annum

(Isaiah 22:15, 19-23; Psalm 138; Romans 11: 33-36; Matthew 16:13-20)

A Student in the School of Forgiveness

Being near a major medical center affords us with not only great medical care, but also a challenge with respect to biomedical ethics at times. As a priest who lives with two hospital chaplains, it also offers us a great responsibility not only to those Catholics within our parish boundaries, but to the many others who enter the hospital closer to death's door than they would prefer. For many of these individuals, the emotions range from sorrow to anger, and the dispositions from forgiveness to resignation. I would like to relate to you once such experience I had with a little boy named Grant.

The day was not unlike many others. There were Masses to celebrate, classes to teach and meetings to attend. I had a school board meeting scheduled for that evening, and was in and out of the office, when Barb, one of our volunteers, who monitors the desk outside of normal business hours, answered a call coming from the hospital. It was the grandfather of a boy who had been in an accident with a horse, and the youngster was in critical condition. The family was requesting a Mass in the hospital room for the boy. This was a unique request. For the most part, when we visit the hospital, or a call comes in for a visit, they are requesting "Anointing of the Sick." But in this case, I was a bit confused. I called the grandfather myself, and he explained the circumstances, the faith of the family, and why the Mass, the highest prayer of the Church, was requested. I notified the principal that I would be late to the meeting, and why I would be late, and then rushed with my Mass kit and oil to the hospital.

I arrived in the pediatric ICU and joined the parents, grandparents and siblings of this seven-year-old boy. He lay there motionless, save for the artificial breath that entered and exited his lungs. I had to catch my breath as I entered the room. I don't think anything can prepare you for that. The family was all there, and eager to celebrate the Mass. I was informed that Grant had already been anointed, and so we proceeded. I was not prepared to preach to this congregation, and yet the Spirit supplied the words. I cannot remember what I said, but the parents appeared grateful. I asked his siblings to pray for him for "although the gates of heaven are resistant to the poundings and thumpings of the mighty, they easily open at the touch of a child."[62]

I left there and joined the meeting already in progress, and informed everyone what was happening and who was involved. After the meeting, the outpouring from the school and parish was unreal. Prayer petitions were going out through even our Diocese, asking prayers for this child. It was decided that the next day, I would give him his Sacraments, as is recommended in the Rite. I returned, and things seemed more dire than ever. Once again, I celebrated Mass, and there, offered him his Sacraments. St. Padre Pio was the saint name for his confirmation, and a drop of Precious blood was placed on his tongue. At this, the parents appeared to be more peaceful. I could barely get the words from my trembling lips.

Grant died the next day. I was there for his passing, and watched as these young parents tried to console their children, while they themselves struggled with the loss of a child. I felt so inadequate in light of the faith that they displayed despite such grief. I said my goodbyes and offered a promise of prayers, which was all I could do before I excused myself and went out by the elevator. I looked for a place to hide so that I could let out this horrible grief, but with nowhere to go, I went to the window and wept. A nurse approached me and asked if I needed anything, and unable to speak, I just lifted my hand to wave her off. Finally the doors to the elevator opened and I entered. Thankfully . . . alone.

---

62 Bishop Fulton J. Sheen, *The World's First Love*, (New York, NY: McGraw-Hill Co., 1952), 92.

It was only after this experience, that I came to understand what happened, and how it was that this young child had been kicked by a horse. They had been visiting an Amish bed and breakfast on a farm. And as children are want to do, they were playing around the farm animals. This is where the accident occurred. Through this ordeal in the hospital, up until the funeral of the boy, there was no talk of litigation or lawyers or blame. There was only talk of forgiveness and surviving the grief.

At the funeral, the front three rows in the Catholic Church, were filled with the Amish family, their friends, and their Bishop who came to offer prayers for this family. It was for me a humbling experience of forgiveness and faith amidst grief.

Sirach says: *"Should a man nourish anger against his fellows and expect healing from the Lord? Should a man refuse mercy to his fellows, yet seek pardon for his own sins?"* The Lord is kind and merciful; slow to anger and rich in compassion. I know, I know . . . we priests and religious are supposed to be leaders at this; and yet, I was shamed through this experience of humility and forgiveness. I went to the hospital not as a teacher, but a student.

St. Paul knew this well. You can tell by his letter to the Romans: *"No one lives as his own master, and none of us dies as his own master. While we live, we are responsible to the Lord, and when we die, we die as His servants."* I'll be the first to admit, I'm no master . . . a student to the end. A student in the school of forgiveness.

When someone is close to death, I have to admit, I ask them, that when they get to the next life, they give me some sign. I know, I know, I have to work on the faith department too! And many times I do get those signs. I never spoke with Grant, and yet I did ask him to send me a sign. Something I would understand.
A few weeks ago, I had a wedding. The evening of the rehearsal, one of the children involved (who didn't appear to be aware of his surroundings and what was going on) just sat quietly in the church, and was sketching a picture in pen on a ratty piece of paper. The rehearsal concluded, and I was tying up loose ends when the mother

approached me and said, "Father, my son drew you a picture."
The picture was of a cross with beams emanating from the middle
outward. I smiled and jokingly responded: "Well at least sign it.
Someday it will be worth something." He signed the cross with
beams, and gave it back to me, and then departed for the evening.
The name in the margin of the picture was "Grant."

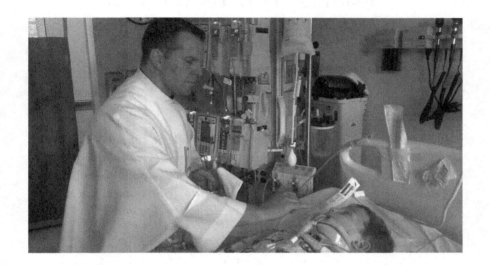

Grant

VIGÉSIMO CUARTO DOMINGO DEL TIEMPO ORDINARIO AÑO "C"

(ÉXODO 32:7-11, 13-14; SALMO 51; I TIMOTEO 1:12-17; LUCAS 15:1-32)

Este hermano tuyo estaba muerto, y ha vuelto a la vida . . .

Escuchen a la carta de San Pablo a Timoteo:

> *"Antes fui un blasfemo y persegui a la iglesia con violencia; pero Dios tuvo compasión de mi porque en mi incredulidad obré por ignorancia, y la gracia de Nuestro Señor se desbordo sobre mí. Puedes fiarte de lo que voy a decirte: que Cristo Jesús vino a este mundo para salvar a los pecadores, de los cuales yo soy el primero."*

Quizas para clarificar una de las historias biblicas más famosas, debemos tomarla y hacerla más facil de entender. A esta escritura, se le llama *"El hijo progido"* y sin embargo podríamos llamarla por otro nombre si entenderíamos al padre. Imagine a su hijo, o si usted no tiene hijos, imagine a un niño o una persona que usted quiere mucho. Este hijo, en quien usted ha invertido su vida; sus recursos; su amor. Alguien por quien estaría dispuesto a entregar su vida, acambio de nada. Piense en ese hijo por un momento.

Ahora . . . imagine el día que su hijo se aleja de usted. Estaba cansado de las reglas, cansado de la vida, y querían comenzar de nuevo. Así, que se fue, y usted tenía que dejarlo ir. ¿Qué pensaba hacer, correr tras de su hijo? ¿Encerrarlo en en cuarto parasíempre? Ya era mayor de edad. Sabía lo que esto implica. Empaco su maleta, y se marcho sin decir una palabra. Usted lo sigue mirando . . . se queda en la puerta principal, y se fija mientras su hijo camina hacia quién sabe donde. Se sintió herido; enojado; traicionado, y no recuerda cuántas horas pasaron antes de que finalmente cerro la puerta. Pero siempre existió esa incertidumbre. Ese temor que lo acompaña al saber, que esta cerrando la puerta a una parta de usted mismo, y la esperanza que quizas en cualquier momento, su hijo regresará y se dará cuenta de lo equivocado que estuvo. Pero hoy, no hubo vuelta atrás; hoy, nadie regreso.

Días y quizas hasta semanas pasaron, y con el paso del tiempo empezo una nueva costumbre. Cada madrugada usted toma una taza de café, o té o jugo y de nuevo abre la puerta, y sólo se queda mirando hacia la calle con esa esperanza que hoy será el día. Hace semanas que no sientes ira, ni traición, pero las oraciones nunca han cesado. La oración comenzaba: "Señor, ayudale a ser feliz y exitoso", pero pronto eso tambien cambia. La oración se ha convertido en: "Señor, permite que se encuentre bien de salud: por favor protejelo y guardalo de peligro." Los días son tan largos sin su hijo, y las noches son un desierto de solitud.

Ahora la oración se ha convertido en plegaria por una vida. Ya no es una oración por su regreso, sino un grito pidiendo: ";Señor, por favor permite que este vivo!" Y, un día . . . después de semanas, meses, y quizas hasta años despues de su partida, aún en ese tiempo, usted esta parado en la puerta, esperando. Y derrepente, en el horizonte, se ve una creatura debil y flaca caminando por la calle. No tiene equipaje, ni zapatos en sus pies . . . sólo un recuerdo de lo que antes era, caminando hacia usted. Usted se pone nervioso, y no puede decir ni una sola palabra. Es todo lo que puede hacer para evitar quebrar la puerta de tela. Antes de que esa hijo mire en su dirección, usted tambien esta corriendo descalzo entre el cesped congelado. Usted toma a su hijo en sus brazos y lo encamina a la casa, donde lo envuelve con mantas y lo toma entre sus brazos. Su hijo lo mira y comienza a hablar palabras de disculpa, de amor, y de arrepentimiento; pero usted pone un dedo sobre sus labios, asegurandole que en verdad no importa porque regreso . . . sino que lo más importante es que porfin regreso. Su hijo esta con usted de nuevo.

¿Acaso usted sabe lo que se siente al pasar por esto? De una forma o otra, todos sabemos lo que se siente. No porque todos somos padres, o tíos, o tías; no porque hemos tenido alguien que nos ha dejado, nos ha traicionado, o han huido de nosotros. El motivo por el cual todos conocemos esta historia, es porque cada uno de nosotros somos ese hijo. Ese hijo soy yo. Ese hijo es usted. Es hora de regresar a casa.

Twenty-Fifth Sunday in Tempus per Annum

(Isaiah 55:6-9; Psalm 145; Philippians 1:20-24, 27; Matthew 20:1-16)

A second chance

Ahhhh! We hate this Gospel. At least, those who don't need a second chance do. There are those people, you know. Those who get through life unscathed or unjaded by the calamities that we all suffer at one point or another. I'm not speaking of the "goodie-two-shoes" whatever that means, so much as I'm speaking about those who never seem to get off track, or veer off the path. You know some of those people, right? I know I do . . . well . . . kinda . . . I mean . . . well, no not really at all.

Granted there are some who at least have made modest mistakes throughout life, or dealt with the consequences of the horrible mistakes and are much better for it. But for the rest of us (I don't exclude myself here) we want . . . we need . . . a fresh start; a second chance. Ah, to be young again, and I would do it all differently, right? Well, I don't know about that. Chesterton has a great quote about this:

> "When one is young, one has these ideals in the abstract and these castles in the air; but in middle age they all break up like clouds, and one comes down to a belief in practical politics, to using the machinery one has and getting on with the world as it is." Thus, at least, venerable and philanthropic old men now in their honoured graves used to talk to me when I was a boy. But since then I have grown up and have discovered that these philanthropic old men were telling lies.[63]

---

63 G.K. Chesterton, *Orthodoxy*, (Colorado Springs, CO, Waterbrook Press, 2001), 61.

He will go on to relate how his ideals didn't change, but his faith was no longer an immature or naïve faith. It now was a faith tested and one that would require an effort for the relationship to work well.

I thank God every day that He is the God of second chance. Because if He were not, how could there be hope?

When I was at Trinity High School as the chaplain, there was a custodian who I would see after school. His ritual was the same every day. As most of the students evacuated the school he would move around slowly, sweeping and scraping the gum off the floor. He would then go into the restrooms and clean up the paper towels that were carelessly dropped on the floor, or the urine that missed the mark. I never once heard him speak. I would go by and he would bow; and I would bow; and then we would part ways.

I moved on from Trinity and was assigned to a parish in Lebanon, called St. Benedict the Abbot. There was a large painting in the sanctuary of St. Benedict. You see, the parish was originally Slovak, but during the nineties, had to consolidate with a Spanish parish. The custom is to change the name when a new parish is formed, so they chose St. Benedict the Abbot. I inquired about this painting and heard the story from one of our priests in the Diocese.

When the parish was created, he commissioned a work of art from a man in one of his previous assignments. This man came over from Vietnam during the war, with a shipload of many others. He was responsible for rationing the soup for his people, who were starving in the bowels of this ship. Because he was responsible for the rationing, he would often give his spoonful to the pregnant women or the children, and by doing this, had saved countless lives during that journey.

I went to the parish, where this man had painted many more portraits of saints. I thought to myself, "Here's this hero, with a great story, and he is a very gifted painter. I wonder where he is and what he's doing now." You can imagine my surprise when the pastor told me, "He's a custodian. He cleans up at Trinity high school. That's his job."

We all make mistakes. And yet our Lord gives us opportunities again and again. Here is a man who was given a chance to make a difference, and didn't think twice about it; even when it meant his life. Even when he is not a renowned artist in the United States. Even as he cleans the gum off the floor. Because he understands. The first will be last, and the last will be first.

So what about us? Are we still waiting in the marketplace for someone to make life easier for us? Or are we ready to go into the field again? So often people have this perception that they're in too deep; that they're too far away from God ever to return. Jesus makes it clear that the same reward can be obtained by those who come at the eleventh hour. The question becomes, when is the eleventh hour?

Now is not the time to wait. Now is the time to act. We have a God of second chance, but we must want to try again. This will not be forced on us. He is rationing the soup, and yet he is willing to give us his portion. *Seek the Lord, while he may be found, call to him while he is near.* For, *the Lord is near to all who call him.*

VIGÉSIMO QUINTO DOMINGO DEL TIEMPO ORDINARIO AÑO "C"

(AMÓS 8:4-7; SALMO 113; I TIMOTEO 2: 1-8; LUCAS 16:1-13)

¡Nunca olvidaré jamás ninguna de estas acciones!

No les parece interesante, sin embargo, como miramos hacia el futuro todo el tiempo. Continuamente dejamos las cosas hasta el último momento. Somos una generación de indecisos.

Había alguien que dijo una vez: "Me gustaría ser un gran procrastinador, pero lo sigo aplazando." La gente que el pobre de Amos tiene que soportar, todos estan mirando hacia el futuro, mientras que continuan viviendo como si tuvieran todo el tiempo del mundo para hacerlo correctamente: tienen todo el tiempo del mundo para oprimir a los pobres, para tratar a la gente como basura, para poner su vida en orden. Un profeta del "pesismismo" es uno para aquéllos cuyas vidas no merecen la vida enterna. Aunque, auizas, es Jesús quien actua como el profeta para quienes más necesitan escucharlo.

Nosotros escuchamos el Evangelio, y para la mayoría de la gente, esta parabola del administrador deshonesto es preocupante. Parece que Jesús esta premiando estas acciones deshonestas. Parece que Jesús lo esta ensalzando como si fuera un ejemplo positivo, este administrador engañoso y egoísta. Pero si lo vemos con lente del vigésimo primer siglo, claro que nos confunde. Pero si nos ponemos el en lugar del administrados del primer siglo, el significado de esto comienza a ser más claro.

Jesús no menciona donde se encuentra este administrador, pero la gente del *Antiguo Oreinte* compredía muy bien este sistema. Los caminos que Jesús recurrió pasaban por un puesto de avanazada, quizas nosotros lo llamaríamos "las afueras" de una ciudad. Los señores de alta sociedad eran dueños de mucho terreno, porque la tierra era fértil; más aún, no habia vida en la ciudad, y seguramente no era un gran metrópli dentro del mundo Palestino. Entonces, estos señores ricos, confiaban sus terrenos y productos a un administrador. Este se encargaba de entregar ciero porcentaje de las ganancias a su partron, y él se quedaba con lo que sobraba. De esta manera ganaba su dinero, de la comisión que les exijía a los clientes.

Sin embargo, estos señores ricos no eran tontos, y se dieron cuenta de que tenían que sacar adelante su negocio. Con el tiempo el patron se enteró que su administrador no estaba haceindo "buenos negocios" y decidió reemplazarlo. Aquí es donde se hace un poco confuso. El administrador estaba intentando de ofrecer un poco de compesación para poder asegurar su sutento. El llama a todos los empradores que tienen deudar con su paratron, por causa de los precios altos, y comienza a reducir los gapos. ¿Cómo puede hacer semante cosa? Porque lo que les estaba eliminando de su deuda, era su comisión. De nuevo, su patron se dio cuenta y para su sorpresa, el patron está contento, y se da cuenta d elo inventivo que puede ser. No con dinero sino el suyo. NO hay nada más aleccionado que una ejeción . . . especialmente si es la suya.

Jesús reconoce por dos cosas. La primera es porque no se quedó con los brazos cruzados ni se convirtió en una carga, sino que se ocupo de este asunto y utilizo sus dones para pensar en el futuro. En segundo lugar; él esta diciendo que es bueno que sacrifico su comisión para poder guardar un tesoro que no se puede ver ni tocar. Un tesoro que puede guardar de los ladrones. Y es, es el mensaje para nosotros. No debemos esperar hasta los últimos días para prepararnos; ya habrá sido demasíado tarde. Es necesario usar hoy los dones, que se nos han confiado, para construir el reino donde habitaremos un día.

Twenty-Sixth Sunday in Tempus per Annum

(Ezekial 18:25-28; Psalm 125; Philippians; Matthew 21:28-32)

What is most authentically human about us . . .
our ability to love.

Jesus presents us with a wonderful metaphor today. We say we believe, we go to church, we tell our children what to do and not to do. But let's face it; we don't always do that ourselves. It's the phrase that I've actually heard adults say to their children, or those in their care: "Do what I say, not what I do." That's a tough sell, because they don't have to believe what we say . . . but they *will* believe what we do.

I've seen this first hand, having been a high school chaplain for over seven years. High school students often have rebellion in their hormones at that point. I mean, come on, we were all teens at one time, right? Well, most of us then. The fact is, that in a Catholic School setting, at times, the subject students test the most, *is* religion class. You know as well as I do, that if we don't like a teacher, or don't respect a teacher, then we're gonna give them a hard time anyway. But the Catholic faith is not an easy faith to adhere to. Especially when there are any number of churches out there, who will let you believe what you want, how you want; and live your life in a way that is most comfortable for you. Not so in our church. Nope, we still have the monopoly on sacrifice. But to get back to my point, they will challenge everything from Church teaching on morals and scripture, to the history of the church in Europe and the middle ages. But I have spoken to many of these students; I've seen them pray (even when they didn't see me); I've seen how they care for each other. They are like the son in the Gospel. They say "no" and then go and do it in secret anyway. Such was the case my last year at the high school.

The Trinity High School community experienced a great tragedy on May 8th of that year. One of our students, a freshman, James, died unexpectedly. Needless to say this was a terrible tragedy, and yet even in the darkest of tragedies we see the best in people. On Friday, the day after his untimely death, in our morning prayers at Trinity we prayed for James. On this particular day, only the freshmen and sophomores were at school. The upperclassmen had the day off, because many were taking AP exams. The faculty had been prepared late the night before, and six of the local Catholic priests were present at school that day.

The announcement was made in homeroom that morning. The response to this news was instantaneous. The students turned to prayer. All of the religion classes reported to the chapel that day and prayed the rosary, read the scriptures, recited psalms, and sat silently in the presence of the Blessed Sacrament. Students were meeting with priests and counselors all day long, asking difficult questions and seeking consolation.

By ten o'clock that morning, we had decided to celebrate the Mass, the highest prayer of the Church. The students took great efforts to be an active part of the celebration. Some would proclaim the Word, others set up the altar, while still others created art or poetry that would enhance the Liturgy. The Mass was without music; it was quiet and solemn.

What I had not known at the time, and only came to really understand as the Mass began, was that a text message had been sent by the students to the upperclassmen, who sent it to others. When I entered the auditorium at the back of the procession, I was speechless. The auditorium was filled, not only by the students who were at school that day, but by many of the upperclassmen who came to school on their day off for one reason . . . to celebrate Mass with us, for a member of our family.

At this time of crisis, all of the other subjects we spend so much time on in school, failed to give them consolation and peace. The One that they all turned to; the only One who could make any sense out of such tragedy, was God. Despite their rebellions and their challenges to the faith; despite their unwillingness to pray at times, today was different. It was seen in their prayer; it was seen in the four classes coming together to pray for the soul of one of them. What is the consolation offered to those who wish God were not; those who even deny Him and try to eliminate Him from our culture? You see, that day time stopped for all of us. That day we were pared down to what is most authentically human about us: our ability to love, and our longing for something greater than this world can supply in our hour of grief. And to those who would say otherwise, the only response is pity. Because they just don't understand. As for me, I thank GOD . . . because I can![64]

---

64 Part of this homily relaying the events of that day were sent that week as a letter to the editor of the *Patriot News* in Harrisburg. It never showed up in the paper.

VIGÉSIMO SEXTO DOMINGO DEL TIEMPO ORDINARIO AÑO "B"

(NÚMEROS 11:25-29; SALMO 19; SANTIAGO 5:1-6; MARCOS 9:38-43, 45, 47-48)

"En el nombre del Padre, del Hijo, y del Espíritu Santo."

En ese tiempo, Juan dijo a Jesús:

> *"Maestro, hemos visto a uno que expulsaba a los demonios en tu nombre, y como no es de los nuestros, se lo prohibimos." "No hay ninguno que haga milagros en mi nombre, que luego sea capaz de hablar mal de mí."Dense cuenta del cambio aquí. El apostol dice: "Ellos no son de los nuestros." Jesús está diciendo: "Ellos no nesecitan seguirlos a ustedes, sino a mí."*

Esto es importante. Lo que parece motivar a Juan decirlo no es que la persona fue un atrevido ante el maestro, sino que esta persona no estaba entregando lo que tenía; no los estaba siguiendo; no estaba siguiendo el ejemplo de Juan. No hay alguien que cumpla un gran hecho en mi nombre. Estas son las palabras que son tan importantes.

Esta frase *"En mi nombre"* se usa veinti ocho veces en las escrituras. Diesisiete de estos casos, suceden en el *Nuevo Testamento*. Jesús dice:

> *Recibe a un pequeño en mi nombre*
> *Cumple un gran hecho en mi nombre*
> *Pide algo en mi nombre*
> *El Padre enviará el Espíritu Santo en mi nombre*
> *Muchos vendrán en mi nombre*
> *Donde hay dos o tres reunidos en mi nombre*

Entonces comenzamos a ver algo distinto entre: seguirnos a **Nosotros** y seguir a **Cristo**. Hacer algo en nombre de esa persona es hacerlo por ellos. ¿Podremos hacer muchas obras virtuosas, pero por quien lo hacemos? Si lo hacemos en nombre de Jesus, entonces Jesus es el centro . . . y nosotros, no. Debemos ser un cristal transparente, para que los demas vean a Cristo atravez de nosotros. Los apostoles estan gozando de una parte de la gloria que acompaña ser un disipulo de Cristo; puesto que ellos no compartian en la gloria de esta persona, lo condenaron.

De los siete *pecados mortales*, el sexto es la *vanidad*. Haciendo estas cosas para que otros te vean. Pero va mas allá que eso. A veces, nosotros queremos que la gente nos siga a nosotros, y no a Cristo. No estoy hablando del deseo de evangelizar a los Cristianos que no son catolicos, o quizas a los que no son Cristianos. Estoy hablando de alejar a otros miembros de nuestra comunidad Católica porque ellos no ven las cosas como nosotros lo vemos. Porque ellos no rezan como nosotros; no reciben la Eucaristía como nosotros; no participan como nosotros, etc. Alguna lecciónes que yo hé aprendido como sacerdote han sido engaños cuales se han convertidos en devociónes con frenesí.

Debemos tener mucho cuidado de no caer en la trampa de los Israelitas en el desierto, quienes condenaron a los que no fueron presentaron con los demas. Debemos tener cuidado de no condenar al extangero porque no parece ser de nuestro grupo.

Cuando eramos pequeños nos enseñaron: "Si pones un escapulario en el poste de tu cama, y si mueres mientras duermes, iras al cielo." Tambien nos enseñaron que si mueres mientras duermes, la Virgen Maria rezara para que tu vayas al cielo." Algunos han recibido papeles llamados "La Novena Irresistible" o "La oración que te garantiza la salvacion." La gente esta bajo la impresion que si se ponen una medallá o si tiene devoción a un santo particular, entonces no tendran que preocuparse del infierno, porque seran salvados. Los no-Cristianos estan enterrando estatuas de San José en su patio para venderla . . . y lo han puesto de cabeza.

¿Diganme cómo les ayudaria vender una casa si entierran a un santo de cabeza en su patio? (Esta bien si se quieren reír, reconociendo que usted lo ha hecho . . . no juzgare . . . mucho.) Intenten pedir a un santo que interceda por usted. La gente dice "funciona." Tambien funcionan los horóscopos. Yo propongo que nosotros haróamos mas obras buenas para nuestra fe de la iglesia si ponemos nuestra confianza en Cristo, y usemos lo sacramental en una manera que nos guíe hacia El, y no hacia nosotros.

¿Se dan cuenta del problema? Por el mal uso de los sacramentales que la iglesia utiliza para el aumento de nuestra fe, nosotros le estamos quitando el poder a Dios. "Si haces esto, entonces sucedera." Estamos prestando mas atenciín a un ídolo envez de buscar a Dios. Nosotros condenaríamos abiertamente a cualquier religión que hace esto; y aun así condenamos a nuestros hermanos catálicos que no lo hacen. Ni Dios lo quiera que ellos nos sigan a nosotros. Ellos no actuarian en nombre de Jesús, sino en nuestro nombre. Nosotros debemos ser una ventana por la cual otros puedan ver a Cristo. Pero cuando nos atravesamos en el camino de Cristo, lla no somos una ventana, sino una pared.

TWENTY-SEVENTH SUNDAY IN TEMPUS PER ANNUM
(ISAIAH 5:1-7; PSALM 80; PHILIPPIANS 4:6-9; MATTHEW 21:33-43)

Preparation and Disposition

The readings for today paint a very interesting picture. We are heading to the end of our church year, and the readings reflect a kind of "final lessons" before the year ends. In a few weeks, we will begin a new church year with Advent (So make sure you have a copy of *61 minutes: Homilies and Reflections from the Year of Mark.*)

Jesus is directing his words to the leaders of the people, in the hopes that the message they relay to their people will be one of **truth** and not personal preference. The words to us are about tradition. So often we think that the tradition is handed over to us, to modify as we like, or as the elders, *"to make something that is of their preference."* Not so. Tradition means a *handing down*, but we cannot make the mistake of believing that the tradition of the Church is handed down to us . . . **we** are handed over to the tradition!

St. Paul writes to the people of Philippi:

> *"Finally, my brothers, your thoughts should be wholly directed to all that is true, all that deserves respect, all that is honest, pure, admirable, decent, virtuous or worthy of praise. Live according to what you have learned and accepted, what you have heard me say and seen me do. Then will the God of peace be with you."*

This tradition over to which we have been handed, is our faith. And the center of our faith is the Eucharist. Jesus' body, blood, soul, and divinity, which has been given to us, not that we might do with it what we will, but that we might be handed over to Him, as he was handed over to those who ultimately took his life.

It was a custom of primitive peoples that when they encountered a worthy adversary, upon killing him, they would consume part of the warrior's heart, so that part of the heart of this warrior might be within them. The Eucharist is not so different for those who believe. Our Lord who became one of us, and triumphed over sin and death, has not spilled his blood to no purpose, but given it to us, that what enabled him to overpower sin and death might fortify us in our struggle.

The Eucharist is the central dogma of our faith, and that which continues to strengthen us. This is what makes us different from other Christian assemblies. We have the body, blood, soul, and divinity of Christ in the Eucharist. We can't just celebrate a "worship service" but must have the Mass. That's why we cannot have a "Mass" without the Eucharist. And that's why for Catholics, we must attend Mass on Sunday, and not just attend any church: because we have the Eucharist. Even what others call "communion" is not the same. This is not just one belief among many, but this is the cornerstone on which our faith is based. *The stone which the builders rejected has become the cornerstone.*

Concerning a gift that is so special, there must be some specific way to receive it, right? We are receiving, for a gift cannot be taken. How is it then, that we are to receive this wonderful gift from Christ? Over these next two Sundays, I want to focus on three aspects of that reception: The way we prepare to receive the Eucharist; the way we actually receive the Eucharist; and then what we do after we receive the Eucharist.

I have a piece of bread here. These are the round discs of bread we use for communion. Now I want to stress here, this is not consecrated; it is not the Body of Christ, even though it looks like it. But what if I take this and throw it on the floor? Now what if I take my foot and stomp on it? Or I crush it up? Or I throw it in the dirt? Now, granted this is just bread, but some of you gasped when I did this. What if someone took the Eucharist and did that? I would suggest that when we come to receive our Lord in the Eucharist, and we are not properly disposed to receive our Lord, we might as well take it and toss it away like so much refuse.

So to prepare, I do as I would if I were receiving company that day at my home. In the ancient world, the heart was called the house, or the *domus*. That's where we get the word ab-domen (away from the home). So if the Lord is about to enter my *domus* in the Eucharist, I would want to make sure it is clean. Imagine, if Jesus in his person, appeared and said, I plan on coming to your house today. I don't know about you, but I would have to rent a house for the day. My philosophy is that dirt protects things (now you won't want to visit), so you can imagine the work I would have to do to prepare. So if the Lord is coming to our house today, what should we do to prepare? Maybe we should consult Martha! It's one thing if we have a guest arrive unexpectedly . . . it's entirely another, if we know they are coming and we do not prepare.

When we know we are receiving the Lord and we are in a state of grave sin, or a perpetual state of sin, the house is not clean, and we are not ready for such a guest. If we do not believe that the Eucharist is truly the Body of Christ, but we belong to some other Christian group, or non-Christian group, then we are not prepared to receive such a guest into our *domus*.

There is also a fast before receiving. So often, we can become minimalists. We look at the shortest distance between the two points. Consider anyone who is an expert in their craft, and you might see them do things in a certain manner. You can see a simpler way that requires less effort, and although it would appear you get the same result, it is slightly different. "Yes, you can do it that way . . . but that's not the right way to do it." A high school student approached me in the hall and asked: "Father, can I go to confession now for something that I'm going to do tonight?" NO!

People will sometimes ask, when we speak of the one hour fast, is that one hour before Mass or before Communion? Come on! This also includes the time during Mass. Some will chew gum during Mass. I know, I know, you don't believe me, but it's true! Their logic is that they aren't really eating anything, because they're "chewing" the gum. On a chemical level, glucose is entering into your system, and therefore technically you *are* eating. Just because you push it aside, when you're ready to receive the Eucharist doesn't, negate the fact. What is the intention? I mean, "for the love of God," we can sacrifice for an hour . . . for the love of God.

Finally, the preparation for communion. Did I arrive at Mass just before communion, and now am going to receive? Now, it's one thing if we got a late start today, there was an accident on the way, the baby threw up in the car: it's understandable that sometimes we will not make it on time . . . but *every* time? It becomes more of a pathology when a person can get here late at exactly the same time every week. I used to have this problem when I was pastor at a Spanish parish. The weddings would begin thirty to forty minutes late. They assured me, Padre, it's cultural. We can't help it. I then made it policy for them to put down a $200.00 deposit for weddings. If they arrived fifteen minutes early, they got back $100.00. It's amazing how quickly "culture" can change.

If we are constantly showing up after the opening prayer and introductory Rites, then we probably should not receive communion. I understand the exceptions to the rule, but not a consistent disregard for our Lord. We would not be late for a concert or a boxing match or a movie. Is my soul ready? Is my house clean? Is my stomach empty? Am I on time to the celebration? The Eucharist is the center of our faith: the body, blood, soul, and divinity of our King. This is not a reluctant giver, but one who gives with extravagance to those who have done nothing to deserve such love and devotion. The gift is here; the fourth King, brings a gift not for a child, but for a world hungering for that grace that can only come through the Sacrament. The gift is here. Are we prepared to receive it?

Twenty-Eighth Sunday in Tempus per Annum

(Isaiah 25:6-10; Psalm 23; Philippians 4:12-14, 19-20; Matthew 22:1-14)

Reception and Redemption

The problem of atheism and unbelief is not so much that the existence of God is denied by certain persons, but that God is absent from the ordinary consciousness and lives of believers, God is not enough alive, or important in ordinary consciousness.[65]

We are heading to the end of our Church year, and the readings reflect a kind of "final lessons" before the year ends. Jesus is directing his words to the leaders of the people, in the hopes that the message they relay to their people, will be one of **truth** and not personal preference. The words to us are about tradition. Last week, we spoke about what it means to be properly disposed for our reception of the greatest gift our Lord has given us: himself in the Eucharist. We must have the house clean, and empty in order to receive our king. We must be on time to the feast and as the words from Jesus reflect in this week's gospel, properly dressed for the banquet. (That's a discussion for another time!)

Having prepared ourselves for the reception of this gift, it would now be prudent to speak about how we receive our Lord. Isaiah speaks to the people in exile: *On this mountain the Lord of hosts will provide for all peoples a feast of rich food and choice wines.* We are invited to this wedding banquet, and having prepared ourselves, we are ready to enter.

---

65 Ronald Rolheiser, OMI, *The Shattered Latern: Rediscovering a Felt Presence of God*, (New York, NY, The Crossroad Publishing Co., 2001), 20.

The *General Instruction to the Roman Missal* says this about reception
of communion:

> The norm for reception of Holy Communion in the dioceses
> of the United States is standing. When receiving Holy
> Communion, the communicant bows his or her head before the
> Sacrament as a gesture of reverence and receives the Body of the
> Lord from the minister. The consecrated Host may be received
> either on the tongue or in the hand, at the discretion of each
> communicant. The priest raises the host slightly and shows it to
> each, saying, "the Body of Christ." The communicant replies,
> "Amen," and then receives the Sacrament either on the tongue
> or . . . in the hand.[66]

Now let's unpack this a little bit, because there are some specifics
that will lead to a better understanding of what we do; and what we
should be doing. In my experiences, and those of my brother priests,
we have seen as many varied ways of receiving Communion as there
are people. Part of ritual is uniformity. It doesn't mean "conformity,"
as though we are automatons who cannot think or act independently,
but "communion" of gesture and intention. When we enter into the
ritual, we live out the tradition to *which we have been handed over*.
Our gestures and responses should reinforce the ritual. What so
often happens is we fall into bad habits, and our egos keep us from
relinquishing our personal gestures or words, for those of the ancient
ritual.

There are many methods of receiving our Lord, but only one is
called for in this ritual. I have observed the "grab and snatch"
method. I believe this occurs most often with non-Catholics, who are
receiving communion in our church. In many of the non-Catholic
assemblies, they take communion in that manner. The other way
people approach the Sacrament is with an attack! They don't extend
their tongue, but open their mouth, and when your hand approaches
their mouth to place Communion in their mouth, like a great white
breeching, they attack. A third method is more of a bait and switch.

66 General Instruction of the Roman Missal. #160-161

They approach with hands out, and then at the last moment drop their hands and stick out their tongue. That's a bit worse than the multiple choice where they both, stick out their tongue and extend their hands. Some will drop back their head and open their mouth like a baby bird, while others will extend their hands and then bow their whole body at the waist, so that like a trap-door, their hands fall out of the space in which our Lord was being placed.

Now I say these things, half in jest but all in earnest. The reason the Church offers a uniform posture for receiving communion is to maximize the reverence, and minimize the possibility that the Sacred Host will fall to the floor or be denigrated.

If you wish to receive communion on the tongue, approach the minister; bow your head (not at the waist, but a simple bow) and stick out your tongue so that the Sacred Host may be placed securely on it. If you wish to receive communion in your hands, place the left hand over the right to create a throne. Make a slight bow, and the minster will place the Sacred Host on the hand which is on the top. Step to the side, with your right hand, take the Sacred Host from your left and place it in your mouth. Then (looking both ways to ensure you are not going to cut someone off) go back to your place and offer thanksgiving. We do not need to make a sign of the cross to bless ourselves, we have just received our God into our body, which is much more powerful than any gesture! That's all. Not complex; not overly burdensome, but it requires us to relinquish our "personal style," and conform ourselves to a communion.

Finally, the response to the ministers: "Body of Christ" is "Amen." It is not "I believe" or "thank you" or "truly" or "it is." The word amen comes from the Hebrew word *emeth*, which is like an Aramaic "right on!" It's a statement about our communion with our brothers and sisters, saying that I believe everything that the church teaches as truth, not just that this is the Eucharist. It reinforces our statement about being *in communion* with the Church and the Body of Christ. That is why we cannot allow just anyone to receive communion in our Church.

Our preparation and disposition is not enough. We must be united with our brothers and sisters in word and gesture. To receive the Eucharist, the greatest gift of our Church, with reverence; and to accept the graces that come with this gift, we must not only be disposed to receive our Lord, but we must also give thanks. This is a choice. C.S. Lewis would say, "I would much rather say that every time you make a choice you are turning the central part of you, the part of you that chooses, into something a little different from what it was before."[67] The nature of the gift is that it does change us; but we must be open to that change.

Finally, what do we do after we receive the gift? What do we do after receiving any gift? We offer thanks. Imagine going to someone's home. They have prepared a celebration for you; offered you company and hospitality. You come and eat a meal, not speaking to the host during the meal, and leaving directly after, without offering thanks. I don't know about you, but I would think twice about inviting such a person again. But so often, you know as well as I do, people eat and run. They get Communion, and the host is still in their mouth as they head out the church door. If we would not appreciate that in our home, why would we presume for a minute that "the Lord understands"? After we have received, we offer thanksgiving at our place. We kneel (if we are able) until the tabernacle doors have closed and our Lord is no longer exposed. Then the final act of thanks is the closing hymn. Not the prayer after Communion; not the announcements; not the final blessing. The final act of thanks is the closing hymn. So we don't leave until after that . . . and even then you can stay longer.

If we are being offered a gift that this world cannot supply; and we offer thanks for worldly things, why would we not offer MORE thanks for this gift. This gift of the Eucharist; *Eucharistia*, from which we get our word, Thanksgiving.

---

67 C. S Lewis, *Mere Christianity*, (San Francisco, CA, Harper Collins, 1996), 92.

TWENTY-NINTH SUNDAY IN TEMPUS PER ANNUM

(ISAIAH 45:1, 4-6; PSALM 96; I THESSALONIANS 1:1-5; MATTHEW 22: 15-21)

God and Country

Is it God and Country . . . or Country and God? Who is looking out for us?

> The real problem at this moment of our history is that God is disappearing from the human horizon, and, with the dimming of the light which comes from God, humanity is losing its bearings, with increasingly evident destructive effects.[68]

Listen to the first reading:

> *Thus says the LORD to his anointed, Cyrus, whose right hand I grasp, subduing nations before him, and making kings run in his service, opening doors before him and leaving the gates unbarred: For the sake of Jacob, my servant, of Israel, my chosen one, "**I have called you by your name, giving you a title, though you knew me not.**" I am the LORD and there is no other, there is no God besides me. It is I who arm you, though you know me not, so that toward the rising and the setting of the sun people may know that there is none besides me. I am the LORD, there is no other. (bold, mine.)*

This speaks to us of the Glory of God. Which of us could create another? Which of us could save another? What could we purchase that could prolong our life for one minute, or give our soul peace?

---

68 Letter of His Holiness, Pope Benedict XVI to the Bishops of the Catholic Church concerning the remission of the excommunication of the four Bishops consecrated by Archbishop Lefebvre

Nothing! It is to God, therefore, that we offer the glory. How do we glorify God? By our very lives, we make God present. What is the sin of the Pharisees? That they need not the God who made them. The question is, in whose image are we created? Because as the prophet says, at some points it appears as if "we know him not!"

> *The Pharisees went off and plotted how they might entrap Jesus in speech. He said to them, "Whose image[69] is this and whose inscription[70]?" They replied, "Caesar's." At that he said to them, "Then **repay**[71] to Caesar what belongs to Caesar and to God what belongs to God."*

Repay to Caesar . . . what did Caesar give to them that they need to repay? Nothing! But repay to God what belongs to him . . . what has He given us? Everything!

Man and woman he created them . . . in his image and likeness he created them.

People will say, "Father, aren't you concerned with those who leave Mass early? Aren't you concerned with those who receive communion and shouldn't be? Aren't you concerned about the cell phones that go off during Mass? Aren't you concerned about those who come to Mass late? Aren't you concerned that there are people who don't sing or pray with the community? And I have to respond, that I cannot be consumed by that concern, because if I do, I might forget those who do *not* leave early; the ones who do *not* come late; those who *are* worthy or those who *keep* their phones silent.

---

69 **Tzelem**, an image (not necessarily three dimensional) which has been formed to resemble a person, god, animal, etc.—'likeness, image'.

70 **Dᶜmut**, likeness or inscription of the inscription, *to be inscribed upon*.

71 **Pay back**, implying payment of an incurred obligation (Mt 20:8); **2.** LN 38.16 **reward**, pay back, recompense, whether positive or not (Mt 6:4, 6, 18; 16:27; Ro 2:6; 12:17; 1Th 5:15; 1Ti 5:4; 2Ti 4:8, 14; 1Pe 3:9; Rev 18:6; 22:12+).

None of us is perfect, but sometimes we use that as an excuse to be less than we can be. When all the Lord asks is that we are faithful; that we glorify Him with our life; because without him we would have no life.

Vatican Council II said this about the universal call to holiness:

> Therefore in the Church, everyone whether belonging to the hierarchy, or being cared for by it, is called to holiness, according to the saying of the Apostle: "For this is the will of God, your sanctification." However, this holiness of the Church is unceasingly manifested, and must be manifested, in the fruits of grace which the Spirit produces in the faithful; it is expressed in many ways in individuals, who in their walk of life, tend toward the perfection of charity, thus causing the edification of others; in a very special way this (holiness) appears in the practice of the counsels, customarily called "evangelical." [72]

Our Lord wants us to keep our priorities in order. None of us is perfect, but that does not mean we give up. None of us will have an easy road ahead, but that doesn't mean that we give up. Our country, our town, our family, might want to make life easier by placing their desires above the desires of God, but we cannot adopt that as our own rule of life.

Our post modern culture might ask, "Is it ever possible . . . to consider as universally valid and always binding certain rational determinations established in the past, when no one knew the progress humanity would make in the future?" The response comes to us from article fifty-three in *Gaudium et Spes*:

> [M]an is not exhaustively defined by that same culture . . . This nature [human nature], itself the measure of cultrure and the condition ensuring that man does not become the prisoner of

---

[72] *Lumen Gentium*, 39

any of his cultures, but asserts his personal dignity by living in accordance with the profound truth of his being.[73]

We are all called to a higher holiness. Not country and then God; not family and then God; not occupation and then God, but God first . . . without whom we would have nothing! Without whom we would *be* nothing! And whose law is written in the human heart. This law, which is truth . . . objective truth. This is not a limit to freedom, but ***true*** freedom. And the truth will set you free!

---

73 *Gaudium et Spes*, 53.

Vigésimo Noveno Domingo del Tiempo Ordinario Año "C"

(Éxodo 17:8-13; Salmo 121; II Timoteo 3:14-4:2; Lucas 18:1-8)

Dios clamó: "Denme justicia."

No les parece interesante, que Jesús cuenta una parábola sobre la persistencia en la oración, como si pudieramos controlar a Dios por medio de lo que decimos, o por nuestro empeño en ser escuchados y respondidos. Muchas veces, esta mujer acude al juez por su propia cuenta para pedir justicia. Tengan en mente que la justicia es un deber. Por lo tanto, pedir justicia no es algo excesivo de su parte. Ella simplemente pide lo que se merece. Si acaso ella estuviera pidiendo un veredicto a su favor en un caso que no parece estar en su favor, eso seria algo diferente. Pero aquí sólo esta pidiendo lo que se merece. Jesús habla sobre un juez injusto. Algo sucedió esta semana que voltea el Evangelio al revés . . . al menos así es para mi. Y se que eso no es un accidente. Creo que esta es una de las formas en que Dios usa el Espíritu Santo.

Era un domingo por la noche cuando recibi una llamada, mientras me estaba preparando para dormir. La llamada era de una alumna en la escuela superior. Esta alumna me dijo que su amiga le habia llamando y le confesó que estaba embarazada. Esta noticia no es una de sopreza porque, como usted sabe, esto sucede con frecuencia. Puede ser qer que cada uno de ustedes conoce a alguien que quedo embarazada inesperadamente. Pero lo que dijo después fue lo que me detuvo por completo. Ella dijo, "y esta planeando ir a la clinica manana para abortar a su bebe." No me contaron esto en confesión, ni en una consulta privada, pero siempre prefiero mantener cierto nivel de discreción.

Casí no dormi esa noche; si acaso fueron sólo unas cuantas horas las que descanze. Desperte, reze y después me fui a la primera conferencia. No pude enfocarme en lo que decía el presentador. Y durante ese tiempo, algo agitaba mi corazón. Me pregunté: "Si ella tuviera un niño de un año y lo quería matar, ¿qué harías?" Reflexioné sobre esto esto por un minuto y después pensé . . ."recuerda todas las mujeres con quienes has hablando y han abortado . . . a las que preguntan, ¿podré llegar a sentirme mejor un día? ¿podré olvidar? ¿podré sanarme de esta herida? Y continue intentando de enforcarme en lo que decia el presentador. Y denuevo pense, "Si acaso ella quisiera tomar su propia vida, ¿qué harias? ¿La apoyarías en esa decisión? ¿Le ayudarias a quitarse su propia vida?" Me levanter, y sali del cuarto . . . busque el numero de telefono y llame a sus padres. Conosco a sus padres y la familia, y sabía que ellos la apoyarian. Sabia que esta jóven, quien le habia confesado a su amiga, cuya persona favorece la vida, lo hizo porque necesitaba ayuda . . . se sentía sola . . . desesperada . . . en verdad necesitaba ayuda. Sus padres reaccionaron como sabía que iban a reaccionar, hasta cierto punto, y tomaron el asunto en sus manos.

Digo esto ahora no sólo porque me afecto muchisimo . . . sino porque fue una experiencia en la cual El Señor me permitio comparir, para que yo entendiera el Evanagelio de una manera distinta. No pienso que Dios es semejante a este juez injusto. Pero nosotros si lo somos.

El lunes pasado, tres veces Dios clamó: "*Denme justicia.*" Fueron tres veces las que Dios exigió justicia, y debo admitir que en la batallá entre la discreción y la vida, tres veces me tuve que preguntar, antes de estar listo para sacrificar mi reputación de amistad y lealtad no sólo por una vida, sino por dos. Nosotros no somos los únicos que rezamos y pedimos por nuestros intenciones. Varias veces al dia, todos los días, Nuestro Señor reza, y pide que se le haga justicia. Nos sentimos tan agotados porque creemos que Dios no escucha nuestras oraciones. Me pregunto como se ha de sentir la frustración Divina, cuando todos los dias, varias veces al dia . . . nosotros rechazamos las plegarias de justicia que Dios nos hace.

THIRTIETH SUNDAY IN TEMPUS PER ANNUM

(EXODUS 22:20-26; PSALM 18; I THESSALONIANS 1:5-10; MATTHEW 22:34-40)

Who is my neighbor?

I was assigned for a summer, to the parish of *St. Francis of Assisi* in Harrisburg. This area used to be the envy of those living in Harrisburg. This was "Allison Hill" or the rich district. By the time I arrived there for my seminarian summer assignment, it was the *diaspora*. The rich had fled and left this part of town to drugs and crime, and unfortunately those who were unable to afford much more than that. And in the midst of this town, existed a hundred-year-old church that really *was* the center of life, for the *anowim* who existed here. Although this was a crime-ridden, drug-infested part of town, I was never afraid there. I was cautious and prudent, but for the most part, it appeared that a majority of the people had a respect for the Church, if not her priests.

I recall meeting Fr. Daniel Mitzel formally, shortly before I arrived. I asked him to write the forward for this book. He had a reputation that preceded him, for St. Francis was a *right of passage* for any seminarian in the Diocese of Harrisburg. He was a strong pastor, with a compassionate heart for the poor. This was an experience of the poor and underprivileged; and an exposure to *Social Justice* lived through the Church that has left an indelible mark on me, and the countless others who ministered, and were ministered to, here on Allison hill.

I have to admit, though, I felt much like Amos . . . but in an ironic sort of way; the opposite. He was sent from the country to the rich and famous; I was sent from a suburb to the periphery. I was intimidated by everyone I met, and yet, few gave me real reason to be intimidated. The parish had also made the shift from an English

252

speaking parish, to a bilingual parish as one group moved out and another moved in. The community as a whole was *mezcla* (mixed).

When I first arrived, another seminarian and I were assigned to accompany the youth group to the beach. Every year, about seven parishes in the Harrisburg area, went down to Rehobeth beach Delaware together to spend the weekend. They would pack a U-haul truck with all of the food and supplies, and then descend on Cape Henlopen state park. The irony was that these were the same barracks I stayed in, with my youth group, when I was in high school.

Cast aside, right now, any preconceived ideas you had of a "youth group." The group that I was taking down could not be conceived as in the most moderate stereotype of a "youth group." Although the guy in charge was very capable, knew the kids, and had their respect, the rest of us were a *ragtag, mishmash,* of people . . . *mezclas.* Our van driver was a guy from the local Catholic Worker house, who appeared like a carry-over from the "sixties." He saw his role as driving the van and being an "adult" in the group, but as far as discipline or order, it was all "groovy" which to any group of youth, was "groovy" too! The other chaperone in the van with me was a woman in her late sixties named Rosa; who most certainly had the respect of the kids, if not fear, but was also a grandmotherly figure. And then there was me: the former teacher, now seminarian, who was concerned about the permission slips; medical forms; meds, and the lyrics that were on the CD's that kept floating to the front of the van, which the *hipster*, without taking his eyes off the road, casually placed in the CD player. I would hear one or two words, or look on the CD case for the "parental warning", and the disc was ejected as quickly as it was put in. The guy driving could've cared less, but there was usually a uniform outcry from the back of the van. Pretty soon another CD would surface. This was the ride to the beach.

Shortly after we arrived at the beach and got unpacked, a priest got up and began to expound on all the things that the teens were **not** permitted to do during this "weekend retreat." He went through many more regulations than the Israelites ever had to follow. You could see the looks on the faces of these kids, most of whom came from the suburbs, as though fun was as distant dream they once thought possible on this weekend away. The looks on the faces of *our* group was different. Now bear in mind, our "youth group" had some eighth graders, high schoolers, and one twenty-year-old who could go because he was still a senior in high school. Our kids were accustomed to being told "no" and had a clear understanding of what disobedience got you. In the same respect though, they also had vivid imaginations, and were very creative, because of their station in life; they were survivors.

When the talk had finished, we went into the "mess hall" to eat. You could already see the dread on the faces of the kids who thought they had been tricked. For our group, they were happy to be having a meal together; happy to be at the beach, which for some, was their first time; and happy to be with others their own age.

We have these moments in life, every now and then, when we are dragged, kicking and screaming, from our comfort zones. It could be a crisis, or it could be a "trick," or some event that was unplanned that leads us there; and yet when we emerge from this experience, we are changed. This weekend was one of those experiences. I looked at this "ragtag" group of inner-city kids with caution and distrust. I was just waiting for someone to smoke or use drugs; I was biding my time for one of the *suburbites* to have "lost" their CD player or their phone, and one of our kids to have found it in their bag. I was intimidated by these "street smart" kids and perhaps that was colored by my previous experiences with inner-city kids, or new insecurities. But one of those moments; those "aha" moments was about to happen and there was no warning.

Amidst the whining of the other kids in the camp about how this weekend was going to be "lame" or how it "sucks" because they weren't able to "do" anything, one of our youth mentioned casually, "They didn't say we couldn't make a bonfire." And he would have been correct. Of the 613 law codes the priest had offered to our flock, there was nothing about bonfires. So, that is what they did. They lit a bonfire. Another took a plastic trashcan and turning it over, took two small pieces of wood, and using them like drum sticks, began to pound out a beat. Before we knew it, there were over two hundred kids dancing . . . to these sticks pounding against the trashcan. There was no music, no lyrics, just this beat. And looking around at this formerly dejected group, smiles were in abundance. Everyone was dancing. Even those who normally did not, were dancing away.

The psalmist sings words of love to God. You can almost see him dancing and crying out. These kids were free; and much like David, danced with abandon. There came a moment after awhile that they began jumping *over* the fire, and then we had to step in. But they were corrected and then went back to dancing. They pushed the envelope, and we guided them back. This would set the tone for the entire weekend. The other parishes would look to *our* kids, those on the margins, to be the leaders, and to make this experience one they would not soon forget.

The next day at the beach, I watched in amazement as these "macho" boys, carefully covered each other with sunscreen so that their Hispanic olive tint was replaced with a pasty white. And then, again, watching them charge toward the water only to quickly retreat, shrieking as the waves chased them down. It was like watching five-year-olds who have come to the beach for the first time. For many of them, it *was* their first time. The other youth were more interested in romancing members of the opposite sex, but surprisingly, these guys had no time for that. As soon as their bare feet touched the sand, they regressed to childhood. It was so refreshing, and a poignant reminder of what is possible. My impression was beginning to change.

Exodus speaks to us of not oppressing those who are different. Those who are on the margins or do not think like we do, or act like we do, or speak like we do. To love our neighbor as our self. Isn't it refreshing that right when we think we have it all figured out, God breaks our glass house and shows us reality? Our group was the one that the others aspired to be like. They were not concerned with what others thought; they were not insecure; they were survivors. To be a survivor is to hope in people and experiences. That hope, became contagious.

The last day, the group of over two hundred youth were truly a family. They had learned from each other. Promises were made that they would bridge the river that separated their churches (the Susquehanna is a real river) and keep in touch. Whether that happened or not, I cannot comment here, but everyone who spent that weekend in Delaware was changed . . . for the better.

We headed back to the parish in Harrisburg, having made only one stop for lunch at McDonald's. Our group was one group again, and they moved tables together in the restaurant so they could sit together. After lunch and hour had passed, and we were only ten minutes from home, crossing the bridge that separated the other five churches from our own. Then one of the kids (the oldest) stood up, and made a speech thanking all of the adults for their part in the weekend. At the end of the speech, they all went toward the front of the van, and offered vases of flowers to Rosa, the older woman who was with us as a chaperone. She was in tears. It was a wonderful way to end the trip.

I spoke to Rosa about their devotion to her, and saw the flowers, wondering to myself when they had picked them up. And then I saw the five vases, holding the flowers; each with "the golden arches" etched in glass. They had "lifted" them from our lunchtime stop. Well . . . it was a good weekend, and they did change a whole group . . . but perhaps there's still room for conversion!

THIRTY-FIRST SUNDAY IN TEMPUS PER ANNUM

(MALACHI 1:14-2:2, 8-10; PSALM 131; I THESSALONIANS 2:7-9, 13; MATTHEW 23:1-12)

Pope Francis changes the Church law!

We like "sound bytes." We do. Little blasts of information like a one word summary of what's happening in the world. Sound bytes can be dangerous though. If we look back fifty or even a hundred years, it was like each town had their own town newspaper. That was all you had, so you could read it from cover to cover. These were the years before the "Foxes" and "CNNs" and news feeds on the internet, amidst countless other sources of news. With all of those to choose from, I think it's rare that anyone reads a paper from cover to cover. We look at the sound bytes and the quotes out of context, and then move on to the next thing. We have to be so careful though, especially about the important stuff, that the byte doesn't become the whole story.

We forget sometimes that the job of the media is not to *inform* us, but *to form* us. It is to put a taste in our mouth for news, so that we will go again, and again, and again, to them. In order to do this, the morsels they offer must be savory ones. This is not limited to the secular press. Even the Catholic news agencies tempt us with a word or phrase that guarantees further reading. In that vein, sometimes we are like children. I don't know about you, but when I was little, we were like little litigators ready for court. "Mom said we couldn't have cookies for dessert . . . . but she didn't say anything about ice-cream." "Dad said we could not shoot the bb gun in the back yard . . . but he didn't say anything about shooting it in the house!" So we find the morsel that will most satisfy our hunger and take that as our truth.

This is why Jesus' statement, is so important. The Pharisees and scribes, who were the guarantors of the truth, were twisting the truth to make it the best for them. Jesus comes along and begins to combat what has gone on for too long, so you can imagine the people started to take his words out of context in an effort to break down God's law. You can almost hear their voices echoed in our own. So Jesus comes forward and says, "The Law is good. Follow it! Just don't follow their examples." That is just as true for us, as it was for them.

A few weeks ago, Pope Francis gave an interview to the press. This new Pope is phenomenal, but different. I would say he's made more work for us priests in the last few months, than we've had in the last few years. It's like riding a tandem bike with someone in the front who is going a mile a minute, and we in the back are just trying to catch up. But it's good! Because we have to preach about it. In his humble style, he is one of the first popes, in a long time, to go without prepared notes when he speaks to the press. I mean, they must be in journalistic heaven. They just wait to pounce on politicians who have prepared notes . . . you can imagine how whetted their appetite is for one who speaks "off the cuff." Our Holy Father takes seriously the Gospel which says: "Do not worry about what you will say. The Holy Spirit will give you words that they will be unable to refute or deny." Well . . . the Holy Spirit's putting in a lot of O.T. with this one (and I don't mean Old Testament).

The interview with the Holy Father, which really should be read in its entirety, raised a lot of concern in the Catholic community because of the sound bytes. These words or phrases, were taken out of context, and decorated the space reserved for headlines in many of the world's papers. He spoke about being so focused on issues, like abortion and same-sex unions, that the other issues of concern have been lost. He further went on to say that with this single-minded attitude, we are becoming increasingly efficient at driving people away from the Church, because while we exercise very well Catholic judgment, we are severely lacking in Catholic forgiveness and charity. He is right.

We can be so Pro-Life, like that is the only issue for us. We want to ensure that children have the opportunity to be born; but heaven forbid they make a peep or a cry out during Mass. The one who carries a sign at the March for Life, becomes the same one who gives the "leer of death" to the parents of the disruptive child. We can boycott companies that openly promote same-sex marriage, but do nothing to nurture marriage within our Church, and support those who are struggling in their marriage.

On the other end of the spectrum, however, we can also concern ourselves so much with Social Justice and the poor, that we ignore the laws of the Church. "Let's take care of the physical needs first, and then we can worry about the law later." That does not appear to be what Jesus would want us to do. *". . . therefore do everything and observe everything they tell you."* Not the sound bytes, but everything.

Remember *Vatican II?* How many constitutions? How many wonderful theological reflections on the Church? How many do *you* remember? I imagine you remember that we no longer have to abstain from meat on Fridays; that the fast was no longer from midnight the day of Mass; and that Mass was no longer celebrated in Latin, but English. You remember those things because they were the little bytes. The reality, in regards to just those three issues go like this: We are permitted to eat meat on Fridays if we offer some act of equal or greater value in place of that. We no longer have to fast from midnight on, but an hour before Mass. Finally, Latin was never eliminated. Quite to the contrary, the common language (vernacular) should be used in place of the Latin at different places in the Liturgy. Not thrown out, but English, thrown in. Now I know you're probably thinking, "I never heard that before." But have you read the documents? Or just the headlines that replaced those documents.

My point is, that over the next few years, God willing, our Holy Father, in his relaxed style, will say many things. And we, the Catholics, have to be sure to look further than headlines created to whet public appetite. We have a law based on the objective truth of God, which does not change with the seasons. *"Have we not all the one Father? Has not the one God created us? Why then do we break faith with each other, violating the covenant of our fathers?"*

We have to be better than that. We are not children trying to find our ways around the truth we know to be true. We are not those who are trying to steal our loyalty with nuggets of phrase. We are the sons and daughters of the Most High. We must be wholly (and holy) Catholic people. We do not focus only on one aspect of the faith to the exclusion of the rest, but are wholly Catholic. We do not only judge, as we are called to do, but forgive; and love . . . as someone who is wholly Catholic will do.

The tandem bike, pedals on; but we cannot be passive riders. So stretch out them legs; grab your water bottle and saddle up . . . because this Pope doesn't show signs of slowing down.

Trigésimo Primer Domingo del Tiempo Ordinario Año "C"

(Sabiduría 11:22-12:2; Salmo 145; II Tesalonicenses 1:11-22; Lucas 19:1-10)

"Hoy vendré a tu casa."

Cuando Dios nos creó, Él hizo una inversión eterna. Desde el momento de nuestra creación, Él nunca ha dejado de contemplarnos, no nos ha olvidado . . . nisiquiera por un segundo,"La creación significa que Dios, desde toda la eternidad, ha anhelado este ser único. El anhelo de Dios por este momento fue tan intenso que precisamente este ser humano llegó a la extistencia, para vivir una vida eterna."

Esto aparenta ser imposible. Así es que usted puede imaginar, si tuviera el poder de crear un ser, y esa creatura se alejara de usted, ¿como esperaría con anticipación el regreso de esa creatura? Pero al regresar esa creatura . . . y se haya arrepentido, usted tendra una opción . . . ¿se divorciaría usted de esa creatura, recordandole que "lo abandonó", y que ustede no puede ofrecerle su perdón? ¿O quizas lo abrazaría, estando agradecido por su regreso, y a la misma vez se asegura de que la creatura este plenamente arrepentida . . . y le daría la oportunidad de ser mejor persona?

Por eso a los que caen, los vas corrigiendo poco a poco, los reprendes y les traes a la memoria sus pecados, para que se arrepientan de sus maldades y crean en ti, Señor. Quienes somos padres no castigamos por nuestro beneficio, sino por el bien de nuestros hijos. Por eso no significa que debemos rechazar a quienes se han alejado y desean regresar. Es nuestro deber recibirlos, estando de acuerdo que ellos lucharan por ser mejores. Pero eso no nos libra de las responsabilidades. Porque muchos de nosotrs hacemos lo necesario; vamos a misa, rezamos, excetera . . . pero, ¿acaso creeemos que nuestra casa sea digna de recibir a Nuestro Señor?

Pablo dice a los Tesalonisenses, pero tambien podría dirigir esta carta hacia nosotros:

> "*Oremos siempro por ustedes, para que Dios los haga dignos de la vocación a la que los ha llamado, y con su poder, lleve a efecto tanto los buenos propósitos que ustedes han formadao, como lo que ya han emprendido por la fe.*"

Esta es la oración de Zaqueo. Imagine si él no hubiera subido a esa rama. Quizas Jesús hubiera continuado su jornada por el pueblo. Dios nunca hubiera visitado el hogar de ese hombre, y Zaqueo hubiera quedado porbre . . . porque nunca hubiera regalado la mitad de sus bienes a los pobres ni hubiera pagado cuatro veces más a quienes había robado. Pero en medio de la multitud, aquél quien parece ser el hipocrita y el menos digno, es quien recibe al hijo de Dios. Y la salvación entra a esa casa. Me parece que todos tenemos un gusto por Zaqueo. Ese hombre medio torpe y de baja estatura. Quizas por su conversión humilde, quizas por su transformación generosa . . . o quizas proque vemos un poco de él en nosotros mismos. Pero todavía no hemos subido a la rama de ese arból, todavía no hemos dejado nuestras comodidades.

¿Qué pasaría si Jesús te diría: "Hoy vendré a tu casa"? No se lo que harian ustedes, pero yo me ocuparía de limpiar mi casa lo antes posible . . . de hecho, ¡creo que alquilaría una! En el mundo antepasado, esto era tu casa . . . el *domus*. De ahí sacamos la palabra *ab-domen*, cual significa "lejos de la casa."

Nuestro Señor nos habla mientras lo recibimos en la Sagrada Eucarstía. Recibimos a Dios en nuestra casa. Pero, ¿acaso nuestro hogar esta en condiciones para recibir a Nuestro Señor? Cuando respondamos esa pregunta, entonces podremos comenzar a entender porque Dios facilmente puede ofrecer la bienvenida a un pecador . . .

a su inversión eterna. Porque ese pecador, humillado por sus errores; agradecido con su Dios amoroso . . . Ese pecador existe detro de cada uno de nosotros. Todo lo que se nos pide . . . como Zaqueo, es que hagamos a un lado nuestras comodidades y subamos a esa rama.

THIRTY-SECOND SUNDAY IN TEMPUS PER ANNUM
(WISDOM 6:12-16; PSALM 63; I THESSALONIANS 4:13-18; MATTHEW 25:1-13)

The belief is so big that it takes a long time to get it into action. And this hesitation chieflyarises, oddly enough, from an indifference about where one should begin.[74]

"Why should a dog, a horse, a rat, have life, / And thou no breath at all?"[75] Father Delp, a Jesuit hanged by the Nazis in 1945, wrote this from prison:

> In the course of these last long weeks life has become suddenly much less rigid. A great deal that was once quite simple and ordinary seems to have taken on a new dimension. Things seem clearer and at the same time more profound; one sees all sorts of unexpected angles. And above all God has become almost tangible. Things I have always known and believed now seem so concrete; I believe them but I also live them."[76]

I think it's important to mention at this point, that this is not a funeral homily; although, I'm sure you're not so naïve as to think I was just filling space with the quote above. Life is the precursor to death, is the precursor to life. We would be putting the cart before the horse to discuss what awaits us in the next life, before we can get out of *this* one. We are approaching the end of the Church year, and I like to visualize this, much as we do the seasons.

---

74 G.K. Chesterton, *Orthodoxy*, (Colorado Springs, CO, Waterbrook Press, 2001), 121.

75 King Lear, exclaiming after the death of Cordelia, in the *Saint's Guide to Happiness*, Robert Ellsberg, (New York, NY, Northpoint Press, 2003),152.

76 Delp, Alfred, S.J. as written in Ibid. 153.

In Autumn, many things are beginning to change, and with that comes death, or a dying of sorts. Some plants and critters actually will die, or at the very least, go dormant. The leaves falling from the trees is the most obvious sign for us that summer is over. Shortly after this season, as the cold which chills to the bone moves slowly in, we celebrate winter. I know it seems kind of strange to celebrate a season of death, but let's face it; aside from the snow (which some people love) we also celebrate a birth . . . and a new year as well. Winter for many, then, is the precursor to spring, and spring is where life blooms in abundance. But if we, like the snowbirds we have in the parish, decide to omit autumn and winter (which they do by going to Florida) then how can we appreciate spring?

Death is inevitable. But for those who believe, death is Spring's Winter. Not only the people from Thessalonica had questions regarding salvation, but Paul's letter, specifically addressed to them, tried to calm their fears. Thessalonica was like a ship without a captain, because of the persecution from the synagogue officials and those who were the false prophets. Imagine being in their shoes, with no one to tell them that the persecution in this world would lead to consolation in the next. In this letter he specifically addresses their question about Christ's second coming, and whether or not they are blessed if they die before that occurs.

St. Paul wants to reaffirm that indeed *"we who live, who survive until his coming, will in no way have an advantage over those who have fallen asleep."* We all have to go through the autumns and winters to enjoy spring. Having said thus, however, we are not to preserve ourselves so that we might live as long as possible, as though death is the ultimate evil, lest we *might yield to grief like those who have no hope.* Hence, we enter the wedding banquet as described in Matthew's Gospel.

Jesus refers numerous times throughout the Gospels to the "wedding banquet." Whenever he mentions this, it appears to be an allusion to the final consummation of the covenant, which will occur at the end. In the Ancient Near East, the banquets could vary from district to district, but there were some parts which appear to be consistently present in all of the celebrations.

After the day has been spent in dancing and other entertainments, the wedding-feast takes place at nightfall. The bride is then accompanied with torches to the bridegroom's house. Finally a messenger announces the coming of the bridegroom, who had to keep outside the house; the women leave the bride alone and go with torches to meet the bridegroom who appears at the head of his friends.[77]

See, when the Bridegroom comes, the time for change is over. The time for conversion is past. There will not be time to get oil in the lamp. There will not be time to go to the market to buy some. There will be no salvation that anyone can offer us; there will be no "get-out-of-jail-free card" that can be obtained. That will be the end.

This time of waiting is not an idle waiting. We have this *Tempus per Annum,* or Ordinary Time, so we can prepare for the final consummation with our Lord. This time through the year is an acceptable time to lose the things that have crept into our lives over time. This is a time to put to rest old grievances, and this is the time to prepare for the banquet that can come at any moment. For those who did not skip autumn and winter, but used them to change themselves, and rid themselves of what was dead and of no use; for them, spring cannot come soon enough. For the others, an eternal winter awaits.

77 Klein, F. A., & L. Bauer, in Joachim Jeremias, *The Parables of Jesus,* 2nd Ed. (Upper Saddle River, NJ, SCM Press, Ltd., 1954), 173.

Trigésimo Segundo Domingo del Tiempo Ordinario Año "C"

(II Macabeos 7:1-2, 9-14; Salmo 17; II Tesalonicenses 2:16-3:5; Lucas 20:27-38)

Se que mi Señor esta allí . . .

Las lecturas a lo largo estas semanas pasadas se han enfocado en el fin de los tiempos. La lectura de Macabeos e incluso el Evangelio nos hablan sobre los últimos tiempos, y esto es natural mientras nos acercamos al término del año liturgico. Los profetas nos hablan sobre el mundo por venir. Por lo tanto, esto continua con semjante testimonio, lo que provoca hacernos la pregunta, "¿Cual es el motivo por el que vivimos?"

Esta es una pregunta muy poderosa, en medio de todo el sufrimiento que hay en el mundo, y en medio de las pruebas diarias en nuestras vidas. Podemos concentrarnos en los deseos dentro de cada uno de nosotrs . . . los anhelos en nuestro interior que nunca han sido cumplidos, y si acaso encuentro en mi un deseo que ninguna experiencia en este mundo puede satisfacer, la explicación más concreta, es que no fuí creado para este mundo . . . sino para otro. Y por eso esperamos ese "otro mundo" con gran fe.

Un teólogo ofrece esta reflexión:

> Imagine si usted pudiera hablar con un bebé en el vientre ántes de nacer. Al nunca haber visto la luz de este mundo, conociendo sólo los confines, las comodidades, y la calidez del vientre, el bebé (me imagino), sería escéptico sobre la existencia de un mundo más allá de la matríz. De hecho, si pudieramos hablar con esa creatura, quizas se nos hará dificil explicarle que hay un mundo afuera mucho más grande y que es en su

mejor interés nacer. Si el bebé estuviera conciente, tendría que hacer un verdadero acto de fe, para creer en la vida después del nacimiento. Tendría que tener una gran esperanza para poder tomar ese paso.[78]

Y así es con nosotros. En el pasado, los santos llamaban su día de muete, su *dies natalis*, su "día de nacimiento." Pero sólo uno quien tiene esperanza en algo más allá de este mundo . . . puede anticipar tal nacimiento.

Pienselo. La única manera que estos siete hermanos pudieron aceptar tal sufrimiento es porque tuvieron esperanza en algo más allá de este mundo. Ellos no escucharon la musica de este mundo . . . pero bailaron. Según dice Pablo: *"Nuestro Padre Dios nos ha amado y nos ha dado gratuitamente un consuelo eterno y una feliz esperanza . . . que podriamos ser fortalecidos hacia nuestro nacimiento a la vida eterna."* Si creemos en la resurrección el temor no es necesario . . . porque alli esta la promesa del Maestro.

Mientras se preparaba para salir del cuarto de examinación, un hombre enfermo le pregunto a su doctor: "Doctor, tengo miedo de morir. Digame, ¿qué hay en el más allá?" El doctor le dijo en voz suave "no lo se." "¿No sabe? Usted, un hombre cristiano, ¿no sabe lo que hay en el más allá?" El doctor tenía su mano sobre la manija de la puerta; y al otro lado de esta, se escuchaba un ruido de rasguños y lloriqueo. Mientras abría la puerta, un perro brincó adentro del cuarto y saltó encima de él con alegría. Mirando a su paciente, el doctor le dijo: "¿se fijó usted en mi perro? Él nunca ha estado en este cuarto. No sabia lo que había por dentro. No sabía nada más excepto que su dueño estaba aquí, y cuando abrí la puerta, saltó sin temor. Sé muy poco de lo que hay más allá de la muerte, pero si sé una cosa . . . sé que mi Señor esta allí, y eso es suficiente."[79]

---

78 Based on reflection by Ronald Rolheiser (Translated N.S.)
79 Internet Forward (Translated N.S.)

Jesús nos recuerda que quienes son dignos de recibir el fin de tiempos no pueden morir. Porque han nacido completamente; porque han pasado por las pruebas y en el sufrimiento han encontrado lo que ántes estuvo fuera de su alcance . . . y por eso son como los ángeles que bailan no por la música, como lo hacemos nosotros, sino que bailan por la alegría completa!

THIRTY-THIRD SUNDAY IN TEMPUS PER ANNUM

(PROVERBS 31:10-13,19-20,30-31; PSALM 128; I THESSALONIANS 5:1-6; MATTHEW 25:14-30)

To know God . . .

Being a priest, I sometimes get to lead these "Marriage Encounter" weekends. These are weekends designed for couples in order to help them to grow in communication; love of each other; and to make prayer the foundation for their relationship. I recall one such weekend, that the issue which kept rising to the surface was: "Who wears the pants in your family." This issue just would not die, so having been a scientist before a priest, I thought, "What a wonderful opportunity for an experiment." And so it began.

I said: "All you husbands who feel as though you are oppressed. You feel like your wife wears the pants in the relationship. That she has absolute authority and you are at her beck and call. That she holds the books; that the kids even come to her because they know where the authority is. You have no freedom to do what you want. All of you men who feel that way, line up on the right side of the church." I then said: "Now, all you men who feel like YOU are in absolute control. You wear the pants in the family and your wife is at your beck and call. That you hold the checkbook and the finances, that even the kids come to you for stuff, because they know that you have authority. All of those men, line up on the left side of the church."

Then I watched. On the side where I told the men to stand who felt powerless, the line reached to the back of the church. On the other side, where I told those men to stand who were in charge, who had absolute authority, there stood one man, and he was kinda hunched over and sheepish looking. So I looked over to him and said: "You are the envy of every man here. How is it that you have absolute authority, that your wife is at your beck and call; that you wear the pants in the family . . . . how is it that you can stand in that line?" And he replied: "My wife told me to stand here."[80]

The first reading is often used for weddings. It speaks of a worthy wife (not unlike the one who was married to the man from the story above). Now if we can get beyond *"She puts her hands to the distaff, and her fingers ply the spindle,"* like I know so many of you do, we can see that this reading, like the others with it, is not limited to those who are married; but to all of us, who are married to the Bridegroom.

Jesus will often speak about being alert for when the Bridegroom returns. He is the Bridegroom and the Church is the bride. Therefore, if the Church is the bride, and we make up the Church, then we are the bride. So now let's read Proverbs, or Sirach, or any of the other parts of Sacred Scripture that refer to the marital covenant and insert our name where appropriate.

In the Old Testament, the sin of the "chosen people," turning toward other idols in worship, was characterized by the terms "fornication" and "adultery." Both of these terms, typically used with respect to unmarried but betrothed, or married people, were the terms chosen by the prophets who were the spokesmen of God. Further, the prophets will state that the people "do not *know* God." This *da'ath Elohim*, is a deeper *knowledge* than just knowing *"about"* God. This word "know" is the same word used in the Annunciation when Mary asks the angel Gabriel, *"How can this be, since I do not **know** man?"*(my bold).

This whole parable that Jesus relays to us about the talents, regards our own insecurity and unwillingness to invest ourselves, which is always a risk. Again, C.S. Lewis speaks of our unwillingness to love:

> To love at all is to be vulnerable. Love anything, and your heart will certainly be wrung and possibly broken. If you want to make sure of keeping it intact, you must give your heart to no one, not even to an animal. Wrap it carefully round with hobbies

---

80   Based on a joke from an Internet Forward

and little luxuries; avoid all entanglements; lock it up safe in the casket or coffin of your selfishness. But in that casket . . . safe, dark, motionless, airless . . . it will change. It will not be broken; it will become unbreakable, impenetrable, irredeemable . . . The only place outside of Heaven where you can be perfectly safe from all the dangers and perturbations of love, is hell.[81]

Our investment is not always going to get us dividends of five more or two more. In fact, sometimes we might not even end up making anything . . . but, what we invest will never be taken away . . . what we invest. That is the sin of the last one. Jesus says: *"Those who have, will get more until they grow rich, while those who have not, will lose even the little they have."* Is Jesus saying this? Does St. Luke know about it?[82]

I was preparing for Mass one Sunday when I got a call from the hospital, that a man was dying and wanted, "the Last Rites." It's nearly impossible to park at the hospital and this is always compounded when you're in a hurry. So when I had to go on short notice, I would take my motorcycle. I went over there and got my usual parking place, and ran inside to the medical ICU. There as I rushed in, I saw six Harley Davidson guys surrounding their comrade, and his wife nestled next to him. They noticed my helmet and one of them asked, "What you ridin' pastor?" I coughed out "Kawasaki." They all bowed their heads. The man in the bed then responded, "I'll let you bless me anyway!"

I had a wedding later that Saturday, and so I asked the two of them. "What advice would you have for a young couple?" Without missin' a beat he replied: "Marriage is not fifty-fifty. Anyone who tells you that, has never been married. We have been together for over half a century, and I'm here to tell you that marriage is 150% and 150%. Because there were days when she could only give 50%; and I pitched

81 C.S. Lewis, *The Four Loves*, (New York, NY, Harcourt, Brace and Company, 1960), 169.

82 Luke's Gospel has a special focus on the poor and how they will one day be rich in the kingdom. 16:19-31 ff.

in the other 150%. And there were far more that I could only give 50%, and she compensated." Wow! That is Jesus' parable in a nutshell. If we give all we can give . . . and **can** is the important word, then God will do the rest and more. But if we do not give what we can give, then even what we have will be taken away.

Any marriage is give and take. Our marriage with the Bridegroom is much the same. But make no mistake; he will always give more than he takes. If in our other relationships we held that same standard, imagine the possibilities!

Trigésimo tercer Domingo del Tiempo Ordinario Año "C"

(Malaquías 3:19-20; Salmo 98; II Tesalonicenses 3:7-12; Lucas 21:5-19)

El mundo necesita hereos . . . testigos a la fe.

Faltaba sólo una semana. Los sacerdotes de la diócesis de Harrisburg estaban en un taller anual para sacerdotes en Hunt Valley, Maryland. Fue una gran semana, y siempre la disfrutamos. Si podemos sentirnos orgullosos de cualquier cosa, legitimamente, nos enorgullecemos en los sacerdotes de la diócesis de Harrisburg. Tenemos un gran presbíterado, y por eso, esa semena fue una gran oportunidad para estar juntos. Todos nos vestimos casualmente la semana entera; no usamos las vestiduras negras de costumbre. Estabamos apunto de asístir a la última conferencia, y el padre Daniel Mitzel, me habia pedido que le ayudara a llevar algunas flores a su coche, para que él las pudiera usar en su parroquia. Estabamos llevando las flores a su auto, cuando se desarrolló un drama.

Mientras cargabamos las flores, nos dimos cuenta que una pelea estaba sucediendo en la colina donde estaba el hotel, cual se dirigia hacia el estacionamiento. Mi primer instincto fue pensar que sólo eran los estudiantes del colegio luchando o jugando, pero en un momento, esa primera impression cambio drasticamente. Derrepente, escuche a alguien gritar " ¡Detente!", y despues vi a un hombre que vestía una sudadera con capucha, y tenía un montón de billetes en sus manos. No se lo que estaba pensando en ese momento, pero derrepente solte las flores y corrí tras él. Corrí hacia el estacionamiento lo más rapido que pude y pronto lo alcancé. Lo agarre de los brazos y le dije que se tirara al suelo, pero él siguio corriendo. Me estaba quedando sin aliento, así es que use lo último de mi energia para derribarlo. Los dos caímos al suelo, lo agarré de los

274

brazos y lo mantuve en el suelo. Me quede allí, sosteniendolo, hasta que escuche los pasos del Padre Mitzel, quien llegó para apoyarme. La policía llego un poco después, con armas desenfundadas. Fue entonces que escuche en sus aparatos de comunicación, que el ladrón "pretendia tener una arma." ¿Qué quería decir eso? Significa que el ladrón poseía una arma, o al menos eso dío a entender.

Los billetes se estaban desparsando alrededor de nosotros, casí volteandose por la brisa. Solté al ladrón mientras el policía se acercaba para arrestarlo. Él se quedo sentado y prendio un cigarrillo, como si nada hubiera pasado (y quizas así fue para él). Después, el policía pidió mi nombre para el reporte, "Me llamo Padre Miguel Rothan" les dije. "Espera un momento . . . ¿tu eres un sacerdote? Esto es increible, le tenemos que avisar a la prensa sobre esto." Me llamaron para entrevistarme sobre lo que habia pasado y les dije lo que sabia. La adrenalina todavía estaba corriendo por mis venas. Ese mismo año recibí el premio de ciudadanía de la ciudad de Baltimore por haber atrapado un ladrón. La ceremonia duro diez minutos, y me presente vestido de sacerdote. Fue una buena oportunidad para dar una impression positiva para el sacerdocio.

Creo que es chistso, hasta loco, que algunas personas vean a quienes tienen fe como debiles o cobardes. ¿No les parece interesante que aquéllas personas que parecen ser muy fuertes en la fe son jusgados como comformistas o quienes no pueden pensar por si mismo? Ellos son quienes se acobardan ante una pelea. Los que deben ser humildes; lo cual se ve como un vicio en este mundo. Ellos son quienes, según el mundo, deben tener la mentalidad de "solo los fuertes sobreviven" y que esa debe ser la regla del dia. ¿Donde pertenece el Católico fiel en esta sociedad? No pertenece en ningun lugar. Ellos existen en oposición a semejante socidad.

Vamos a enfrentarlo . . . hasta hoy, esa sociedad es la mayoría . . . y semejante menoría enfrentandose a una mayoría no refleja cobardía ni debilidad, tanto como refleja el heroismo.

No me malentiendan, no quiero decir que todos debemos atrapar a un ladrón, pero si debemos saber quienes somos, y lo que representamos. Tomen esto en cuenta; nuestra iglesia no necesita cobardes . . . necesita heroes y los heroes no son quienes pueden volar, ni manejar autos invisibles, ni quienes tiran redes de sus manos. Los heroes son quienes viven en este mundo, pero no son de este mundo. Ellos son quienes se presentan costantemente como autenticos Católicos Cristianos, condenados por la fe, cual dicen ser suya. Estos no son quines huyen a las montañas, sino quienes desde antemano no se preocupan por su defensa. Ellos confían que todo lo necesario viene de Dios, y no temen a quien puede dañar al cuerpo, sino a quien puede condenar el alma al infierno.

Este mensaje evangelico es para los heroes, quien aún en su entusiasmo sienten miedo. "Los traicionarán hasta sus propios padres, hermanos, parientes, y amigos." Se que hasta yo tendría miedo. Pero esto nos exije determinar si en verdad somos verdaderos testigos a nuestra fe, o si acaso no lo somos, la cual viene de la palabra mártir. Si nos quejamos de los inconvenientes más pequeños en nuestra fe, ¿qué haremos cuando en verdad seamos sometidos a la prueba? A esto me refiero cuando hablo sobre la cobardía. ¿Acaso repetimos en nuestras confesiones que se nos ha olvidado abstener de la carne durante cada viernes del año, al menos que lo háyamos sustituído por un acto de cardial? ¿Acaso nosotros somos quienes nos quejamos de los días de obligación, o acaso tratamos de evadir nuestra obligación porque estamos de vacaciones? ¿Usamos vestimientos regulares para misa, para no sentirnos incomodos, o acaso podemos salir de misa sin cambiar nuestra ropa y continuar nuestro día? ¿Acaso nos quejamos porque la cermonia no nos entretiene lo sufficiente o no guarda nuestra atención? ¿Acaso nos quejamos porque hay niños en misa quienes hacen ruido? ¿Somos quienes salimos de misa inmediatamente después de comulgar para poder ser los pimeros en salir?

El motivo porque quizas se estan riendo ahora es porque usted conoce a alguien así . . . ¿verdad? Porque Él Señor bien sabe que nosotos no somos así. Pero en verdad preguntese: alguien que actua de esta manera . . . ¿en verdad estarían dispuestos a morir por la fe, o al menos sufrir en un nivel menor? ¡Claro que no! No necesitamos más cobardes. Necesitamos heroes. Pero, ¿cómo es que sabemos cuando somos heroes? Jesús nos da la certeza cual nos indica, con respecto al mundo, cuando los somos . . . el mundo nos contradecirá: "todos te odiaran por causa mía, sin embargo, no caera nigun cabello de su cabeza." Como el Obispo Fulton Sheen diría." Busca la religión que es más perseguida por el espíritu del mundo . . . y has encontrado una religión que es divina." El mundo necesita heroes . . . ¿esta usted listo para ser uno?

THIRTY-FOURTH SUNDAY IN TEMPUS PER ANNUM

(EZEKIAL 34:11-12, 15-17; PSALM 23; I CORINTHIANS 15:20-26, 28; MATTHEW 25: 31-46)

The Life Body, Blood, Soul and Divinity

It seems so ironic that we are celebrating *Christ the King of the Universe*, and the readings suggest that the universe as we know it, is ending. When we come to understand, however, that we are living in a world that was never meant to last forever, then we can appreciate what it means to be "King of everything!" Jesus' rule does not end with this world, but spans time and space. The kingship he enjoys, however, is not one of an overlord, but an *underlord* . . . one who humbled himself as a man, so that he might further place his very self in a piece of bread and a cup of wine; that man might allow our *Lord*, to assume the role of the *servant*.

Jesus will say, *"I came not to be served, but to serve, and give my life as a ransom for the many."* The word ransom (from the Greek *apalutrosen* which comes from *lutron*) is the payment for a death sentence. In other words, you are at the gallows, preparing to meet your Maker, when your Maker approaches with his own gold and riches, and offers them for you; and the executioner loosens the noose and sets you free! Our salvation, however, is not a once and done event that saved us just that one time, and now we're on our own. We are "being" saved. He gives us this ransom again, and again, and the strength that came to the early Christians through this event, comes to us in a very real way every time we partake of the Eucharist.

Today the center of our celebration *is* the Eucharist. It is the central dogma of our faith and that which continues to strengthen us. This is what makes us different from other Christian assemblies. We have the body, blood, soul, and divinity of Christ in the Eucharist. We can't just celebrate a "worship service" but must have the Mass. That's why we cannot have a "Mass" without the Eucharist. And that's why for Catholics, we must attend Mass on Sunday, and not just attend any church; because we have the Eucharist. Even what others call "communion" is not the same. This is not just one belief among many, but this is the *crux* (pun intended) on which our faith is based. A faith based in the sacrifice of the *Lover*, for the *beloved*.

There is a story I saw on the internet a few years ago which illustrates this idea of sacrificial love.

> Many years ago, when I worked as a volunteer at Stanford Hospital, I got to know a little girl named Liz who was suffering from a rare and serious disease. Her only chance of recovery appeared to be a blood transfusion from her five-year-old brother, who had miraculously survived the same disease and had developed the antibodies needed to
> combat the illness.
>
> The doctor explained the situation to her little brother, and asked the boy if he would be willing to give his blood to his sister. I saw him hesitate for only a moment before taking a deep breath and saying, "Yes, I'll do it if it will save Liz."
>
> As the transfusion progressed, he lay in bed next to his sister and smiled, as we all did, seeing the color returning to her cheeks. Then his face grew pale and his smile faded. He looked up at the doctor and asked with a trembling voice, "Will I start to die right away?"
>
> Being young, the boy had misunderstood the doctor; he thought he was going to have to give his sister all of his blood.[83]

---

83 Some will say this is an urban legend. I received it as an internet forward. But in the words from the movie: *Second Hand Lions*, "There are somethings worth believing. Whether they're true or not."

LA FIESTA DEL CRISTO REY
AÑO "C"

(EZEKIAL 34:11-12, 15-17; PSALM 23;
I CORINTHIANS 15:20-26, 28; MATTHEW 25: 31-46)

El Dominio y la Dominación

No es interesante que muy seguido a Jesus se le llama "Señor." Quizas pensamos de esta palabra en una manera teológica, pero por un minuto piensa como alguin que no conoce en Dios. Esta palabra aún tendría un sentido de gran significado e importancia. El "Señor", o "Rey" era el soverano de los pueblos. Pero me gustaría sugerir dos clases de reyes; dos estilos de governar, *Dominio* y *Dominación*. Al distinguir entre los dos; debería ser evidente porque celebramos esta fiesta como la corona del año liturgico.

La primera lectura viene del segundo libro de Samuel: *"Aquí estamos, hueso tuyo y carne tuya somos; ya antes cuando reinaba Saúl sobre nosotros, fuiste tú quien sacabas a Israel y entrabas con él."* Se necesita mas que una corona para ser rey. Se trata de relación. Este verso de la segunda carta de Samuel es muy parecido a este, de Genesís: *"Esta sí que es hueso de mi huesos y carne de mi carne! Se llamará Mujer, porque ha sido sacada del hombre."* En ese declaración, Adán habla sobre Eva como mucho más que una simple compañera o ayudante. El habla acerca una relación. Y la alianza significa una relación.

El rey, que se invierte en su pueblo y les ama, ejerce el dominio. Dominio significa que él es responsable de atender a las personas que estan bajo su cargo. Debe asegurarse que ellos tengan hogares, alimentación, y protección. Esta relación, sin embargo, no es parcial. La gente que vive dentro de los dominios del rey, tienen que estar de acuerdo de cuidar el reino, a defenderlo y prometer se obediente al rey. Así es como funciona la relación en una alianza. No se les hace extaño que despues de crear Dios al hombre, tambien le entrego el dominio. "Entonces Dios dijo, *'Hagamos al hombre a nuestra imagen, según nuestra semejanza; para que domine sobre los peces del mar y las aves del cielo, el ganado, las bestias de la tierra, y todos los animales que se arrastren por el suelo."* El dominio.

La Dominación es diferente. La dominación existe cuando alguien decide, y actúa de una manera que se entroniza a si mismo. El poder esta en el servicio de su egoismo, en comparación con el servicio del amor. El dominador se aprovecha de las personas a su alrededor para su propio beneficio; ordena leyes y mandates, que sirven en su interes, y hace lo necesario por mantener esta manera de vivir. Esta Conciencia Real busca crear dentro del pueblo un orgullo por sus logros; una esclavitud de los demás para construir el reino y un silencio de los que se oponen. Un reino de la dominación necesariamente incorpora una Conciencia Real dento de los suyos.

Jesús habla de la Conciencia Real cuando se encuentra con dos partidos: Los fariseos y Pilato. *"Los Fariseos se impusieron sobre ellos; pero no será así entre ustedes. Cualquiera de ustedes que sea el Maestro, él es quien servirá a los demas."* Los fariseos necesitaban mantener la dominación, ya que sin su poder, serían como los demas. Pilato comparte un diálogo con Jesús sobre el poder. Para Pilato, el poder significa tener la habilidad de liberar o crucificar a un hombre; el poder es el respeto y reconocimiento de Roma; el poder se trata de tener control. Pero para Jesús, el poder verdadero simpre se encuentra en el servicio del amor. Y de esta manera se cierra el diálogo. No se les hace extaño que Pilato obligo el epitafio de la cruz permaneciera: *"Este es el Rey de los Judios."*

Vemos dentro de la realeza los dos modelos que se han aplicado a traves de los siglos: La Dominación y el Dominio. Se le entrego el dominio a Adán, y aún así se aferro a lo que no tenía derecho de poseer, él cruzo la línea y nacio la dominación. Ahora Jesús es el nuevo Adán, y ofrece una segunda oportunidad a todos bajo su Señorío. Les ofrece protección, les ofrece alimento, les ofrece hogares; y les ofrece la vida eterna. Sólo faltaba una cosa por hacer para que el Rey garantizara todas estas gracias a sus sujetos. El único requisito, era el sacrificio de su propia vida. El dominio es la realeza que viene del amor puro, lo que el poder absoluto entrega. Por eso Cristo ES el Rey.

281

APPENDIX I

HOLY DAYS AND FEASTS WITHIN
THE CHURCH YEAR

FEAST OF THE IMMACULATE CONCEPTION
(GENESIS 3:9-15, 20; PSALM 98; EPHESIANS 1:3-6, 11-12; LUKE 1: 26-38)

December 8

Mary is the mother of Jesus . . . Jesus is God . . . therefore, if Mary is the mother of Jesus, and Jesus is God, then Mary is the mother of God. The mother of God . . . the one who gave birth to Jesus could not have been of sin. When the angel approaches her in Luke's Gospel he says (in Greek) *karikatomene*, which means full of grace. If grace is a share in God's divine life . . . the very presence of God within us, and Mary was full of grace . . . then there was no room for anything else. She was full. Therefore, she must have been sinless. If one has sin, they can never become purely sinless, because some remnant of sin remains. If Mary is full of grace, there is no remnant of sin, and, therefore, there never must have been any sin, which means even from her birth, her very conception, there was no sin. Therefore . . . her conception was, in a word, immaculate.

La Fiesta de la Inmaculada Concepción
(Génesis 3:9-15, 20; Salmo 98; Efesios 1:3-6, 11-12; Lucas 1: 26-38)

Deciembre 8

María es la madre de Jesús . . . Jesús es Dios . . . por lo tanto, si María es la madre de Jesús, y Jesús es Dios, entonces María es la madre de Dios. La madre de Dios . . . el que dio a luz a Jesús no pudo haber sido del pecado. Cuando el ángel se acerca a ella en el Evangelio de Lucas dice (en Griego) *karikatomene*, lo que significa llena de gracia. Si la gracia es una participación en la vida divina de Dios . . . la presencia de Dios dentro de nosotros, y María llena eres de gracia . . . entonces no había lugar para nada más. Ella estaba llena. Por lo tanto ella debe haber sido sin pecado. Si uno tiene el pecado, nunca puede convertirse en purly sin pecado, porque algunos restos de pecado permanece. Si María es la llena de gracia, no hay ningún vestigio de pecado, y por lo tanto nunca debe haber habido algún pecado, lo que significa que incluso desde su nacimiento, su concepción no había pecado.

Por lo tanto . . . su concepción fue inmaculada en una palabra.

SOLEMNITY OF MARY
(NUMBERS 6:22-27; PSALM 67;
GALATIANS 4:4-7; LUKE 2:16-21)

January 1

The feet of Mary hold fascination for me. I have yet to see a picture of Mary with shoes or even sandals. In the *Pieta*, she is bare-footed. Beneath the cross her feet are covered. Even in the manger scene, it appears that she is kneeling, or seated, and her feet are shrouded with her garments. The feet of Mary hold fascination for me, because they walked the path laid out for us, without sin!

Can you imagine the temptations she must have endured? Sinless yes, without temptations, no! We are in a battle that, at best, is difficult at times, and at worse nearly impossible! Every turn of ours is one that could lead toward temptation. Not because we pursue it, necessarily, but because it pursues us. Now imagine . . . being the mother of God! If one cannot destroy the soul of the chosen one, surely they can destroy the soul of the one who brought him here. Right?

How many temptations of pride, "He's my son?" How many temptations of the flesh, being a virgin in a world that scorned it? How many temptations toward gossip, or self-pity, or desperation, knowing all that she experienced? How many times could she have questioned even her own son, and his work, and his words? And yet . . . she was faithful, despite her humanity.

I believe her feet fascinate me because bare feet can be tender; and yet they crushed the head of a serpent; they trampled the thorns that Paul speaks of in his letters; they kicked the dust from them in protest against a town that did not offer peace; and they also made the trek to Calvary feeling every splinter; every stone; every stubbed toe, wishing only to take the place of the *One* making the journey.

See, her life . . . her mission . . . her purity did not end with the birth of her son, or even with his death. She continued to walk the path, regardless of its incline or decline; stones or thorns; stumbling blocks or sharp turns. She was faithful. And we are to be the same. It doesn't mean that the temptations will abandon us . . . but that we will be able to walk over them; through them; crush them; with her as our guide to the journey's end; her Son.

San Francisco
6·13·10

The Pieta, sketched at the church of
Santa Clara, Queretaro MX.

Ash Wednesday

(Joel 2:12-18; Psalm 51; II Corinthians 5:20-6, 2; Matthew 6:1-6, 16-18)

Now is *an acceptable time*

An elderly woman walked up to a little old man rocking in a chair on his porch. Though he looked weathered and feeble, he had a content smile on his face. "I couldn't help noticing how happy you look," she said. "What's your secret for a happy life?"

"Well, I smoke three packs of cigarettes a day," he said, waving a wrinkled hand through the air, with a smoldering cigarette between his thumb and finger." "I also drink a case of whiskey a week, eat fatty foods, and never exercise." "That's amazing!" said the woman. "So, how old are you?" He answered: "Twenty-six."

If the condition of our souls could be seen from the outside of our bodies . . . I wonder how old we might look. Perhaps we've been putting off the change we really need during Lent. Maybe we've been putting it off for forty days, or even forty years . . .

Put it off for forty more? Sure . . . there's always time, right? But you better be sure.

Miercoles de Ceniza
(Joel 2:12-18; Salmo 51;
II Corinthios 5:20-6, 2; Mateo 6:1-6, 16-18)

¡Ahora es el Tiempo!

Una anciana camino un viejito en una silla mecedora en el porche. Aunque se veía cansado y débil, pero tenía una sonrisa en su rostro era satisfecho. "Me parece, que tu es feliz, dijo la mujer. "¿Cuál es su secreto para una vida feliz?"

"Yo fumo tres paquetes de cigarrillos al día", agitando una mano arrugada por el aire, con un cigarrillo encendido entre el pulgar y el dedo. "Yo también tomo una caja de whisky a la semana, como alimentos grasos, y nunca hago ejercicio."
"¡Eso es increíble!", Dijo la mujer. "Así que, ¿cuántos años tienes?"
"Veintiséis", respondió.

Si la condición de nuestras almas se podía ver desde el exterior de nuestro cuerpo . . . Me pregunto qué edad nosotros apareceriamos. Quizas hemos estado posponiendo el cambio que necesitamos durante la Cuaresma. Tal vez 40 días, o incluso 40 años . . .

¿Lo pospondra por 40 más? Claro . . . siempre hay tiempo, ¿verdad? Pero es mejor estar seguro.

HOLY THURSDAY:
FEAST OF THE LORD'S SUPPER
(ISAIAH 61:1-3, 6, 8-9; PSALM 89;
REVELATION 1:5-8; LUKE 4:16-21)

"Pray that You are not put to the test."

What is the sacrifice Jesus desires? Tonight, he offers us two great gifts: The Eucharist, and the priesthood. Without the priesthood, there can be no Eucharist. Without the Eucharist, there is no reason for the priesthood. The great feast we celebrate tonight, brings into focus these two great gifts. But . . . what is the responsibility with the gift? What is it that he wants us to do?

"You call me Master, and rightly so . . . you must do for the other." What is it he says at another place in scripture: *"but I say to you . . . love your enemies."* So whose feet does he want us to wash? The feet of Judas! The one to whom he not only gave his body and blood, but also washed his feet . . . knowing, that Judas would be responsible for his suffering and death.

In many of the depictions of the last supper, Judas is on the end. At times, his head is looking down, or away from Jesus; at other times, he is facing our Lord, while he clinches the "blood money" in his hand. But he seems to be on the end. Now, imagine the picture then . . . at the end of the meal, Jesus gets up and dons an apron, and the Apostles turn away from the table on their little pillows or short benches so that their feet are exposed, and then he washes them.

I often wonder . . . was he the first to get his feet washed? Was he the last to get his feet washed? Did Jesus wash his feet first, perhaps, before he got the chance to run off? Did he wash his feet last; to save the best for last! Or was there something that he wanted the other eleven to see; that even amidst betrayal . . . one still must show love.

Perhaps this was a shadow of things to come *"You will be led before kings and governors . . ."*

We receive two great gifts tonight among others. The priesthood, through which we will receive the grace of all the other Sacraments . . . and the Eucharist, which is the nourishment which fills us with sanctifying grace . . . the very presence of God within us . . . the God who washes the feet of his betrayer and wants only, for us, to do the same. *"Pray that You are not put to the test."*

Jueves Santo

(Isaías 61:1-3, 6, 8-9; Salmo 89; Apocalipsis 1:5-8; Lucas 4:16-21)

"Oren . . . para que no caigan en tentacion."

Cual es el sacrificio que desea Jesus? Esta noche, nos ofrecie dos dones grandes. La Eucaristia, y el sacerdocio. Sin el sacerdocio, no hay Eucharistia. Y Sin la Eucharistia, no hay razon para el sacerdocio. La gran fiesta que nosotros celebramos esta noche, aumenta estos dones maravillosos. Pero . . . ¿cual es la responsibilidad que el don require? ¿Que es lo que el desea que hagamos?

"Ustedes me llaman maestro, y dicen bien, porque yo soy. Pues si yo, que soy el Maestro y el Senor, les he lavado los pies, tambien ustedes deben lavarse los pies los unos a los otros." En otro lugar en las escrituras el dijo: *"Pero, yo les digo . . . amen sus enemigos."* ¿Entonces, a quien no pide que le lavemos los pies? Los pies de Judas. La persona a quien das u cuerpo y sangre, pero tambien lava sus pies . . . quando supo que judas seria responsible por su sufrimiento y muerte.

En las pinturas de la ultima cena, usualmente, Judas esta sentado al fundo de la mesa; a veces, su cabesa esta bajada, o ne esta mirando a Jesus . . . a veces, el esta mirando a Jesus mientras sostiene la bolsa de monedas en su mano. Ahora, imagine la pintura . . . quando la cena termina, Jesus se levanta se pone una toya y los apostoles dan la vuelta en la mesa, entonces sus pies estan en frente de Jesus y Jesus los lava.

¿A veces pienso fue la premera persona a quien le lavo las pies? ¿Fue la primera persona a quien le lavo las pies? Acaso, Jesus lavo los pies de Judas primero; ¿Quizas antes Judas huyo? ¿A via algo que el quiso que los demas vieron? ¿Que aun en medio la traicion, todavía necesitamos mostrar amor? Quizas esto fue una sombra de las cosas por venir. Jesus dijo: *"Los entregaran a las autoridades y los golpearan en las sinagogas."*

Esta noche, recibimos dos regales grandes. El sacerdocio por el cual vamos a recibir la Gracia de todos sacramentos, y la Eucaristia, que es el alimento que nos llena con gracia santificada, la presencia verdadera de Dios. ¡Dentro de nosotros! Dios lava los pies de su traidor y solo nos pide que hagamos lo mismo. *"Oren . . . para que no caigan en tentacion."*

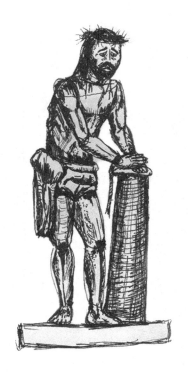

Santa Del Carmen.
6·26·10

Scourging of Christ from the Church
Santa del Carmen, Queretaro MX

Good Friday of the Lord's Passion
(Isaiah 52:13-53; Psalm 31;
Hebrews 4:14-16—5:7-9; John 18:1-19, 42)

The Seven Sorrows of Jesus

I was once assigned to a parish by the name of the *Seven Sorrows of the Blessed Virgin Mary.* The Pastor, Fr. Louis Ogden, used to call me "The Eighth Sorrow," among other things! I imagine, however, that through his lifetime Jesus experienced many sorrows as well, for we know that at one point he even "wept." I would like to propose that Jesus, too, had seven sorrows, but these were concentrated within his passion and death. The seven sorrows are as follows:

"One of you will betray me." The sorrow here was not elicited only by the fact that one of his most intimate followers would betray him, but also by the response of those who were at table with him. *"Certainly it is not I, Lord?"* As each of them repeat this phrase going around the table, we see how truly human each of these men is. The greek root, *mā* (may) is used in the Gospel. This word denotes a question, which is expected to be answered in the negative. It is a strong word. By asking this question the apostles are doing two very normal things: first, they are excusing themselves by the validation of Christ, but also, in a less obvious way, they are betraying their own insecurity. To ask such a question, they must think it possible that they **could** be a betrayer. It was not only the ultimate response of Judas, but that the others thought themselves capable of betrayal, that would have saddened the heart of Jesus.

The second sorrow of Jesus occurs during what has come to be known as the first Sorrowful Mystery of the Rosary: the Agony in the garden. *"He was sorrowful, even unto death."* What brings even a greater anguish (if one can imagine greater anguish) is when Judas approaches for the betrayal. He greets Jesus, *"Rabbouni."* Now, to the observer, nothing appears out of form. Jesus really is, a rabbi of sorts.

But to someone looking behind the text, there is always more. He has been with Jesus for almost three years. He will actually call them his friends. Judas greets him with an act of familiarity, but addresses him as a stranger. Calling him "Rabbi" would be equal to addressing him as "Mr. Jesus." Totally impersonal. Jesus' response betrays the true relationship. He responds in the Greek, "*etaire*" (etai-ray), which means, "My most intimate friend." The only other place this word is used, is in the Old Testament. It is the word Jonathan uses for David. Judas addresses, "Sir," and Jesus responds, "My most intimate friend."

The third sorrow of Jesus was when *"Judas hanged himself."* Even in the most heiness sin, forgiveness is a possibility; a hope. If there was any chance, it died with Judas. We know that Jesus was human, and yet it appears he not only had a special connection with this apostles, but could *see* things even when he was far away from them. No scourging could have hurt nearly as much as the loss of Judas. *"This is the will of the one who sent me, says the Lord. That I should not lose any of those that he gave me . . ."* (John 6:39).

The fourth sorrow dealt with one of the first four followers of Jesus. This was the one on whom the Church was to be built; the one whose name he changed; the one who followed him up the mountain for the transfiguration, and walked to him on the water. This one . . . denies our Lord. In the Gospel of John this denial is spelled out much more clearly than the other Gospels. One could take it, if Peter denied Jesus once; I mean we've all done that, right? Even a second time, if he was caught off guard; but a third time? The Greek is also very clear here. In the first denial, he is like a studdering, scared man. By the third denial, he actually swears an oath and says he does not know the man . . . sadly, that is true.

His level of hurt with the fifth sorrow was obvious as someone who is powerless to stop a mistake made in ignorance. He feels sorry for them. *"They know not what they do."* He forgives them even as they mock him. The words of hurt are responded to with healing; the words of hatred, with love. Even now he thinks not of himself, but the other. Even now it is evident that the kingdom is not reserved only to the "chosen ones" but to "the many" as well. His sorrow then is more of "being sorry for" them, then it is sorrow for himself.

Goodbyes are difficult under the best situations. When we go away from home for the first time, or on a long trip that will separate us from our mothers for an extended period of time. When we might have gone away on a "bad note," and it is not so much a moving on in life as it is fleeing from an uncomfortable situation. Goodbyes are difficult, but when it comes to those who not only brought us into this world, but also raised us up, goodbyes can be torture. Here, Jesus says goodbye to his mother. Where, many years ago, he said goodbye, having left the homestead, now he says goodbye in preparation for leaving his earthly home. Motherhood is one of those gifts that does not end with death: neither the death of the mother, nor the death of her child. Why would this be different with Mary. Whereas we might cause our parents much heartache or stress during our lives, rarely will we insist that they adopt others, who are perhaps worse than we are. This is just what Jesus did. He not only had to say goodbye to his mother, but now, no longer of this earth, he would entrust the world to her . . . and her, to the world. It must have caused much more pain than the crucifixion to leave her to a world that would not welcome her son at the beginning of his life, and would ultimately kill him in the end. This was his sixth sorrow, but surely one of the greatest. *"John, this is your mother."*

Finally, in solitude he prays, *"Eli, Eli lema sabathani."* There are many people "like" us, but no one "is" us. God has created us unlike any other ever. With this individualism comes a loneliness of sorts . . . a solitude. There will be times when we are very much alone, because no one can possibly understand. Imagine being the Son of God. Imagine being completely surrounded by those who cannot understand, at least not yet. But there was always the consolation of the Holy Spirit, and the angels who were sent to console him. He was always in communion with the Father. Because of those long nights in prayer and communion, some solitude would be tolerable. But now here on the cross, he cries out, *"My God, my God,"* and it appears as though, under the burden of the sin of the world, the solitude overwhelms him. St. Paul will say, *"He who knew no sin, became sin for us."* Sin is separation from God. And as Jesus took all of this sin; as he became the sin offering for all of us, he felt that separation in such a way that there was no one . . . he was utterly and completely alone. The seventh sorrow.

These sorrows might lead to desperation, if they did not result in the ultimate joy. And because we have this joy and we believe in the one who promises it . . . because we have this "what," like him, we can endure almost any "How."

THE FEAST OF THE ASCENSION OF OUR LORD
(ACTS 1:1-11; PSALM 47; EPHESIANS 1:17-23; MATTHEW 28:16-20)

The King, Ascends to the Throne

Today we celebrate Christ the King. I know what you're thinking: "No, Christ the King is at the end of the Church year. The last Sunday of the Church year when we celebrate that Christ is king of all. But that's not completely true. The Ascension is not merely "an" ascension to Heaven, but to the throne in heaven. The Psalmist says: *"God mounts his throne to shouts of joy a blare of trumpets for the Lord."* Christ is king, because of his sacrifice. That's why the Gospel for Christ the king speaks of the crucifixion. So, having ascended into heaven, Christ is the king, and ultimately the king of all.

But the irony is, Christ is NOT *our* king. Oh, he is king of the Universe, after all, he was there when it was created, but king of our world? No way.

Why did Paul write letters? Because although people had the message of the Gospel, that had received the Gospel, they had not "received" the Gospel. They had mixed themselves so well with the pagan world, that they were still very much pagan. Christianity was very different from all of the other religions of the day, save for Judaism. Most of the other religions of the day validated some acts forbidden by the law of God, and I don't mean eating pork. Roman law by that time was morally bereft. All you have to do is read Tacitus, or Philo the Jew to see those things that were not only permitted, but promoted in the Roman Empire. And these were not necessarily overly religious guys.

The ideal was an *epicurean* Ideal: pursue pleasure and avoid pain. And yet by persuing untempered pleasures, life was always going to be painful, if not empty. Paul is trying to balance the Ephesians. There are the extremes who want to be called Christian because they are promised resurrection, but want to live as Roman pagans. There are others who want to follow all the prescriptions of the laws and have no love for their neighbor or obligation to the poor. Christ was not their king.

The apostles now want the fulfillment of what they think the promise to be. Now, he will surely take over Jerusalem and kick out the Romans. After all, that's what a king does, right? God chose David as king, because the peoples' king, Saul, ran the kingdom into the ground. But even as God chose David as king, throughout his life, David will also choose "David" over God again and again.

Christ is the king of the Universe, and in the end, we know who the victor will be, there's not another scenario that fits. But right now, he is not king of our world; he is not the king of our country, and perhaps not the king of our individual lives . . . but he could be.

Religious and priests pray this prayer book 5 times a day. In the office of readings (the first prayer of the day) the reading came from Origen, a priest from the early centuries of the church who contributed many great writings. He says this:

> Note this about God's kingdom: It is not a sharing of justice with iniquity, nor a society of light with darkness, nor a meeting of Christ with Belial. The kingdom of God cannot exist alongside the reign of sin.

> Therefore, if we wish God to reign in us, in no way should sin reign in our mortal body; rather we should mortify our members which are upon the earth and bear fruit in the spirit. There should be in us, a kind of spiritual paradise where God may walk and be our sole ruler with his Christ. All this can happen in each one of us, and the last enemy, death, can be destroyed.[84]

---

84 Origen, priest, "From a Notebook on Prayer", in the *Liturgy of the Hours*, Vol. IV, 577.

I'm sorry to say it, but amidst the spirit of a world who seeks to destroy God, except the one they have created in ***their*** image and likeness; we have lost the battle. We can blame any number of factors that played a part in this loss, but like the ancient Israelites who had to spend years wandering in the desert; and years in exile; like the people of Rome and Corinith and Galatia and Ephesus and Philippi and Collosae and Thessalonica; we have now enmeshed ourselves so thoroughly with the spirit of this world, that no one would recognize us as having any king, but Caesar. We've bought into it.

Perhaps we will be the ones who say *"Lord, Lord"* in the final days, and he will reply, *"I do not know you."* Or perhaps we think the king is dead, like so many thought at the crucifixion. Whatever we believe, will be true for us, and others will see that very clearly in the way we live, the movies we watch, the places we shop, and the company we keep and the various diversions we have used to fill the void where our King once was.

Jesus Christ is not the king of our world . . . But he could be.

That will take more than greed. It will take more than get, get, get. We must start by going beyond the simple pleasures of this world, and ascend, to where he wants us to be.

ASSUMPTION OF THE
BLESSED VIRGIN MARY

(I CHRONICLES 15:3-4, 15, 16:1-2; PSALM 132;
I CORINTHIANS 15:54-57; LUKE 11:27-28)

Blest are you . . .

I never had a real connection with Mary. I never really had a devotion either, but probably because of the "connection thing." I think part of that was reactive. Especially growing up with all the devotion to Mary. At my church we even had the weekly Novena to our Mother of Perpetual help. After all, we were a Redemptorist parish in the heart of Lancaster. I knew how to pray the Rosary and knew the *Memorare*, Hail Holy Queen, and even the *Ave Maria* in Latin. But love . . . devotion . . . it was not there.

It got even worse in the Seminary. Again the stubborn reactivity of being told, "She's your mother," or "You gotta love Mary, because Jesus loves Mary." But all the pictures and icons I saw just didn't inspire that devotion. I remember at times during my stay at St. Vincent, going down into the crypt of the church where they had a beautiful grotto to our Lady of Lourdes. It was always so quiet there and dark and peaceful, but that was it. There was nothing but quiet and dark and peace. She was not there.

And then I recall seeing a picture, for the first time. Look it up! It was a painting by Rossetti that I have now hanging on my wall. Dante Gabriel Rossetti's, *Ecce Ancilla Domini* (Behold the Handmaid of the Lord), was finally an image of Mary I could grasp. It spoke to the humanity of the woman I could never have imagined. All of the statues, pictures or icons I had beheld in the past, showed little reality for what I imagined must have been a traumatic experience of the Divine. Rossetti captured perfectly a Mary who was unsure, scared, and would most assuredly have asked, *"How can this be?"*

304

The Mary we celebrate as Assumed into heaven, was not taken body and soul into heaven because she was perfect. She was not assumed because she was fearless or brilliant or bold. She was taken into heaven body and soul because she was sinless; and in her sinlessness, she was faithful. Sinlessness for us is a dream; but to be faithful . . . even those of us who are rebellious souls, can attain that virtue. Dante brought that to light for me through his portrait. Not a portrait in the usual sense of the word. A portrait usually shows all the greatest attributes of the subject. What this portrait brought to me was the possibility of devotion to a woman who was once a scared little girl . . . unsure of the future, or the present for that matter. And I could be devoted to her; I could follow her to her Son.

Where she has gone, we shall follow. Not soon enough! But we will, because we can. It's simply a matter of seeing in her, what perhaps we need most to develop in ourselves, and follow her *fiat* to faithfulness.

ALL SAINTS DAY

(REVELATION 7:2-4, 9-14; PSALM 24;
1 JOHN 3:1-3; MATTHEW 5:1-12)

Perseverance and Hope

The saints are those in *Beatification* (happiness). It is significant then that today's Gospel is that of the Beatitudes. They speak to us of not being satisfied with who we are, but to always strive for *better* than we are. This means that we learn from our mistakes. That is the difference between the saints and those who are not. Saints sinned, and had aspects to their lives which were far from saintly, and yet they never gave up. They rose up again and again. When we learn from our mistakes, and rise above them to become better, then we are on our way to sainthood.

I think when the apostles, *et alia*, began to follow Jesus, it was for the notoriety, or the miracles and magic, or the power of forgiveness. They stayed with him because it looked as though his *kingdom* would be the one to endure. Then . . . he died. And with him the dream. And yet . . . they stayed. Why would anyone stay? Unless they found more than what they had originally been looking for. Unless, this was the *One*, perhaps, they had been looking for all their life. You see, it was this perseverance . . . this hope, that made them saints.

St. John says, *"We are God's children now; what we shall later be has not been revealed."* We have what we need now, but we must persevere. We must constantly look at the mistakes we made in the past and learn from them. We must see ourselves as the "betrayer," "the denier," "the doubter," the ones who were early disciples, and emerge like they did from the morass of sinfulness into the hope of future beatitude.

Perhaps you've heard of the not-too-bright fellow who saw an advertisement for a cruise. The sign in the travel agency window read "Cruise—$100 cash."

"I've got 100 dollars" he thought, "and I'd like to take a cruise." So he entered the door and announced his desires. The fellow at the desk asked for the money, and the not-too-bright guy started counting it out. When he got to one hundred, he was whacked over the head and knocked out cold.

He woke up in a barrel floating down a river. Another "sucker" in another barrel floated past and asked him, "Say, do they serve lunch in this cruise?" The not-too-bright fellow answered, "They didn't last year."[85]

Do we learn? Imagine if we did, the change that could occur. Roger Garaudy, the famous unorthodox-communist philosopher in Poitiers, is said to have made a remark about Jesus of Nazareth in this vein: "I do not know much about this man, but I do know that his whole life conveys this one message: 'anyone can at any moment start a new future'." This is the message of Christ. This is the message of John: *We are God's Children now* . . . who will we later be?

---

85 Internet Forward.

Todos los Santos

(Apocalipsis 7:2-4, 9-14; Salmo 24; I Juan 3:1-3; Mateo 5:1-12

No es para los débiles de corazón . . .

Nuestra fe no es para los débiles de corazón. Hay muchos quienes dicen ser "católicos" o "cristianos. Ellos van a misa, cuando les conviene . . . rezan cuando les conviene . . . son activistas y protestan cuando les conviene . . . pero cuando se sienten incómodos dejaran caer su fe como un cigarillo desgastado. No estoy hablando de un cobarde, porque almenos el cobarde reconoce sus miedos y le teme a algo. Estoy hablando de alguien es apático . . . noten la raiz "patético." Necesitamos personas que están listos para ser mártires y misionarios . . . el futuro pertenece a estas personas, no a los débiles de corazón. Pero el mundo les hace pensar diferente. "Si el mundo no nos reconoce, es porque tampoco lo ha reconocido a él . . . . Todo el que tenga puesta en Dios esta esperanza, se purifica a sí mismo para ser tan puro como él."

¿Qué significa ser mártir y misionario? Quiere decir que estamos comprometidos y somos condenados en nuesta fe. Hoy en día se acostumbra tener pulseras o esos imánes en nuestros coches. Algunos tienen tantos imánes que no se sabe que es lo que representan, sino que simplemente apoyan la industria de los imánes. El hecho es que aún con pulseras, marchas, o incluso imánes, no hay compromiso. Se pueden quitar y poner como un accesorio. Un compromiso hacia algo o alguien no es un accesorio a la vida . . . es una vida. El futuro no es para los débiles de corazón . . . es para los que estan comprometidos. Sin embargo, no es suficiente estar comprometidos . . . ¿A que nos estamos comprometiendo?

"Ellos son los que han pasado por la gran persecución y han lavado y blanqueado su túnica con la Sangre del Cordero." Comprometernos a algo significa verdaderamente creerlo . . . entenderlo . . . ver lo bueno en eso. ¿Pero cuantas cosas defendemos hasta la muerte que no valen nuestro tiempo? He dicho que los que son fragiles protestaran cuando les conviene . . . ¿Qué significa esto?

¡Es hora de despertar! De comenzar a comprometernos a El que tiene poder sobre nuestra alma. Los que no estan comprometidos tienen una cosa en común . . . ellos escuchan la voz del mundo, cual es basía, y aún así siguen su precepto que : "Tu puedes tener todo . . . ambos, y." Sea la persona que representa algo en su vida. No sigan la multitud como un banco de peces, simplemente para estas cómodos. Pero, a esas cosas que usted se compromete . . . sean cosas para mejorar el mundo y a usted mismo . . . no solamente algo que le permite llevar una vida de comodidades.

"Felices los que son perseguidos por causa de la justicia, porque de ellos es el Reino de los Cielos. Dichosos serán ustedes cuando los injurien, los persigan y digan cosas falsas de ustedes por causa mía. Alégrense y salten de contento, porque su premio será grande en los cielos." No hay futuro para los débiles de corazón . . . no hay espacio para los miedosos en el Reino. El Reino es para los que se han comprometido. Para los que están dispuestos a soportar con valentía cualquier persecución que se les presenta porque no son sujetos desatentos de este mundo. Ellos son los que estan "apartados" y por eso es que se les llama sagrados . . . sanctus . . . por esto se les llama Santos.

APPENDIX II

REFLECTIONS

TALK ON THE EUCHARIST AS THE CENTER OF OUR LIVES

Quo Vadis Days, 2005

There is a story of a priest who was captured and placed in a prison camp. Upon entering the camp he was allowed to contact his family once, to bring any necessary items for his incarceration. He requested "his stomach medicine." They knew immediately what he wanted. They took a flashlight, and placed hosts in it, and replaced the label on a bottle of wine with the words, "stomach medicine." He recalls that every day during his imprisonment, he celebrated Mass with three drops of wine and one drop of water in one hand, and a particle of bread in the other."[86] Fr. John Clifford, S.J., recalls spending 888 days in prison. "888 days without receiving communion or celebrating the Eucharist . . . . only a priest can understand such loss and solitude."[87] In the wake of the recent Tsunami, the body of a nun was found. She had been dead several days, and yet because of *rigor mortis* her body was knurled into a ball. As they were preparing her for a proper burial they realized what it was that her hands had clasped. That in her final seconds, as the wave approached she grabbed the most important thing in her life . . . a ciborium within which still remained our Lord. She knew she would be making the journey into eternal life, and so took the one she knew would lead her there, making her body a tabernacle in death as she did in life.

The Mass is the highest prayer of the Church, and within that prayer, the Eucharist is the pinnacle of our worship. What a gift we have been given. That the God heaven could not contain has chosen to rest in our hands; on our tongue; and make His dwelling in our bodies. This is the great gift we have received, through which the only proper response is gratitude or thanksgiving or *Eucharistia*. If we believe.

---

86 Timothy Cardinal Dolan, *Priests for the Third Millenium*, (Huntington, IN, Our Sunday Visitor, 2000), 216.

87 Ibid., 217.

If we kneel here in adoration of a piece of bread, then what we practice is idolatry and blasphemy; and we are the most pitiable of men. But if what we have before us is the God who gives us life and breath; who fashioned us, and loves us, and we do NOT worship; we are the most pitiable of men . . . the most lost of all. Jesus faced this disbelief even before his death. The evangelist John has preserved this discourse which has etched itself into our hearts. I chose this reading for the Gospel because it is the only doctrine over which disciples leave Jesus. They had disagreements at times and confusion, but never left over a doctrine, until now. The issue goes on even today: Is this really the body and blood of Christ that we consume, or is it simply a symbol?

Jesus begins by saying *"He who eats (phagete,* generally eating) *my flesh (sarx,* living breathing flesh) *and drinks my blood has life* (which is translated from the Hebrew, *Nephesh)* or the presence of God within. Now some found this saying difficult and I imagine the apostles were saying: "You know, he uses these metaphors all the time." Jesus must have understood that there might be confusion, even though the Jewish authorities were very upset. So he repeats. This time he uses *"Trogon"* to chew, and *gnaw* and *crunch.* "He who chews, and gnaws, my flesh and drinks my blood." And then goes on to use the word *Alāthās* (true or truly). *"My flesh is true food and my blood true drink."* If this were simply metaphor no one would have left . . . no one would have considered this an abomination; but they did. And many walked away. There were those who believed this saying was too difficult.

Jesus speaks of the thieves who do not pass through the gate, but go over or under it. Those who unworthily try to receive the same benefits as the ones who have gone through the proper channels and who have suffered. If we believe what we say we believe, then we would never want anything less than the best for our Lord. To receive our Lord, as to receive any sacrament, places a responsibility; a sacrifice on the part of the one receiving it. *"Can you drink the cup of which I drink."* And yet sometimes we want anyone and everyone to be able to receive communion.

Isn't it ironic that we won't just allow anyone and everyone to vote in our country; that many institutions have probationary periods, before which, the person cannot share in the club. And yet we would offer our Lord so quickly to those who do not believe what we do, or worse yet, believe, and wish to receive so that they might desecrate the Eucharist. We must come to realize what a great gift this is; that our God has humbled Himself so that we might become intimate with Him in the best way possible. We cannot take that for granted, simply to pacify those who might protest; we cannot compromise the truth, so that all might be included regardless of their disposition. Paul says: *"Those who do not discern the body and blood are liable to condemnation,"* (in Greek, *krisis*); translated in Latin, *Damnatio.* Having heard that . . . . will you also leave? *"To whom shall we go Lord, you have the words of everlasting life."*

Ten Year Anniversary of September 11, 2001

(Sirach 27:30-28:7; Psalm 103;
Romans 14:7-9; Matthew 18:21-35)

September 11, 2011

An eye for an eye and a tooth for a tooth. This was Hammurabi's law from the ancient world. This law is still in effect in many parts of the middleeast and beyond. If you take my eye, I take yours; if you steal from me, I cut off your hand. Seems like justice, right? Why not?

So we go ahead and take revenge . . . then what? We talk back, or insult the other, then what? Recover our honor? Is that what happens? As we commemorate this day, I recall it very vividly. People used to discuss that the day that Kennedy was shot, they could say exactly where they were and what they were doing. I didn't get it. How could something have such an impact as to burn itself into their memories? But for me, this day did.

I was going upstairs to the recreation room in the seminary on the fourth floor, to get some things out of storage, for the school year for us has just begun as well. There were about seven guys huddled around the television, and I saw smoke coming from a tall building. Thinking they were watching some action movie, I was ready to dismiss it when I saw the scrolling text along the bottom of the screen: "United States Attacked." I was frozen for a minute and then took my seat among the others, hypnotized by what I was seeing, until the other plane approached.

I remember where I was, what I was doing; I remember the feelings of anger and the desire for some kind of revenge. I remember wanting to leave the seminary at that moment and go join the military as so many did in the wake of the attacks. Those feelings never went away;

316

I don't think they ever go away, especially if we lost a loved one in that event. The feelings do not go away . . . but they can change.

To feel angry is human; to feel sad or frustrated with the "state of things" is normal; but to harbor hatred and animosity for many years is futile at best. See, we fail to understand at times that hatred does damage to our SELF. It does nothing to harm the other. The old adage, "kill them with kindness" is more true than we probably think. To hate a person takes a lot of energy from us, and does little to affect the other.

The readings for today were not changed to suit the day. They are the actual readings for the day. Think that is coincidence? I don't think so. A theologian once said: "If someone smacks you today, it will hurt. But if it still hurts two weeks later, that is no longer the person, but you." This is true! Listen again to these words from Sirach:

> "Wrath and anger are hateful things, yet the sinner hugs them tight. The vengeful will suffer the Lord's vengeance, for he remembers their sins in detail. Forgive your neighbor's injustice; then when you pray, your own sins will be forgiven. Should a man nourish anger against his fellows and expect healing from the Lord?"

What I think of more is the people who died that day. If they knew it was their last, how might they have lived differently. Who might *they* have forgiven? Who might *they* have asked forgiveness of? Who might *they* have told, "I love you."

When I was in college I went on a retreat, and during this retreat our friends and neighbors and parents gave testimonies of their love for us. What a powerful image to see these videos of our loved ones saying, "I love you." It reminded me of when I go to the hospital at times, and there is someone with their family around them. And they are giving their last words to them. And then they die . . . they can do nothing to change it. They missed an opportunity to do something that perhaps they could have done ten years ago. We have that opportunity that they do not . . . that they did not. Don't miss it!

Because if we learn nothing from this tragedy; if we are not changed because of it, then they died in vain.

Cinco de Mayo

Today is cinco de Mayo. For some reason, it always falls on May 5th! It is a celebration by the Mexicans (especially those of Puebla) of the day when they fought and won against the French army. The French army was yet undefeated, and had double the numbers of their Mexican enemies, and yet they lost. Some believe that the French were trying to move through Mexico, in order to break up the union in the U.S. Because of this act in Mexico, the French went no further north.

We never know all the ways that events will affect, even those who seem like they are not involved. Sometimes, we worry too much about what others will say. We are not proud of our religion and what we profess, and because of this, many will see our example and not desire to become Christian. When we are proud, as Jesus tells us to be, and we are witnesses, then we also have an effect. Perhaps if we fought for our faith, as the Mexicans fought for their country, a world might finally be converted!

Cinco de Mayo

Hoy es cinco de Mayo. Es una celebracion de Mexico (Especialmente para los que viven en Puebla) Recordamos el dia quando lucharon y le ganaron al ejercito frances. El ejercito Frances fueron derrotados y tuvieron muchos mas soldados que sus enemigos, pero, fueron derrotados! Algunos personas creen que los frances, estuvieron tratando de viajar hacia el norte para destruir la union de EEUU. Porque el evento de cinco de Mayo, los Frances no pudieron avanzar.

Nosotros no sabemos todas las maneras por las cuales eventos los afectaran a otros. A veces nosostros estamos preocupados sobre lo que otros hablan. Nosotros no sentimos orgullosos de nuestro religion, y lo que creemos. Entonces, a veces muchos veran nuestro ejemplo y no desean ser cristianos. Quando tenemos orgullo en nuestra religion, somos testigos; y son efectivos. Quizas, si luchamos por nuestra fe, igual que los mexicanos lucharon por nuestra pais, Nuestro mundo sera convertido!

Homily Given at the Basilica in Washington D.C. for the close of the Marian year.

La Gozosa, La Dolorosa, La Gloriosa mysterios de Maria. "No es una isla en si misma, sino el estrecho mas valiente de la humanidad, exendiendose hacia un mar de divinidad." Maria es nuestra madre por adopción; ella es nuestra hermana a través de la creación; es nuestra intercessora porque la elegimos.

Quisiera concentrarme en los misterios de la vida de Maria. Maria vivio el gozo, al ser elegida la madre de Jesús, y aún así, para que ella alcalzara la gloria, tuvo que sufrir dolor.

<u>Maria la Gozosa</u>

Maria, en sus primeros años debia haber sentido una gran alegria, como cualquier otro joven de su edad. Mas, sin embargo, imaginense . . . sin la sombra del pecado original en su alma, lo diferente que debe haber sido su vida. Que ella vivio la alegria de la salvación antes de haber dado luz al redentor. Seria dificil explicar este gozo, y quizas pensariamos este gozo inalcanzable . . . si nosotros mismos no hubieramos sido testigos.

Creo que por este motive, Dios elegio a una joven para ser la madre de Su hijo. Debido a que ella no habia sido endurecida por el mundo . . . se lleno de gozo, porque estaba llena de gracia. Es posible para nosotros vivir este gozo con quien se ha redimido . . . o quizas todavía, no sabemos que somos redimidos. La felicidad de Maria, no fue un gozo alocado, tampoco un estado de ser feliz todo el tiempo," sino una paz. La paz que viene de un entendimiento apropiado de la libertad. El pecado es una falta de comprensión de la libertad. Pero con un entendido adecuado de la libertad, uno mismo siente paz . . . una paz que nos acompaña incluso atravès de nuestras amargos dolores.

La Dolorosa

Si recuerdan los siete dolores de Maria, queda claro que ella no vivio sin sufrir. Por lo contrario, ella sufrio muchisimo durante el transcurso de su vida. Y sabiendo esto, propongo que la causa de su sufrimiento fue el abuso de la libertad por parte de los hijos de Dios. Ella conocía la historia, sabía que hace solo unos cuantos años habian dejado de ofrecer sacrificios humanos a los dioses en Canaán. Pero ella tambien, se dio cuenta que los recien nacidos todavía serian sacrificios en su epoca . . . no para agradar a cualquier dios, sino para hacer la vida mas facil. Esta matanza de los inocentes, sucedio en su epoca; mucho antes que Herod lo habia ordenado . . . y por eso llora; aún hoy, en nuestro tiempo.

Ella presencio las influencias Romanas en su propia sociedad de campo al ver a niños de su edad esclavizados por motivos perversos, y por el deseo de las parejas quien buscaban otro estilo de vida. Ella fue testigo de la pena de muerte que recibieron algunos criminals, y el abandono de los ancianos y viudos. Ella fue testigo del fracaso de los escribas y fariseos quienes no eran lideres fuertes ante la corrupcion y falta de moralidad. Ella presencio todos estos pecados, y sin embargo lo que le causo gran dolor fue ver la poca paz que tuvimos, al seguir nuestro propio camino.

En la Pietà, ella ve mas allá que el cuerpo de su hijo . . . nos ve a nosotros en el aquí y ahora. Ella sufre con nosotros, en el rostro de un niño con hambre; en el incesante dolor que siente un artrítico; en el rechazo de la voz de los inocentes; en el corazón aislado de las victimas del abuso; en el alma solitaria del picador, y en el pensamiento desgastado de los maltratados; ahí, esta el dolor de Maria.

En cada acto contra la justicia, cada violación de la dignidad; cada ataque contra la vida; en cada acto de asesinato, fornicación, violencia, cada ofensa contra los inocentes, ahi, se encuentra el dolor de Maria. Y apesar de todo esto . . .

La Gloriosa

Ella vencio su dolor, no por parte de sus abilidades y talento, sino porque fue elevada . . . ascendida a la gloria por aquél que le habia entregado todo su ser. La asunción la robo de la muerte, el resultado del pecado, y la llama hacia la gloria. Sin el gozo, sin el dolor, no puede haber gloria. Sin la pietà, no hay presentación. Maria tuvo paciencia con un mundo, que no la considero . . . y que todavía no lo hace.

Hoy en día, nos encontramos en el centro de los problemas munidales. Estamos en el lugar central, donde se imponen decisiónes. Y aun así, vivimos en un mundo que, no simplemente neiga la existencia de su hijo, sino busca destruirlo. Vivimos en un mundo, muy parecido al que ella vivia en los primeros siglos de la iglesia. Este es un mundo que, no reconoce que el sufrimiento es una oportunidad de acercarse más a Dios, sino que, lo evitan por falta de compresión de la libertad. Y como resultado sufren sin descanso dentro de la carcel que ellos mismos han creado. El dolor de la Bienaventurada Virgen Maria todavía siguen en pie, y sin embargo . . . su Gloria, tambien, sigue en pie . . . La gloria de la que fue elevada y coronada, no por sus meritos, sino por su fe. "Bendita eres tu por creer que se cumpliría lo que El Señor proclamó."

Su deseo es que vivamos en libertad al ser hijos de dios. De vivir el gozo, que es la paz de una vida llevada en la libertad verdadera. De aceptar con valentía el sufrimiento, que sentimos porque no estamos dispuestos a adaptarnos al mundo. Nosotros y nuestros hijos nos renunciamos a perder este mundo por causa de la cultura de muerte, sino que, por Dios lo tendremos denuevo. Somos fieles Catolicos. Nosotros somos sus hijos, encomendados a ella. Consagrados a ella por ser nuestra madre . . . nuestra protectora. Ella siente nuestros dolores, y nos desea su gozo, para que un dia nosotros tambien podamos vivir, la gloria.

APPENDIX III

WORLD YOUTH DAY
"THEY CALLED IT D-5"

They called it "D-5." This was the tag we all wore for World Youth Day. The tag we were given at the very beginning, and told not to lose, for fear of death . . . or merely not being able to participate in the festivities. One of our kids was so careful that he put his tag, along with his passport, between the mattresses in Lourdes so it wouldn't get stolen . . . and he left it there as we traveled to Madrid! We did get both by the time we needed them, because, after all, those tags were important. After all . . . the whole reason for being here, was the Mass with the Holy Father and the festivities . . . right?

We traveled a far distance in order to make a pilgrimage to some place. That place would be the culmination of our travels. The area set aside for all the pilgrims at WYD. The place we would congregate after a week's travels to pray and camp and awaken to a Mass celebrated by our Holy Father on the last day of the celebration.

From Lourdes we would pass through Burgos on our way to Madrid, and the ultimate site which was D-5. I guess we knew that we would not get close enough to see him as he arrived in Madrid, or witness his prayer during the *Stations of the Cross*, but that was okay. We knew that our patience would pay off as we entered the "reserved section," right near the front. D-5 would be our ticket into history. So as long as we kept our tag; and remained as a unit, before we knew it we would enjoy the celebration of His holiness and our own pilgrims. That was the plan.

"You duped me, O LORD, and I let myself be duped." I love Jeremiah, because he always says it like it is . . . even to the Lord. *"You were too strong for me, and you triumphed."* I have come to understand the humanity that Jesus dealt with in his time on earth as a man. I understand it far greater than I have at any other moment, and through any other event in my life. I find it humbling, if not

fascinating, that at times the Lord will take such an event . . . an experience, as tragic or uncomfortable as it is, and He will hold us hostage and make us endure it that we might grow; might come to understand something in a way that otherwise might never have been possible. Because of this experience we might come to some revelation or enlightenment that otherwise might not have been accessible. That miracle for me . . . was D-5.

In fact following this event, the young people who attended WYD would come to understand the term "D-5" in apocalyptically symbolic terms. "Don't make me go *D-5* on you." Etc. But it all began with the final leg of our pilgrimage . . . our journey from the Hotel on *Calle de Jorge Juan*, to the abandoned air field, which would become the largest church in the world for a day. In past years, the dioceses of the U.S. who were attending WYD, would celebrate a U.S. Mass before arriving at the site for the main celebrations. Our plan was to check-out of the hotel, leave from the U.S. Mass and travel the hike to the air field. Having been told that we had a designated spot and that we would have space, we took our time after the Mass in order to eat, get plenty of water and then begin our journey. We weren't worried about finding room. After all, we had our clearances . . . we had not lost our tags and were ready to redeem them for the care we took all week long to keep them in pristine condition.

The first part of the journey to the airfield allowed us to take the *Metro*. We arrived at the station and there were not many people waiting for the train. This should be easy, no? It was when the first train arrived that we understood why the place was so empty. I didn't know it was possible for a person's body to change shape so easily, but with the way these people were squeezed into this rectangular train car, my incredulity quickly changed shape as well. Each of the successive trains bore the same resemblance to a double packed sardine can with no room for mustard or oil. We would never make it as a group, so we split up into three groups of four. We knew the stops and just had to be vigilant with our bags. I warned the kids ahead of time that they would probably be groped in some fashion because of the close quarters.

I could tell the kids felt uncomfortable. They clung to their backpacks as they witnessed fights erupt between two Italian men. They watched in horror as the French woman got on the train after having been rejected twice a place, and spit on the people close to her, who quickly made accommodations. And for the first time the words escaped from the lips of one of the youth with me. "Are these people Catholic?" Surely it couldn't be. Good Catholics would not spit on each other; or pummel each other for a place on the train. Good Catholics would not step on each other to see the Holy Father; Christ's representative on earth . . . would they? Could they?

For the first time in a long time, I thought about the conditions in which Jesus lived. The times when he had to get into a boat to preach off shore; the times when he raced on to the next town; the times when the paralytic could not get near the house, so they had to climb up the roof; the time when Zacheaus had to climb the tree in order to see. Now it made sense. How must it have been in Jerusalem when they made the pilgrimage to the temple? Even reflecting on the story when Jesus got lost in the crowd as a child after being left behind in Jerusalem.

Finally we arrived at the station and poured forth from the car like water through the hole in a dam. Out of the packed car and into the packed road on our march to the final destination. That would be the end of trying to fit in anywhere, because soon we would be part of the D-5 family, where there was a place for everyone. As we walked, people in the high-rises along the road would toss buckets of water down over us, or spray their shower streams down on us to cool the desert walk. Finally we arrived at the bottleneck, through which all pilgrims passed. Our ticket into the desert sanctuary would be our orange card with the letter/number combination. This made the whole trip worthwhile. We passed through one security access point and then another. At the second point they were checking our bags and passports. All of us made it inside the security gate. We gathered together, thankful to have made it and then began the dusty walk to our home for the next twenty-four hours.

The lines of people like ants, went on for miles it seemed. This vast airfield became very small and tight very quickly. People were everywhere and yet there still was not enough space. We were shoulder-to-shoulder with people on the road to our designated area. People were pushing as much now as they had on the cattle-car that brought us here. There were metal fences like parking barriers around these designated areas which had now transformed with tents and mats into an improvised campground. The odor was horrible. Was it sewage or body odor, I couldn't tell, but it was bad. We looked for the water stations which were to be along the perimeter of the area, but all we saw were fire trucks at various locales, spraying the crowds to keep them cool. There was not a tree in sight . . . no shade . . . only our hats and sunscreen to guard against the menacing sun and unrelenting heat of the day.

We would pause from time to time, looking for our section, and then always, one of the green-shirted *voluntarios* would move us along. Finally we arrived. The orange flag was like a beacon, waving a welcome to travelers who had come from miles away. *"But there was no room in the inn."* We looked over the vast crowd in hope of spotting our reserved area where we could finally sit down and rest, but there was not even a small swatch of land. Where were we to spend the night under the stars with our Holy Father? That was not a rhetorical question . . . it was a real question! The other chaperone and I split up to go around the perimeter looking for a small area where the few could at least sit down. There was none. Not only that, but there were no walkways into the camp. People had filled every nook and cranny with bodies, and therefore not only was it not navigable, it was a panic trap!

I was getting nowhere with the *voluntarios* and so I approached a police officer. I asked him to make an announcement that the people should move in and make more room for the groups for which this area was reserved, but he responded that they already did that. That there are too many people and they don't listen. I responded that it was unsafe because there is no walk way to get emergency aid in to the people and he just looked at me and then made it clear what had happened. Apparently they had prepared for a million people . . . and there were two million. There would be no moving in; there would be no walkway made; and we were unable to go to another division. We were stuck. I had erroneously thought D-5 would have been the U.S. dioceses or something, but it actually consisted of about 25,000 people. All here to see the Pope. Even now the battles were beginning over territory. Even now sleeping bags and mats had dry dusty footprints on them from the pilgrims who had stomped through camp looking for a little patch of real estate.

There was a small patch along the road on which we entered, and we staked it out immediately. The *voluntario* said we could not remain in that area and made us move on, but when a French group came and did the same, and he did not object, we set up camp, with little more space than would fit four people comfortably. We decided to ask the group what they wanted to do. Did they want to stay, or go? The one chaperone had his two children with him, so they didn't have much of a choice. So he and his two, plus Vincent, stayed behind. Now this was Vincent's first big trip and I was worried the whole time about losing him. I was reluctant to leave him behind, but I knew the chaperone would take care of him.

The eight of us journeyed back to the hotel; everything was less packed now, and settled in; we drank some water and turned on the TV in the lobby of the hotel to see what was going on out at the airfield. I was told that we wouldn't have to go back for the Mass the next morning as we had planned, and that they would send a bus out to collect our people. Then I began to watch the TV and saw the massive crowd beyond counting spread out over this, now seemingly small airfield. The commentary by the news people said that water was running short and that the bathrooms were backed up because they couldn't handle the numbers of people who were there. It was then that I decided to make the trek back out there and at least take water to our kids. The assistant youth director for the Diocese was heading out there because she felt like she should be with them, and when I found out that she was going alone, I volunteered to go with her. During this time, the Bishop called and told us to get our groups out of there. He was mostly concerned about us getting our flight the next day amidst millions, but upon finding out about the massive numbers and the water issues, the message was clear.

We made our way up the once grassy hill toward the entrance I remembered from earlier in the afternoon. The area, however, was obscured this time with bodies . . . thousands of people waiting in a line that rubbed the perimeter of the security area, with a human fence constructed of *voluntarios* who were shoulder-to-shoulder. The rain had now begun to fall a bit harder and as the wind whipped up, the dust from this bowl was beating into our faces. Guarding our faces from the sand, we pushed our way through the line which was fifty deep, to one of the *voluntarios*. I began to ask him in Spanish if we could pass, and he spoke English in return. He said they were not allowing anyone else into the area . . . it was full. "You don't understand," I tried to explain "We want to bring people out. Our kids are in there and we need to bring them out." He said no one was allowed in. Needless to say, I was not happy, but as we continued to argue, the crowd around us began to count. One, two . . . the *voluntarios* and the police yelled to each other as they locked arms making a human fence readying itself for a stampede. Three . . . .
these five thousand or so people stampeded the police, the *voluntarios*, and ran for the security gate.

I yelled to the assistant director for the Diocese that we needed to get out before we got trampled, but as we pulled back we witnessed the mass of people storming the gate, knocking over the metal detectors, and police, and volunteers. The gate was now open. Anyone could enter or leave, and that was much more dangerous than the lightening which was now illuminating the navy gray sky. We had to go in there and get our kids. Anyone could enter now, with anything they wanted to bring along. I heard the police shout that they were calling the riot team and the SWAT. We ran through the gate.

I stationed the assistant director at a kiosk near the entrance, and told her that when I found groups I would send them to her. I prayed a prayer to St. Anthony asking that I might find Vincent and the others I had left behind. With the rain and wind now, mixed with the lightening, the Pope had paused the holy hour service. They requested the people to reflect in quiet prayer, but they would just begin to get quiet, and suddenly an air horn would go off, or a chant would begin. The Pope did not speak. I went back several times to D-5, but my people were not there. I looked over the perimeter thinking that perhaps they went for a better seat, but to no avail. Finally, I texted another chaperone who was attending a Mass of anticipation and said to go to our hotel to see if they had returned. I ran into the youth director for the Diocese who had stationed himself at the corner point of D-5. He asked if I would go and find our groups, and that is what I did.

I plowed through the hordes now leaving because of the weather and the new infiltrators who had stormed the gate. I saw a brigade of police, two by two in a long line heading for the entrance. I found one group, and then another, none of whom knew anything about the lack of water or numbers of people. I led them to the director and then out the gate, only to return again. Finally I received the text from the hotel that my group left when the clouds started rolling in and they were safe and sound . . . thank God! One group was left. I knew *about* where they were, but it was impossible to navigate through the bodies and sleeping bags, camping mats, and tents. Amidst this holy hour, many were in the tents doing things that are inappropriate in any public place. Others continued to chant despite the request for silence. The question that the boy had asked me at the subway reappeared in my mind: "Are these people Catholic?" I was hoping that I would catch a glimpse of the missing group with the intermittent strobe of the lightening, but it was so dark, and against the stage all I saw were silhouettes.

And then, right as I thought the Pope was going to speak, he merely made a motion, and through the stage came a monstrance the size of a small car with the Blessed Sacrament inside. As it rose, many fell to their knees, like the wind running across a field of grass. And then, silence. He who calmed the storm and rebuked the wind now did it again! And I was struck. This whole week I was unable to pray, and now in the midst of this chaos, I felt the urge to fall on my knees as well, and offer thanksgiving. And that is exactly what I did.

331

After a moment, I got up and looked around. And there they were! The Pope offered benediction and then began to leave; and as he did the crowds ran to where he was leaving, which opened the path for me to get this group and get them out. They asked people not to spend the night there, but to leave and sleep somewhere else and come back. Yeah right . . . 1.5 million people! We checked in with the Director and then I led the remaining pilgrims out to the kiosk, and returned to look for one more small group. When I left the grounds, it was after midnight. I was informed when I returned to the hotel that we had recovered everyone safe and sound.

Then Jesus said to his disciples, "Whoever wishes to come after me must deny himself, take up his cross, and follow me. For whoever wishes to save his life will lose it, but whoever loses his life for my sake will find it."

I saw these millions of people; stepping on the faces of their brothers to see . . . . the representative of Christ on earth! These people storming the gates at the possible peril of others . . . and I thought, "These are Catholic people?" Then what kind of Catholics are they? They are much like Peter, who said, *"God forbid Lord, you will never suffer."* Those who don't like the sacrifice, but focus on the self. These are the *cultural Catholics*. Those who attach the label to their name, but have no more investment in the faith than that.

After WYD in Toronto the headlines read: "We love the singer, but hate the song." I think that says it all. We love the ideal, and the ideal *is* possible, but this is *not* the ideal. We hate how it plays out. What we witnessed was a *European party*. An excuse for young adults from all over the world to get together and do what they do. It is a shame too, because many *were* there for the right reasons. Many *did* sacrifice to get there and sacrifice daily within their lives. These are the *true* Catholics whose faith is not based on the latest trend or how they feel at the moment, but live a true sacrificial faith! They do not step on their brothers, but lift them up! That was the problem with this experience. Not everyone was there for the right reason.

We have to decide whether we are the ones who use faith as an accessory when convenient or easy, or whether we are in it for the long haul. Whether we are a cultural Catholic who adapts the ideal to their living standard, or the true catholic, who allows others to see what could be possible, by the way they live their life now!

APPENDIX IV

My Mexican Adventure

QUERETARO
JUNE 7, 2010 AT 5:43PM

We landed on the tarmac of the Queretaro airport. This airport had not been there two years before. As we exited the plane, there were men in military fatigues with automatic weapons. This was something I had not seen since Rome. We entered the customs post and filled out our paper work. It was about nine pm, so the only light was coming from the city. We had arrived. I went through the scanners, pushing my luggage with two-months-worth of cargo packed inside. I had on a clerical shirt but tan linen pants. Granted, although my sisters might argue, I would never wear this outfit together in reality, but it was cool and airy.

I approached the guard who took my passport. "¿Tu es sacerdote?" he said. "Sí," I responded. And he waved me through. A van dropped off the different seminarians to their host families, and only I and the other priest were left. We were dropped off at this house, jammed between two others in the dark. The ten foot high front doors opened, and out came the sweetest Mexican man and woman who embraced us both.

Concepcion, or Chepita, and her husband Adan, grasped our hands and kissed them. We entered through the front doors into a large, open-air atrium, with stairs that ascended to the heights. The breeze was cool and dry, a perfect evening. With my suitcase and carry-on in tow, we reached the top floor and were shown to our rooms. Each was a small suite, separate on the top of this four story house. Beyond, all that could be heard were the city sounds and . . . what . . . no, it couldn't be . . . yes, it was . . . a train. Right behind the house was a train that ran through about every few hours. I was not still in Lebanon was I? Perhaps, and perhaps not. Because the Mexicans I had encountered in Lebanon were such beautiful people, and here . . . it was much the same. Perhaps there were more similarities than differences.

I woke up . . . to the sound of the train in the morning and a rooster, just next door . . . on the roof? Of course! I pushed on my door and it seemed reluctant, as if something were set in front of it. I peeked wearily through the crack in the door and there, lying on the floor in front of the door, was a big brown boxer. He lifted his head as if to say, "Can't a guy get some sleep around here?" and then lazily moved to the stoop across from my own. I walked around the right corner of my suite and there was a flat stone roof, with a black barrel for the water. Clothes were snapping in the soft morning breeze on a line dried with sun and age. I walked over on the roof, sat on a rugged short wall separating the two roofs, and prayed the office. Glorious!

I went to breakfast at 6:30 am, and there was Adan, cutting up mango and brewing coffee. He held up a can, and showed me these foreign beans that were a tannish stain. Coffee beans . . . he took them raw and roasted his own beans, only to grind them and make a fresh pot of coffee. I really don't like coffee, but *this* was good. We sat down and talked about spiritual things. I'm sure I only caught half of what he said, and said only half of what he heard, but he is truly a spiritual man. What a gift to see the two of them, seemingly very much in love after so many years.

I went to school with the rest of the group, and then we were split into classes based on our ability. My ability was sketchy. I only studies Spanish for one year in the Seminary and then the rest I gleaned from the people at St. Benedict's Parish. I got into a class with three others, and it was not long before we were speaking. There was one fella having a bit of trouble, and I felt awful for him, so I would try to help. The instructor (who was probably a little more than twenty years old) would ask a question in Spanish, and he wasn't getting it, so I would kind of give him some hints. Well . . . needless to say, my first day of class, and I got yelled at by the teacher who was younger than I! It was a long day, but *la comida*, or the midday meal made everything okay. After a short (next to non-existent) *siesta*, it was back to the school. It was then that I discovered something that I had not known prior to this journey . . . something that would necessarily impact my experience, and that of the other students on this trip.

Celebret. It is a little card about the size of a driver's license, and the Spanish call it a "*licencia.*" I had gone to the school to begin planning where we would celebrate daily Masses, plus the excursions that we would do. This card, "*celebret*" means "he celebrates." And without it you cannot celebrate Mass in a foreign place. My first thought was that they would be more lax here about the laws, because the people do seem liberated. I was wrong. Therefore, without this card, I would be able to do nothing!

Every priest I encountered or called was very gracious and hospitable, until I told them I had forgotten my celebret at home. Suddenly, they would shut down and respond that when I showed them the *licencia*, I could make the plans. Are you kidding me? Obviously not. I told the other priest with me about this dilemma and he remarked: "Oh, don't you carry that everywhere with you?" (Thanks mom!) Hmm. Obviously not. I called my parents to see if they could get the card from my truck and scan it, so that it could be emailed to me. They decided to spend the day at Ocean City. So now what? I called my sister. As I called them, though, something felt different. I was aching a bit, in my neck, and limbs, but that could've been *anything*. Right?

I lost a whole day.

It's evening now.

I remember a little over ten years ago when I laid down my motorcycle on a rainy night around my house. I had some abrasions and cuts, but was wearing a helmet. When I woke up the next day, from my head and neck, to the tips of my toes, my body was a mountain of hurt. I could not move without being in pain. This morning was worse. What had happened?

I had not eaten from the roadside stands, or forgotten to wash my hands. I hadn't opened my eyes or mouth in the shower, or even really eaten a lot since I was here. My water was all bottled. My sleepless night was spent curled up and shivering, in a place that is never "not hot" while my trips to the *baño* were frequent. My head was swimming, and my stomach was following suite. What could it be?

I went into the kitchen in the morning, just to get some dry toast, and there it was. Lying in the sink was half a lime. Their limes are much smaller than ours, and the woman making the food, cutting various meats and vegetables had picked up half a lime and gave it to me. Without thinking, I popped it in my mouth, just for a few seconds. Apparently that was enough.

I went to two hours of classes this morning and rushed back to my house to sleep only for an hour, because of a meeting scheduled at one, with a seminarian from *Juano Juato* who had ties to our parish in Lebanon. After the meeting, I curled up my shivering pile of pain and slept. But not before receiving my sister's email with the *celebret* attached. I printed it out and now was able to make the plans.

I know tomorrow will be a better day. It has to be . . . doesn't it? For the main meal today I had another piece toast, which by the way is bread, toasted at the factory and sealed in bags. I came back to the school amidst the firecrackers and music in the streets anticipating the feast of *San Antonio*. I don't know what happened, but I know now what **not** to do.

In the Garden of Eden, I don't think Eve ate the whole fruit . . . all it took was a bite. See, a bite may not kill you, but you'll feel like death when it's over. And to think . . . I didn't even know who Montezuma was.

I wish I'd had my camera when I went to the Mexican Wal-mart! **June 12, 2010 at 7:27pm**

Just let me say that I wish I had brought my camera to the Mexican Wal-Mart . . . yes, even here the *paga aquí por menor* ("buy" or "pay here for less") is in Mexico. Before you click your tongue or think to yourself "*lo que sea*" (what-everrr) listen to this. I walked into the place, because I needed detergent to do my wash. (Talk about showing your dirty laundry, my rooftop lounge doubles as a clothes drier, story for another day.) There was a greeter at Wal-mart, which is not so uncommon in Wal-marts in the EEUU (Estados Unidos or

United States abbreviated). But this greeter was a bit different . . . well wait . . . first I need to tell you about the trip there.

In Mexico, I imagine it is much like it was in the first Christian centuries, in that all the buildings are adorned with crosses or statues of our Lady of Guadalupe built right into the façade of the structure. There are rosaries hanging from the rear view mirror of almost every car. People go in and out of the *templos* (churches) all day long. That was part of the problem today.

We were supposed to concelebrate Mass at the *Cathedral of Querétaro*, but we were told the time was 8:30am. Well, contrary to popular belief, the Masses in Mexico *DO* start on time. The Mass was 8:00! The seminarians started to arrive, and I sent a sentinel outside the church to warn them. I waited until the end of Mass, and then ran to the sacristy to see if I could celebrate Mass privately, with the guys in the cathedral. Well, it happened that the bishop was coming to the cathedral today for confirmations at 10:00am. There would be people in and out, and they would be setting up, so it wouldn't work. The priest said we could go to *Santa Clara* (a beautiful, pictures without flash, church). We went there, but they were getting ready for a wedding at 9am. The priest with me said to join a Mass in progress. No! I needed to celebrate Mass, or at the very least, concelebrate.

We spoke to the sacristan at Santa Clara, and he offered their chapel to us. What a beautiful chapel! He prepared everything and it opened to the street. It was like so many other shops along the *calle*, (street) that people visited to get some treasure. But the treasure here . . . well, it was the pearl beyond all price. And cost nothing. So various passersby came in to worship on this feast of the *Immaculate heart of Mary*. When we have private Masses, we still celebrate in Spanish, but chant everything in Latin (seminairans, sems for short, are great to have along).

As the other priest and I walked out, an organ began to play. Was that the wedding next door? How could that be? We would never be able to focus. But no . . . it was too close . . . no, it was the chapel organ. I looked up and the Spanish woman smiled and played the opening hymn. What a beautiful Mass! She played all the Mass parts and the guys sang along beautifully. Afterwards we were offered this chapel, for our private Masses whenever necessary. I walked back through the plaza, where hundreds of beautiful Mexican children were gathered with their families playing, and causing trouble, and eating . . . wonderful.

My holy hour isn't the same here as back home, where the church is dark and locked. I still take my walk in the morning and pray as I walk along. I make the morning hour with a seminarian, whereas the others opted for the afternoon holy hour with the other priest. Either is fine. But during the holy hour people come in and out constantly . . . they walked in . . . made a visit, and left. . . . And another comes. Dropping coins in the vigil box; praying the stations; talking gently, one to another. I just thought the other day . . . *oh to have a silent church* . . . to have the solitude! And then I was praying the *Divine Office* and the Psalm read: *"I rejoiced when I heard them say, let us go to the house of the Lord."* The reason it wasn't silent . . . there was no solitude . . . is because the people were there! They started their day with the Lord; and finished it with the Lord. And somehow . . . that holy hour was sanctified. I don't mean it's easy. I don't mean it's not distracting . . . but it *is* Holy.

So . . . back to the Wal-Mart. The greeter was giving samples . . . which might not be uncommon in the states as well . . . but the samples he was offering were in little cups. You had the choice . . . Tequila or Rum! That's right! Free samples? You better believe it! They were standing in front of two aisles with familiar American names . . . Jack and James . . . Johnny, etc. and various wines and beers! At the Wal-Mart! . . . So they really DO have everything.

What was it I said . . . "Much like the Christian centuries" . . . yes. Because all the cars have rosaries hanging from the rearview mirror. Police cars have them; buses have them; I even saw a *smart car* with a rosary ring around the support for the mirror. And now I know why. How do I know you ask? All it took was one ride in a taxi, five minutes to the Wal-mart.

Some questions are better left unanswered. And imagine . . . of all the cars in this great city, this cab didn't have a rosary. (That should have been my first sign.) But what he did have, was a picture of the *Sacred Heart* on his glove box, as big as the glove box itself.

That's not to say I probably should have had a sample cup from the happy greeter at Wal-mart before riding back, but I knew Christ would not let me down on this the feast of His Mother. *Immaculata Corazon de Maria . . . ora por mi. Sagrada Corozon de Jesus, ten piedad de mi.*

I made it back. And I was right . . . about that anyway.

Crucifix at Santa Clara in Queretaro MX.

Isn't there a reality show called "Lost?" Well, this is episode 4
June 15, 2010 at 5:28pm

I was wrong! What a costly mistake. *San Francisco*, a beautiful church, within which we have celebrated several Masses, is on the cusp of a walkway skirted with vendors of all kinds. These little *niñas* (actually *lindas* would probably be the best word, because they *are* beautiful) approached me to buy some cookies. I asked her if she made them (at least I think I did) and she smiled. "*No, mi abuelo.*" I said no thank you and moved on . . . and was cursed for the rest of the day . . . . well, almost for the rest of the day.

At the end of this walkway is a park where I answer most of my emails, because in every public park there is *Wi-Fi* for free. The park is on *Cinco de Mayo* street. If you're wondering where this is going, just be patient. I took a different way after exiting the church from Sunday Mass, and began walking along narrow streets with little room for one car to drive, let alone two. I finally ran into *Cinco de Mayo* street. Perfect! I knew exactly where this street ended up, and therefore, I turned onto the *calle* and began the walk back to town. There was only one problem.

At this juncture, I had a few landmarks I used to tell where I was. And I was getting better at orienting myself. As I walked on Cinco de Mayo, I was so thirsty, and it is easy to get dehydrated if you're not careful. I walked into a store after an hour of walking. Surely I was getting closer to town. I got a Coke (they're crazy about Coke here, and it tastes different because it's made of real sugar and not corn syrup.) I was getting hotter, wearing these black pants and dress shoes from Mass earlier, and was hoping to get home soon, so I could rest and refresh.

The sun was now dipping toward the horizon. I had given my map to one of the seminarians that morning to write on, and didn't think . . . well . . . he didn't give it back to me, alright? I had turned several times, because I realized my path had taken me out of the city . . . and you don't want to be outside the city . . . especially in the dark.

Finally, I reached a highway-looking-road, and took a break. I reached into my backpack to get my phone, and there it was . . . the map!

I opened it, and anyone nearby would've heard my gasp. I was off the map. Now what? I could back track, but didn't know where I had come from. I should've taken those cookies, because I hadn't realized how hungry I was now. It was around six o'clock now. I had walked for two hours, and didn't know where I was. The town of *Centro* (where I live) is a cereal bowl with mountains around it. I was on one hill of the bowl, but knew not where. Then I saw it. Over a hundred feet high, big stone arches to carry water into the city in the days of yore . . . an aqueduct.

This thing was huge, and when I looked at my map, eureka! Finally a landmark. It looked as if the aqueduct was going downhill, so I decided to follow it. It must have been two miles long at least. I got to the end of the aqueduct and was no closer to getting home, when I saw a sign for *Centro*. It pointed towards the other end of the aqueduct. I was right there and hour ago! I walked two miles back to the other end.

Meanwhile, the clouds were growing dark and ominous. It rains here every night, and about every other night, there is a thunderstorm. There is no drainage system in the streets, and at first I was confused by this. Centuries old brick roads with no drainage. But the first morning after a storm, I discovered why. By ten o'clock, all the water's dried up by the sun. There's no need for drainage. Anyway, I made it to the end of the aqueduct and saw a sign for the Armory. I knew where that was. I was so tired, but began to climb the small *colina* (hill) to head towards town.

It was then that I heard the singing. Beautiful singing, coming from the top of the hill. A church? Well, no doubt about that, but what church? Where was I? Long story short . . . I was at the Church of *Santa Cruz*. What a beautiful place! There is a tree there, the thorns of which grow in a cross. As I approached the church, the weirdest thing was happening. People were walking out of the church . . . backwards! I thought to myself, okay . . . too much heat . . . too much walking . . . not enough water, they're obviously going in reverse. But this wasn't crazy at all!

They were having Eucharistic adoration in the church, and no one would turn their back on the Lord, as they exited the church. I just stood and watched. It must have been like this with shepherds and kings as they visited the child in Bethlehem. Backing away, not wanting to take their eyes off of him, lest he disappear. I was lost that day, no doubt about it . . . but what I found was a treasure . . . a moment. There are no accidents with God.

I don't know how long I stood there watching, but it was dark by the time I got back.

I turned the corner of *Heroes de Nacorzani,* and there was the taco stand, just like every other night. Charlie was his name. How do I know? Because, I asked. He said "Charlie." I responded, *"mucho gusto Carlos."* *"No Carlos,"* he said. *"Charlie."* I walk past there every night, smelling the tantalizing bouquet from the meats, cheeses, and onions sizzling on the grill. And you know what? I think tonight might be the night. Maybe tonight, I'll take a chance and try just one . . . one little taco. What would the price be for something that smells so good? Some might call it "running with scissors", or Russian roulette. And perhaps it is "playing with fire." After all, it only took one bite of the apple for Adam and Eve. But man . . . if Charlie, the taco vendor had been there, one bite would not have been enough!

And we thought our sports fans were nuts!
June 18, 2010 at 8:09am

We approached the corner. Dark clouds had blanketed the sky earlier like an omen. In fact, it might **have been** an omen, if it didn't happen every night. Rain in the evenings, late, and then by morning everything is gone. Bright and sunny every day. There was a fingernail moon visible behind the passing clouds, like the clear image on the placid lake, just before the breeze comes and ruffles the top. But the fragrance . . . the aroma was in the air.

Every day I pass Charlie's taco stand and pretend like I'm disinterested. As if afraid to even look on the feast inviting . . . enticing; like the poor mariners answering the song of the sirens. For only a few pesos; a pittance really, this coveted morsel could be mine. I keep my eyes on the ground until I am beyond the grasp of the sirens' song. And yet . . . one cannot escape. Because once up on the roof, the perfume of the city envelopes me. And the predominant scent delivered by an eastern breeze beckons me . . . "Just one amigo . . . just one couldn't hurt."

When we first arrived here, we met two great girls and their mother. They were from Houston, Texas, and one of the three was here to learn Spanish like me. The other (and her mother) were taking a little vacation to celebrate the elder's graduation. They were both homeschooled for most of their lives, and although they had turned out to be wonderful ladies, I believe we still have the best homeschoolers in my parish. But I digress.

We talked about many things during the *cena* (evening meal which is smaller than the *comida* or midday meal). But then something changed. The one girl mentioned going to the taco stand at the corner . . . Charlie's taco stand. There was a moment when all of a sudden I felt like Golem from the Lord of the Rings. I thought about the food there, and my lips were forming the words, "My precious." (Not really . . . but it does add dramatic effect.) It would be me, Mr. Frodo and Sam in our quest for that which was forbidden. At least for those with weak stomachs . . . or non-Mexican stomachs.

They wanted to take a late night jaunt to get a taco. Now only days before I had been sick (if you didn't know, I'm telling you now). I never wanted to be sick like that again, but two things were playing against me. First, I wanted to try a bite of the apple that was *verboten* up to this point, and secondly, (and perhaps more importantly) I didn't want them to think I was more chicken than the *quesadillas* we had that night. What to do?

Today was insane. You think fans of PA sports are out of control, just be in Mexico, when Mexico is playing France . . . and wins!! I'm not much of a fan of any sport, but when you're in Rome . . . and let me tell you, it was intense. Today . . . everyone is Mexican! I watched part of the game and it was pretty good. I mean, of the many sports, at least soccer is constant action for the most part. I don't know the players, the rules, or even the teams at times, but you couldn't but be infected by the crowd. It was intoxicating. The unity of the team . . . of the country.

All afternoon, people were honking their horns down the streets. Beep . . . . beep . . . . beepbeepbeep. Again and again. People cheering in the streets. I had to go to the plaza to check email, and as I approached, the main roads were closed. The Mexican SWAT were out with their modified AK-47 guns and gear. The *policia* were everywhere. In fact, at one point a truck filled with fans, and flags, and painted faces tried to get past the barricade. You could almost see the regret on the faces of the officers as they had to turn them away. Their hearts were divided, because they were celebrating too . . . , they won too. And this wasn't even the championship!

In the square, thousands of people were shouting; singing; kicking soccer balls high into the air and waving flags every chance they got! Where was I, anyway. The chants went out: "Ooooolé, olé, oléééééééééééééé! The jerseys were everywhere, and painted faces, the norm. They would see someone who was not Mexican, and go over and dance around them. The mob moved as one body. They cornered some Germans, some Aussies, and then . . . . well, then they looked at me. Oh come on! It was in the plaza right near *San Antonio*, so as I saw their gaze meet the next target, I darted into the church. Even in the twenty-first century, it appeared that the Church still offered asylum for anyone who was fleeing.

Well, let's put it this way. I made a second holy hour today. When the Lord wants to see you, He'll find a way. Even if he needs to use rabid fútbol fans to do it. And I had much to thank him for.

The three of us walked down the street, the aroma filled our nostrils, drawing out the primordial creature in all of us. I mean, my mouth really did begin to water. Pavlov could've used me as a willing volunteer. And then, the moment of truth. I turned to Dorothy and said: "What if I get sick again. I mean, you're pressuring me into doing this so . . ." "What do you want?" she asked. "How about if I get sick, you pray the rosary for me for the next thirty days . . . the whole rosary, all twenty mysteries." "Twenty?" she said. "I'll pray the original fifteen." "Oh so you don't like JP II?" I mused. She sighed, and with that sigh, promised if I got sick, she would pray the fifteen decades every day for thirty days. Wow. She must have had great faith . . . in the Lord, or Charlie, I don't know. Either way though, it worked.

I ate a taco and to say it was wonderful falls terribly short. Two bites and it was gone (they are smaller than typical tacos, before you start forming your opinions of my anaconda-like eating habits). But now I wanted some more. Hmmm. Fool me once, shame on you. Dorothy flew out the next day and left her sister Leah to learn Spanish with us for the next seven weeks. Tonight's another night and the sirens beckon once again: "*Quiere taco? Quizas . . . solamente uno.*"

Not for the faint of heart . . . it's a long one.
June 21, 2010 at 6:15pm

Most of the time in Mexico, I can look to a situation (or the way I handled it) and find some comedy in it. In the Greek dramas, there were *comedies* and *tragedies*. We often think of these two as opposites, and actually in a sense they were. The Greek idea of "Comedy" was not something meant to be funny. Over centuries it has come to mean just that, at least in our American culture. In the Ancient Greek world, a "comedy" was a drama that ended good, or had a happy ending; whereas a tragedy was the opposite. Thus Dante's *Divine Comedy*, if read in its entirety, as opposed to merely reading the first volumn, the *Inferno*, does end happily in the *Paradiso*. I would speak similarly of my adventure in Mexico City.

There was quite a bit of planning involved in this trip. We were going to a place we had never been before, where a different language was spoken, and where only the day before, a violent protest had broken out right in the square. As I walked to school that morning, my mind was racing. Not only did I have things to tend to regarding parish business, but we still had some last minute details for the trip. One of my frustrations here in Mexico, has been that people will often say "yes" . . . just to be polite, while having no intention of doing what they said "yes" to. I've been told it's cultural. We, as Americans, are quite bold and speak our minds, while many Mexicans are much more "polite" or "proper" and avoid saying "no" at all costs.

What this means is, every day I have to check and re-check with the church, to make sure someone will have it open for us. When we make arrangements, we must check and re-check the arrangements. At times, I have been glad I checked, because they denied having ever spoken to me. But I'm working through this . . . patiently . . . well . . . . I'm working through this.

Our trip would take us to Mexico City, a three hour ride on a pretty nice bus. At Mexico City (*Ciudad de Mexico*, DF) we would get on the metro to our Hotel and then eat dinner. Saturday we were scheduled to visit the Pyramids of the Aztecs, and then Guadalupe. On Sunday, we would celebrate Mass at the Cathedral, and depart for home in the afternoon. The best view of D.F. (Mexico City) for me, was in the rear view mirror.

It is difficult, at best, to use words to describe my experience at Guadalupe, without somehow diminishing the experience of it. I had not intended for this weekend to be a retreat or weekend of recollection. There are certain moments in our life, however, when something so powerful; so overwhelming; so supernatural; reaches inside of us . . . and turns us inside out. As I approached the original basilica from the street outside of our Metro stop, and plowed my way through the countless vendors gating the entrance, I encountered innumerable pilgrims, many of whom were walking on their knees across carved stones, toward the Basilica. A woman holding her sick child kneeling, and then slowly scooting one knee forward by only inches, before following suit with the other. An older couple were holding hands, as they moved on their knees in synchrony.

Our immediate need was to celebrate Mass before it was the Vigil. We had arrived around 3:30 pm, and we still needed to see if we could celebrate Mass. I went to the office at the Basilica, and of course, the lady asked for my *licencia*. I gave her the copy of my *Celebret* and she looked at me as if her mind were saying in English, "Really? Are you kidding me? You don't have the original?" Thank goodness I had my passport too, because she matched up the name and picture, and I was in good shape.

As soon as we rounded up the seminarians, we headed up to the second floor of the Basilica, which is a more modern structure. The second floor has about twenty chapels so one can celebrate a private Mass, but they are not enclosed. It just so happened that at the moment we were beginning our Mass, the Mass in the Basilica was beginning as well. We could barely hear ourselves. But it was a Mass in the Basilica, and we celebrated it. I celebrated this Mass for a special intention, and that was the first time I felt it.

During the Mass my heart was deeply moved, so much so that I stumbled on the words . . . and they were in English! My heart hurt. We concluded our Mass, and then each went their own way. I was tired, but wanted to make a holy hour here to pray for my intention. I visited the first Basilica, and prayed for a bit, but again, my heart was hurting and I thought it was just too much for that day. You see, before we climbed the steps to the Basilica . . . we climbed up the steps to another temple. Maybe that's what hurt . . . it was just too much.

That morning, we had arrived at the bus station at 9:00 am sharp. Our bus left at 9:30 am (not sharp, don't get me started on that). As we took off from the bus station, he would stop at times to let on vendors. At first it was okay. He let on a guy with water and food. He came on the bus, no one bought anything, and he got off. It was different when the guitarists got on. Now there were people standing in the aisle, and the musicians began to play. We made up a majority of the people on the bus . . . Amercians (blatantly obvious by our trendy and stylish attire). So, they tried playing American songs. "Can't Buy Me Love," will never sound the same again.

We arrived at our destination; got all sun-screened up, and headed out. I really do have to learn more about these cultures. It was amazing. There were three great pyramids, which were originally temples to the gods. Then, along the "Avenue of the Dead," there were smaller pyramids and buildings which once housed the priests, and administrators of the kingdom. The largest of the three pyramids, was to the sun god, and the second to his sister the moon goddess. I wanted to climb them, and knew we only had a certain amount of time. So like the kid who, at the amusement park, runs straight through to the biggest rollercoaster he wants to ride first, that's what I did. 241 steps later I was at the top . . . seemingly the top of the world. (I wonder why the Aztecs never put in an elevator?) For miles around, one could see everything. The stairs at times were steep, and several times I was worried for the children and elderly that were making the climb, but about 25 minutes later, I was at the top.

The whole day was like a pilgrimage for me. I prayed the rosary constantly; as I walked, as I climbed, I prayed. I prayed for all those who were pagan Aztecs who died or were killed. I hauled around the Mass kit and vestments behind me everywhere I went. It was like a 20 lb sand bag on my back for most of the day. I thought, when I got to the top of the sun god's pyramid, of celebrating Mass . . . to consecrate a pagan place as they did with much of Rome. But I was afraid they might toss me off, like they did some sacrifices back in the day. So I finished the Rosary, and sat for awhile before making my descent. Shortly, thereafter, I climbed the moon goddess's pyramid, which was much shorter. I finished up my trip at the entrance building, and had one of the best authentic Mexican meals I had eaten since arriving in Queretaro. We took the hour long bus ride back to the Metro, where we were to embark on our journey to the Basilica. I was worried about all that Mexican food I had eaten, but perhaps the *dos equis* I drank with it killed any bacteria that was present. Guadalupe was what I wanted to see.

After our private Mass at Guadalupe, my chest was hurting, and I thought, if it's not a heart attack, it must have been the food. I was considering my plans to make a holy hour, as the gray clouds began to blow in. A storm? Really? This is the rainy season for Mexico and it is not uncommon to have these clouds looming for an evening without a drop of rain, but this was different. There were too many people . . . there was no silence, there was no freedom from distraction. I would come early tomorrow, and make a holy hour for my intention. As I left the area, forging my way through the walls of people and vendors, I arrived at the metro. The sky was now a charcoal gray, and in an instant the sky tore open like a *piñata* on the last hit. The dome in the sky opened up, and all the water that had been pinned up for days dropped, seemingly all at one time. I changed trains several times, as was necessary, and when I arrived at my destination, the rain was only starting. As people dodged into nearby shelters, I made my way around the corner and into the hotel, the smell of ozone thick in the air.

When the rain stopped for a bit I walked to the cathedral to check Mass times. It was closed! All the churches in Mexico City opened late, and closed early. On the sign it read that Mass was at 9:30 am and 12:30 pm on Sunday. I was so tired, I went to bed early, but was awakened several times during the night by some twenty-somethings upstairs talking. The hotel rooms were oriented around a courtyard. Now where do you think everyone wanted to be? I waited, in the hopes that the noise would stop, knowing in my heart that was unlikely. Finally, in the best Spanish I could articulate and project, at three in the morning, I yelled up at them: "*Vayan al dormir! Bastante.* (Go to BED! Enough!) They looked at me as if I must be speaking to someone else. It was quiet for about ten minutes and then started again. I called the office, and they promised to send someone to deal with it. (See previous note on politeness and getting things done.) It was five in the morning when it finally got quiet.

I got out of bed around 7:00 am (which is late), and got on the train for Guadalupe. I looked all over the room for my rosary, but could not find it. This rosary I had when I went to Rome. I carried it with me wherever I went. In my morning walks in Lebanon, and in Queretaro; my hike up the pyramids, and through the streets of Guadalupe, I took it everywhere. Now it was lost! I searched again, tearing everything from my backpack and suitcase. I looked under the bed, on the desk, even outside my room door. It was gone, and I had to go if I were to make it back in time.

I slid a note under the other priest's door saying I would meet them for Mass at 12:30, and that I was at Guadalupe. The scene there was much more serene. The vendors were just unpacking their things. I decided the first place I would go, was the chapel, that our Lady asked to be built on the hill. I followed the trail of people leading up the hill to the chapel that our Lady wanted to be built there. 194 steps to the top and the whole city below. The chapel was beautiful, and many entering the marble narthex, were on their knees, and approaching the image of our Lady asking for her intercession. I decided to do the same. I thought that I would want to pray the best I could. The only thing that distinguished me from the others on their knees was that I was not Mexican. I made my way to the front, and on my knees, asked once again. Just as yesterday at Mass, my heart was moved. It was this weird, scary feeling. Not an uncertainty, or fear, as much as a realization of how little I was . . . how powerless, how not-in-control. That's all I can say.

I returned to the old basilica, and prayed there in front of the Blessed Sacrament, in a monstrance the size of me! Finally, I made my way to the image of our Lady of Guadalupe on the humble cloth of *San Juan Diego*. That was the last ounce of energy I had. For the third time, I was moved beyond words, and although many were there around me, I felt alone with Her. A third time I made my petition. And then, it was time to go. I wanted to have plenty of time to prepare for Mass, and organize our concelebration, as I did here in Queretaro.

I arrived at the Cathedral, and saw a Mass in progress. At 10:30? There was no Mass for 10:30! Again, I was so frustrated, because not even the signs delivered like they said. I spoke to the usher, and he assured me that Mass was at 10:30 and 12:00. What! The sign said 12:30. I walked a little ways and found the entrance that was closed the previous night. The sign read, 9:30 am and 12:30 pm. So, I was right? What was this? There was, here in D.F., the Cathedral main church, and then, the Cathedral Parish Church next door. I knew the guys were showing up for the 12:30 pm, so I planned on that Mass. No problem . . . we're still good.

I walked back to the Cathedral by about 12:00 pm, and sure enough, Mass was starting, and there was the other priest, concelebrating . . . with the Cardinal! The cardinal decided to show up for Mass at the Cathedral. It was now 12:10, so I went next door to the Parish Church to arrange Mass. I approached the sacristan to ask if I would be able to concelebrate, and he said: "I'm sorry, but Mass here is cancelled today, because the Cardinal is here. The only Mass permitted is at the Cathedral." "What?!" I ran over to the cathedral and up to the usher, and requested to be able to concelebrate Mass here at the Cathedral. He took my credentials and went to the Master of Ceremonies. They were up to the *Gloria*, so not too far into the Mass. I could just slip in the side. He returned, and said that I was too late to concelebrate.

I could not believe it. I had done my homework . . . I had planned, so I would be able to make my holy hour at Guadalupe and get back in time. I checked and double checked. I did everything I could to ensure these plans, and now, I would have to sit at Mass. I have not missed celebrating a Sunday Mass since I was ordained! I sat there for a minute, on the verge of tears! My one chance to celebrate at the Cathedral in Mexico City, and I missed it. What more could I have done? But I was not going to sit here for Mass. I had to celebrate Mass . . . that's what I do!

We had a beautiful church next to our hotel (which opened late and closed early as well), and so I ran down the street hoping to get there in time for a 12:30 pm or 1:00 pm Mass. I arrived at 12:25, and spoke to the sacristan. I asked him if I could concelebrate, and he told me he would ask the priest celebrating the Mass. He finished lighting the twelve candles; turned on the rest of the lights and walked in the sacristy. The bell rang, everyone stood, and the priest came out of the sacristy. The sacristan walked down to me and said: *"No puede."* (You are not able.) I couldn't believe it. I just could not. My heart was hurting again, but in a different way this time.

I could no more sit through this Mass than I could have the other. In my pack, for the last two days, wherever I went, I carried a Mass kit. I now carried it up to my room, and celebrated Mass for my parents, on Father's Day, alone. Here I was in one of the most famous cities in Mexico, with some of the most beautiful churches, and I was celebrating Mass in this cave of a hotel room. As I began the readings, I almost could not get through the words. I salted my lips with tears, and the words of the scriptures cut to the heart.

Zechariah: *"In those days, I will pour out on the house of David and on the inhabitants of Jerusalem a spirit of grace, and petition; and they shall mourn as one grieves over a first born.*

Psalm 63: *O God, you are my God whom I seek; for you my flesh pines and my soul thirsts like the earth, parched, lifeless, and without water.*

Luke 9: 18-24: *He said, "The Son of Man must suffer greatly; be rejected by the elders and chief priests, and the scribes, and be killed on the third day and raised. If anyone wishes to come after me, he must deny himself and take up his cross daily and follow me."*

The priest is supposed to be the *"Alter Christos"* and *"In Persona Christi Capitis"*, but I never saw it so clearly as I did that day. I felt like I had lost so much that day; physically, emotionally, mentally . . . but there was something else . . . something new. I can't explain it. There are certain moments in life, however, when something so powerful; so overwhelming; so supernatural; reaches inside of us . . . and turns us inside out.

My prayer is different today, and I don't know if that would've been possible with our trip to Mexico City. I hope never to go back there again. Guadalupe, and the pyramids, definitely. Sure, there were more steps at the pyramids than at Guadalupe; but the Sun is behind her, and the Moon under her feet. The best view of Mexico City, is in the rear view mirror; the best view of our Lady of Guadalupe, is at her feet.

Day in the life
June 25, 2010 at 9:31am

It truly amazes me how inventive these people are. The scooters are everywhere! On one scooter, I saw a man taking two kids double (without helmets), and an English bulldog sitting between his feet on the foot platform. A gentleman, every morning, delivers papers. He has most of them stacked on his cargo rack, and the rest, on the gas tank in front of him, between his arms which are steering the motorcycle. Amazing. I have not yet witnessed a single traffic accident here, and yet amidst the one-way streets that seem only big enough for two small cars or an SUV, there are sometimes three lanes during rush-hour.

I discovered "Buen Pan" and fear it will be the death of me. I pass these markets everyday, but rarely stop. One particular morning this week, the aroma was so alluring I had to peek my head inside . . . just a peek. But when the woman offered me some *pan dulce con fruta* (sugar bread with fruit filling) for eight pesos . . . well, the rest was history. I'm sitting on the *azotea* (roof) tonight with *Boss* (the brown, three-year-old boxer).

I remember on the trip to Mexico City, and the rolling *colinas*, which reminded me so much of Pennsylvania. Is it any wonder that so many Mexicans settle in Pennsylvania? We have an optional trip this weekend. It is a day-trip an hour away to Syrianna, to have Mass in the chapel there, and then climb the third biggest rock in the world. That's right, you're envious, I can tell. We will then go to a town nearby, where there are shops and eateries. I have my doubts, having been to *Guadalupe*, that anything will approach the wonder and grandeur I felt there. Time will tell.

We had a cookout yesterday: steaks and hotdogs. And although their hotdogs were different here . . . well, actually, the steaks were too, there was a little piece of home. I received two care packages in the last two days. One of them had a return address . . . for the other one, thanks for the *Absolute Gratuity*. Note to self: When you ask a Mexican if the *salsa* is spicy or not, they're gonna say no . . . they're Mexican. Just be ready when your eyes start to sweat. Tomorrow, we celebrate Mass at the *Templo del Carmen*. The priest loves us there.

Walked seven miles yesterday, through a "not so nice" part of town, to see Toy Story III . . . in Espanol. The characters are just funnier in Spanish . . . go figure. You remain in my prayers as I hope I remain in yours. *Dios te bendiga*.

Toy Story 3: Did "Buzz" speak Spanish?
June 25, 2010 at 9:46pm

I know this is the next day, but Guadalupe was so long, I thought I'd give you a break. Therefore, the last one was short, but I would be remiss if I didn't comment on *Toy Story 3*. What a great film. Please somebody tell me if Buzz, (pronounced "Boss" in Mexico) spoke any Spanish during the film. Because . . . the whole film was in Spanish, and without subtitles. It was great. I always suspected that Dinosaur was really Mexican, but this sealed the deal!

I entered the theatre from the front of the mall it was in. I walked about 35 minutes to get there. Mostly, because I made some wrong turns, and asked some people for directions. Let's face it: it doesn't matter whether you're in the EEUU or Mexico, people don't know anything about where they live. But I got to the theatre, and the girl at the booth was being trained. As if it isn't bad enough, I have to try and buy a ticket to a movie, that in English and Spanish is advertised as "Toy Story 3," (or *doy estory tray*) this girl was new.

I went to the matinee, so it was *mas barato*, (cheaper) but she asked me if I wanted regular or *"todos"* all? I didn't know what that meant, so I said all. It was a bit more *cara*, (expensive) but apparently, the 20 *pesos* extra included popcorn and a large drink. I didn't trust the ice cubes in the gallon of soda that they gave me, but the popcorn was delightful. It was about 3:20pm when I arrived at the theatre for the 3:30pm show, so I figured there would be a minimum of tolerance time for all the kids that would be in the theatre. The movie finally started at 3:50pm . . . *quando en Mexico* (when in Mexico).

My pre-movie-starting observations are classic. When I entered the theatre (by myself), there was one other family present. As it got closer to the time (not the time the movie was advertised, but the time it actually began) more families entered . . . that's right . . . families. Not a mom with ten kids, or two teens or tweens, but whole families entering. And . . . they all sat around me, and each other. It was remarkable. So often, (and I do this) I try to leave a buffer zone around me; but these people wanted to be close to each other. They didn't want to isolate themselves. Incredible!

The chatter of the *niños* (children) was great. Their Spanish was so elementary that I could actually understand them, much better than the CD's the teachers played for us at the school, or even the teachers themselves. And precious; their precious voices formed arguments of why they should have their own soda, instead of having to share with their brother. Or the father who said: "Are we going to see Schrek?" to which the *nene* announced . . . *"no papi . . . doy dory!"* There was no air-conditioning in the theatre, so I was hot at first, having walked several miles, but by the time the movie started, it was quite comfortable.

One family sat directly in front of me, but the father and mother made sure that they were not sitting in my line of sight, as they arranged the booster seats for the children . . . that's right . . . booster seats in this theatre; which, by the way, was immaculately clean. I couldn't believe it! There was no stadium seating here, but the screen was oriented higher on the wall so there was no problem for anyone. The kids were yelling, each to get their voice louder than the other, until finally the movie began. And then . . . it was over.

I'm not going to give it stars, or even give much commentary, for fear of giving it away, but it certainly was truly a delightful experience. I understood the general story, even though Woody spoke faster than most Mexicans. And I was delighted by the families who didn't isolate themselves from the guy seated alone . . . but surrounded him . . . embraced him . . . as this city has, since I arrived.

I can tell the time of day, by which side of the street I'm walking on
June 29, 2010 at 9:19am

I can tell what time of day it is, by the side of the street on which I walk. Most of my walks follow a North to South trajectory. I'll cross from East to West, or vice versa, from time to time, but primarily my walks are along the poles. It is next to impossible to avoid the heat here in Queretaro, without ducking into a jewelry store or a *del Sol* (like our Kmart) the only stores which typically have air-conditioning. Few, if any of the houses have air-conditioning, and yet in their architectural genius, these casas were constructed in a way that takes full advantage of the almost constant breeze.

Some nights, as I sit out on the *azotea*, (roof) I need a jacket and warm-ups because the breeze is so strong and cool. It cools the whole body, like bathing in the creek on a crisp summer morning, (like we've all done at one time or another right? . . . um, no? Well, me neither, but there are some people who do that crazy stuff). So, one cannot avoid the heat; but the Sun . . . there are tricks to avoid the direct light of the sun. An umbrella is handy, or a newspaper, but my technique, consists of avoidance. I walk on the right side of the street to catch the shadows of the buildings, and when the sun is directly overhead, I rest inside or write these blogs . . . inside, with my door open, and the window gaping just enough to allow that breeze through the wind tunnel which is my room.

We had a wonderful weekend. We took a bus to *Soriano* on Saturday. *Our Lady of Soriano* has a great devotion here in Mexico, because of the miracles that have occurred through her intercession. The church is beautifully nestled in the *colinas* of the small town. There was a museum of miracles attributed to her, and two chapels: The *Chapel of the Apocalypse* and the *Chapel of Souls in Purgatory*. I prayed in both chapels, and we were able to celebrate Mass there. I prayed for two intentions close to my heart. Again, the people were walking on their knees across the marble tile of the center isle to the front, asking her intercession for them. The church was magnificent, but I didn't feel comfortable at all taking pictures. I don't know why, as I've taken them in other churches . . . there was just something different.

The Mass was beautiful, with almost a full congregation (for our private Mass), and that was okay. Preaching was in English, but the rest of the Mass in *Español*. We left there for a place called *Bernal*. This place allegedly has the third largest rock in the world, but when you look at the pictures of this thing, it's more like a mountain. And yes . . . we climbed it. We almost made it to the top, but any higher on the rock required rock-climbing gear; and I left mine at the rectory . . . right next to my scuba suit.

The scene was beautiful, and the seminarians seemed to enjoy being together and working together to get to the top. It was a tougher climb than the pyramids, but just as enjoyable. We took our pictures, and descended in half the time it took to ascend to the top. We then made our way back to *Queretaro*, and I barely made it to the bed before my body gave up. I did thank God. I thanked him for the gift of that day; the gift of the men who were studying for His Church; and that I didn't have a heart attack at the top of the mountain, necessitating a less than comfortable scurrying rush to get me back down.

The next morning, we celebrated Mass with the Franciscans at *San Antonio* and I had an experience at Mass I never had before. First I should mention, when we entered the sacristy, (which is unlike any that I've seen in the states) the priest greeted us with warm hospitality. I then asked, "*Como le podemos ayudar?*" (How can we help you?) He responded, "*Quiere praedicar?*" (Do you want to preach?) Ha! Want had nothing to do with it. I responded, apologetically that my Spanish was not that good, unless he wanted me to preach in English. The other priest responded similarly. He ended up preaching, and it was obvious why he asked us to preach . . . he probably had not prepared.

But the experience I had never had before was *intinction*. Intinction is where the communicant receives the Sacred Host and dips it into the *Sacred Blood of Christ* before consuming it. At the time for communion, the celebrant handed me this paten with a cup in the middle of it and hosts all around it. I looked at the other priest and said: "What am I supposed to do with this?" He told me to intinct. So picture this . . . two altar servers with a purificator the size of a bath towel. Each on either side of me, holding the corners so that anything that would drop, could fall into this net. Two other altar servers were stationed with candles on either side of the priests distributing communion. *"El Cuerpo y La Sangre de Cristo,"* was what I said. I improvised.

After the Mass we were invited to have breakfast with the Superior and the priest who celebrated Mass with us. He had only been ordained five years. We shared a delightful breakfast with them for a little over an hour and they were so grateful that we were here, and loved Mexico, and were learning Spanish. We had done nothing for them really. We accepted their hospitality to celebrate a Mass there every Monday at 12:45pm with the sems, and yet they seemed to be so grateful. This was a lesson to me in gratitude. The lesson was solidified when I left the church.

Every day last week, there was a man on the side of the street by the church. Monday, I saw him begging for change, and I asked him what he needed and he said a tamale. I gave him five pesos and he went right over, and got his tamales for breakfast. Each day I saw him again, and it so happened I would have some change and didn't mind giving it to him because he was buying, and eating food. He would say *"Gracias senor, gracias."* That Sunday as I left the church, there he was. He came right up to me with that smile and just said, *"Por favor."* I reached in my pocket, but had put my change in the collection coffer at the front of Church. I pulled out my empty pocket and said, *"Lo siento"* (I'm sorry). Immediately his face changed, and he began to curse me in words I will not repeat here. I thought, *where is the man with the toothless smile who graciously thanked me every day?* He was never there. Because true gratitude, is an attitude that is not changed by the winds of fortune or misfortune. True gratitude is the recognition of a gift that might not have been given; that didn't have to *be* given. True gratitude recognizes that God wants only the best for us; provides only the best for us . . . if we would but accept it.

Perhaps that's the reason why, not coincidently, that the word Gratitude comes from the same root as Grace. I'm glad I'm always grateful and never resentful when things go wrong . . . . right? Hmm . . . maybe we're not so different after all.

I heard the pig squeal . . . and then there was silence. Hmmm . . . wonder what's for dinner.
July 6, 2010 at 9:15am

The five were very discrete. They were walking away from the group with a wheel barrow. I remember hearing the pig squealing, from behind the wall of wood separating me from the rest of the *rancho*, like the piglet I used to feed with a bottle. And then there was silence. That's when the five guys came around the corner; the dead pig in the wheel barrow. They headed toward the big pots filled with water. They did this three more times.

I think I'm getting old . . . in fact, I know I am. I used to seek out the adventures. I wanted nothing more than the high energy, "not-sure-of-the-outcome" situations, where I had to use all the resources at my disposal to overcome whatever odds there were. I welcomed confrontations as a mechanism for opportunity, and couldn't wait for the next bruising or beating, to be pushed beyond my own expectations.

Well . . . "them days is over" . . . I don't look for that anymore. I'm kinda tired, and have to admit, I enjoy the comforts of a nice bed; a digestible meal; and a predictable schedule . . . for the most part. I am happy with my ability to use the English language, whether correctly or not, and the ability to predict outcomes based on earlier experiences. And I have never gotten into anything, I didn't know how to get out of. So I guess, since I am so comfortable, and not prone to adventures any more, the Holy Spirit throws me into these things, much as He threw Christ into the desert.

The plan was simple: a weekend trip with the seminarians to *Guanajuato*. Simple, because there **were** no plans. Get there; find a place to celebrate Mass; and then, whatever the guys wanted to do. This was the plan we made in week two. By week three, I had met a Deacon who was related to a Mexican family in my parish back in Lebanon, and the simple plan . . . predictable . . . simple . . . was drastically changed. Not in *that* moment, did it change, but the weekend of the trip . . . one that would come to be one of my finest memories; my finest adventures in Mexico.

There are certain symbols in this world that elicit an emotional reaction within us. Not necessarily because of the object itself, but because of the people and experiences that are represented by it. This is what the Mexican flag has come to do for me. Because wherever I go, and whenever I see it, I know I'm still here; amidst the people and places, the faith and tradition; and . . . the possibility. I saw it just a few minutes ago on the way back from the bus station; tired and saturated from the weekend; enlightened and moved beyond words, once again.

In *Guanajuato*, lived many who were related to a family in the parish back in Lebanon. Since we would be in the area for a weekend, I had hoped we might get together. You know, perhaps for dinner, or a chat, just to see the people and places I hear so much about. That was the simple plan. I spoke to the Deacon, whose ordination I could not attend because we were in Mexico City, and he informed me that there was a wedding that weekend. He subsequently asked what my plans were, to which I answered, "I don't have anything set."

In the EEUU (*Estates Unidos*), a statement like that leaves one wide open to the possibilities, with the understanding that once plans are made, I will let you know, and we can go from there. In the Mexican world, when one says, "I have no set plans" they take it as meaning you are looking for something to do, and therefore, they will find plenty of activities.

Those I knew in *Guanajuato*, had called me on the phone just before the weekend. My Spanish still wasn't where I wanted it to be, nor where it should have been probably. What's more, on the phone, I had a difficult time hearing to begin with, let alone to be trying to understand Spanish. I thought what I had told him was that I was going to *Guanajuato* on Friday by bus. Well, he insisted that they pick me up with their car. There was no way I was going to take a bus. I was, after all "their priest." Therefore, according to my world, we had agreed they would pick me up in Queretaro at 4pm on Friday. I could then have some quality time with them, and then they would take me to the hotel by 10:00pm. That would be plenty of time for me to get some sleep. I would meet the sems and the other priest there that morning, and then we could make some final plans. I never met the sems that morning.

I was waiting. I was in front of the house, and it was now almost 5 pm. I knew that sometimes there wasn't such a stress on time here, but it was getting late. Here in Mexico, I have my cell phone, but can't retrieve messages. Through classes and meetings, I have it turned off. When I turned it back on that Friday, apparently I had missed seven calls. There was no available number, so I waited for the call again. At about 5:00 pm, I got the call. My contact asked where I was. Where was I? Where were they?

He said, and I'm paraphrasing, "We're here at the hotel in Guanajuato to pick you up." What! I thought they were sending a car. I handed the phone to Adan, the husband in my house here in *Queretaro*. Through their conversation, I came to discover that they thought I was going with the sems to the hotel, and then they would pick me up. I told Adan, I would take the bus. That was the easiest thing. Are you kidding! They were driving to *QRO (Queretaro)* now to pick me up. Aghh. *QRO* is two hours from Guanajuato. Two hours here and back and it was already five o'clock. But, they would not hear otherwise. Before I knew it, the phone was dead, and they were on their way.

We had arrived. We drove up the stony road with no street lights. We passed a *vaca* (cow) on a leash in the field. There were dogs crossing the road like deer do in Pennsylvania. The *Abuelo* (grandfather), a patriarchal figure whose presence was amiable, with a smile that lit the room, opened the gate. He had silver gray hair that was buzz-cut, and was slightly shorter than I, with a solid build. The standard bars that encased the numerous doors in *QRO*, and formed the fences around the playgrounds of the schools were here as well. The large suburban crept forward like a lumbering beast, and I was sure we would have to renegotiate the turn. True to form, however, the driver safely navigated through the narrow gate into the modest courtyard.

What immediately struck me was the coziness of the surroundings. All was very still; the only sound breaking the silence was a frog that was determined to be heard. The driver then went to the back and opened the trunk to unload my *maletas* (bags). I wondered why I needed my bags? Did he not trust the locks on the car? Did he think I wanted to get refreshed, or what? The *abuelo*, who was in the car, guided me through the path to his humble abode. The driver had kept warning me that they were very poor; he kept saying that it was not what I was used to. I had been to some poor places in my time, so I was prepared for the worst.

They opened the door for me, and I was greeted by the wife of the patriarch, who I knew from having seen them at the parish in Lebanon. She seemed overjoyed that I was there and had arrived. It was then, that she showed me my room.

Nope . . . no stuttering here . . . ***my room*** . . . the place where I would ***spend the night*** . . . not in the future . . . not if I ever decided to stay, but tonight! Then, it all made sense. Not only had I missed getting the point across about the pick-up in *QRO*, but obviously I also confused them about where I was staying. The moment I realized this, I almost burst with laughter. What else could I do? Welcome to my world!

I acted as if this were all part of the plan, but made sure that the driver knew I needed to be at the hotel in the morning, tomorrow, to meet the seminarians and the other priest. After all, I was directing this, right? The driver promised to pick me up at 8 am, and upon confirmation of that plan, he departed.

The ride from *QRO* was long, but the people, who were in the car, I knew well from the parish. It didn't change the fact that on a bus, I wouldn't have had to speak Spanish at all. My head was about to explode with the *preterito* (past tense) we had learned (or should I say *we learned*) and a bus ride with nothing but an i-pod or even a movie with subtitles was a welcome gift . . . no gift . . . yet.

They began to show me around, and as they did, the laugh did escape, but not because of the irony of my incipient adventure . . . but because of the pictures I saw of the people I knew from the parish. Pictures from years ago. Pictures are always great, and when I visit any house, I really do delight in looking at the people and places.

I went into my room and got ready for bed. The bathroom was in the other room, and the door was a curtain, so I was reluctant to use the restroom. They assured me that my comfort was their top priority, and it was obvious by the way they coddled me, that their words were true. They were just so gracious to have me in their home, and my heart was moved. There was peace here, and there was joy. They were not well-to-do, whatever that means . . . but they were not nearly poor.

I had fresh *mango* for *la cena* (dinner) before retiring to my room. I went to brush my teeth, and *Abuelo* was in the bathroom. He dropped everything and left, allowing me to have it to myself. I went to brush my teeth, and the teeth were already there! He really did drop everything. He was cleaning his dentures, and had just left them in the sink so I could use it. A laugh finally escaped my lips, and then I just started. I was laughing so hard, no sound came out. Tears were streaming from my eyes, to the point where I thought I was honestly going to die. I didn't brush my teeth . . . I washed my face quickly, drying the tears, and went to bed.

I drew back the covers on the bed. It looked so very inviting after such a long and seemingly frustrating day. I turned off the light, and could not see my hand in front of my face. The clouds had been darkening the sky all night, and I knew it would rain (because that's what it does in *Guanajuato*). I sat down on the edge of the bed, lifted my feet and pivoted to lie down and begin my rest in this strange "hostel." I was immediately sucked into the middle of the bed like a "down sinkhole." And there I remained for the duration of the night.

This was certainly what I would describe as a "coma bed." It had obviously endured many years, and many backs had lain upon it, so that the middle was almost like the bedding of a nest, with the low walls of plume around it. My feet were up, my head was elevated, and the rest of me fit comfortably into the nest. I stirred only twice during the night. The first time was when the bullets of rain starting showering the roof and skylight window that I had in the ceiling of my *habitacion* (room). The second time was when the first clap of thunder sounded. The rest of the night was a blissful blur. The silence was broken at varying intervals only by the frog which I was certain, lived under my bed.

I awoke in the morning at . . . . what! 7:00! I couldn't believe it. I was so drowsy, and yet, just wanted to stay in the bed forever. I struggled to free myself of the feathery quicksand, and moved my groggy frame towards the door. Upon opening my room door, and standing in all my glorious "nest-hair," "dragon breath", "cut-off-sweats pajamas", I saw the family seated at the kitchen table in the main room, as though they had been anticipating the arrival of the bride and groom at the reception any minute.

The response was immediate. *Abuelo* jumped up and offered me coffee. He had a rosary in his left hand, most of which was resting on the table. I had obviously interrupted their morning prayers. I greeted the *Abuela* and *Abuelo* who immediately showed me to the shower. He turned on the water, and I thought, "Ahh . . . a hot shower is just what I need." It was then that he informed me that the water was not hot, but room temperature.

The shower was brief, and after, I was now certainly awake! I had a cup of coffee, as the daughter was preparing pancakes with her mother. I asked about the gardens I had only seen in the dim house-light, late the previous evening, and *Abuelo* stood up with his bright grin and motioned me to follow him. This was not a *jardin* (garden), but a paradise.

I never really considered why we don't do anything for ourselves anymore. I mean, most often we go to the store and buy what we need; or hire someone to do something for us, that we might be able to do for ourselves. Granted, it's good for the economy that we *don't* rely too much on ourselves, but these people did *everything* for themselves. It's something I've found again and again here. Unemployment is high, which means there is a lot of poverty. But what I've discovered is that where there is poverty, there is also ingenuity. They have no money to buy, or to pay someone else, so they do it themselves.

Within this paradise, there was an abundance of fruits and vegetables, spices and seasonings, water catchers and reservoirs. The fruits on the trees were developing in a way that one would be ripe while the other was developing. Harvest would happen gradually, and then start again at another location with another crop. Amazing. This man had many years under his belt, and yet he was spry. I found this out when he easily climbed the ladder up to the roof, and then motioned me to follow. And follow I did.

You could see all around the *rancho* (that's what these homes are called.) In these *ranchos*, as I would find out later, there are sometimes many generations living under one roof, if not on one *campo* (piece of property). It reminded me a lot of the Amish I grew up with; lots of family around. Beside this *rancho*, there were the ruins of a small mission chapel. You could still see some of the tile floor and the sanctuary. *Abuelo* informed me they used to house many priests and even bishops at times who would come out to celebrate Mass. They always took care of them. What a rich, rich tradition. The main house was over a hundred years old. *Abuelo's* parents lived there at one time too. Astounding . . . beautiful . . .

Remember, everything I did or said was all in Spanish. I felt as if I were going mad. The words were all mixed up . . . endings and tenses . . . and yet they responded as if what I said made perfect sense. And they laughed . . . when I made jokes! They got it! I think at this time, I was so delirious that it didn't matter. It wasn't long before my driver came through the gate again.

I went inside and had some pancakes and maple syrup, which were wonderful, and then made my way to the room to pack up. I entered the *sala* (living room area) with my carry-on and backpack, ready to go, and the driver, son of *Abuelo* looked at me and hesitated. *"Necessita tus maletas?"* (You need your bags?) I responded that tonight I needed to stay at the hotel. He began to plead, and I saw another night here in my future, so I explained that as the director, I did have to be at the hotel with the sems and the other priest. He seemed to understand that. He was not happy, but understood.

As we started the trip to the hotel, which was over an hour away, my stomach started to hurt a bit . . . you know . . . not a stomach kind of ache, but another hurt. What could I possibly have eaten? Well, it didn't matter. I popped the emergency pills. I had and prayed that my digestive track would be more patient than I was. We were getting closer to *Guanajuato* and the hotel, and then I would take advantage of a private bathroom . . . but then we turned off the exit. This was not the exit for *Guanajuato*.

"Adonde vamos?" (Where we going?) I asked. To pick up *mi hermano* (my brother), he said. "Um . . . your brother? How much further to GJ (*Guanajuato*)?" I asked. *"Quarenta minutos"* he responded. Forty MINUTES! Impossible. We stopped at his brother's house. It was like a drive-by, but I asked, as calmly as I could muster, if I could use his restroom. The Devil's in the details, so I'll leave them out. Needless to say, his brother went with us, but the rest of the family was at home. I feel a bit of sorrow that I didn't get to really greet them.

We arrived at the hotel, and there wasn't much time because we had the wedding at 2:00 pm. Oh yeah . . . the wedding. We returned from the hotel. I left the Mass kit and my vestments, knowing now with certainty that I would not be back with the seminarians in time for Mass . . . or anything else for that matter. The driver took me to the *rancho* where he was staying. Again he warned me that it was really poor. I felt bad that he wanted to apologize for this, but assured him I would not be put-off by poverty.

We approached the *rancho*, and I could smell the flesh cooking. How do I know what this smells like? I had worked with dead animals in my previous career, and had, at another time cooked pig's feet for a "Fear Factor Night" for the youth ministry. He parked the car, and as I got out, one of the driver's sons ran up and yelled, "*Padre*" in his little Spanish voice and wrapped his arms around me. From that height . . . there is no going down.

The children were everywhere. There were scores of them across the *campo*, playing and running and eating. The people were like ants, each with their own job, working together. The flies were everywhere. I was trying to remember where I had seen so many flies, and then I recalled, when my friend David Fisher invited me to his farm for a dinner one summer. The flies come with the farm. I felt right at home. The flies didn't seem to be on the people or the food, so much as they were just milling around. He took me over to the women preparing the *sopa* (soup), and they each stopped what they were doing to greet me, and of course offer a *beso* (kiss). The aroma was wonderful. He took me out back where there were four campfires with pots filled with water. The pots must have held about forty gallons, and in each there was a whole pig. I didn't know what to think . . . but it didn't matter . . . that was dinner. In the side yard were more camp fires under pots filed with beans and rice.

The driver gave me the tour, and introduced me to what seemed like hundreds of people . . . all of them were somehow related to his wife. This was their *rancho*. Five daughters, three sons and their families; and cousins; and *suegras* (mothers-in-law). I kissed more *mujeres* (women) that day, than I have in the last twelve years! It was the common greeting, and the greetings were not wanting. Everyone treated me like I was some kind of royalty. Then, I met the Patriarch and his wife. I sat down with him at his table, and I believe I could've stayed there for hours. Everyone was getting ready for the wedding and the reception to follow.

The father apologized to me that his dwelling was so poor, and it was at that moment that I just couldn't speak. I remembered what Mother Teresa said: "To be rich is not to have everything . . . but to need nothing." And then the Spirit moved me, and I spoke in Spanish that seemed to flow. It was articulate; expressive; it made sense. I said: "You are so rich. You are not poor. Not many places in EEUU are there so many within one family living together. All: the good, the bad, the sorrowful, the joyful; and all working together for a wedding. They are all working together for a *fiesta* that does not have invitations or guest lists, but an open door for whomever wants to celebrate." He smiled.

It was time for the wedding, so I went with the newly ordained deacon to the little mission church. I had planned on concelebrating. It's simple. I just sit in the sanctuary and offer Mass like I do every day. We were waiting for the priest, because he had an itinerary. He went from chapel to chapel, mission to mission, all day long. He arrived fifteen minutes after two, and we were ready. He had already celebrated five Masses that day, so he asked me what I could do. I said I could do the vows, and the Gospel, but not preach. The deacon was Mexican, so he would preach. I read over the prayers and readings, but I had already witnessed many weddings.

It was time to begin. The sacristan vested me in white with the deacon, and I saw the other priest put on a purple stole. Hmm. I wondered if he didn't have a white one for the wedding. I guess I would be the main celebrant, and he would assist. The wedding began, and he sat down in the sacristy . . . and began to hear confessions! I WAS THE celebrant. He finished confessions before the homily, got in his car and went to the next mission. He had three more Masses that day.

The wedding was beautiful. Of course the bride had an elegant wedding dress, and the gentleman was dressed in a tux. Most of the area of the *rancho*, where the reception was to take place, was mud, dirt and stone. I asked if they were going to change clothes, and I was informed "No way." They only wear the dress once, so why not get it a little dirty. EXACTLY!!! It made so much sense.

They set up a table for us inside, with less flies. I wanted to sit outside, but it was unheard of. They would bring in people, as if I were a head of state, and each time I felt smaller and smaller than these people. Ninety-two year old women; uncles, aunts, children asking for a blessing. I felt like a bum at the Country Club. I felt like I was the poorest sap in the room, though they treated me like a king. They brought the pig, rice and soup to the table with *tortillas* and *molé* (a rich and hot sauce, like gravy.) I ate twelve of those *tortillas* that I had stuffed with the food on my plate and downed two small *cervezas* (popular Mexican drinks).

Everything else after that, paled in comparison. Before I headed back to the hotel, we made two stops. The first was at a church where the Deacon was to celebrate his first Mass. Absolutely one of the most beautiful churches I had seen. The second stop was special. We stopped at the farm (I believe it's called "*Mora*") where the *suegros* of one of the brothers lived. This farm had mostly cattle, and as we approached some dogs made their presence felt. We were greeted by a grandfatherly farmer. He was all grins as we approached, and all but invited me in for dinner as we made introductions. He walked us from there up to the house where his wife was coming out of the house, preparing for the next task, as the thunder rumbled low in the sky. Again, she was just so gracious. She acted as if she had been waiting all her life to see us. I wished I could have stayed there longer, but now the rain began to fall, and we had to get to the hotel. We said our goodbyes (I got no stories from them) and headed to the hotel.

I got back to the hotel, and met with the sems and priest. I did get a hot shower and didn't need anything more to eat. I slept in a hotel bed, and had a mediocre night's rest. My driver and his brother in law had volunteered to drive us to the top of a mountain with a great church the next day. We went in the two suburbans up to the top for an hour, beyond the clouds, and then down again. We celebrated Mass in a little ancient chapel at the hotel, and had a long bus ride back. But nothing else compared to my brief experience of true joy . . . true peace . . . true wealth. I miss it as I write this.

Jesus was poor by the standards of the world, but I wonder if he knew it. This family had no problem getting people to help with projects or events or anything. There were no volunteers there . . . only family. And their family made up most of the parish at this mission. The family fills the parish. What if a parish though . . . **could** be a family. What if they could work together like this humble family, living on a *rancho* on the outskirts of one of the most beautiful cities in Mexico?

I'd choose the *rancho* to the city in a heartbeat. The beauty I experienced, you can't build with stones. I think I'm getting old . . . in fact I know I am. But, I also know I'm not done yet. And I know why they don't often let Diocesan priests go to poor countries . . . because they undoubtedly will want to stay. And if I come back here again, there's no doubt where I'll stay if they'll let me. Rich? Absolutely . . . *because where your treasure is . . . there your heart will be also.* Jesus is asked . . . *"Who is my neighbor?"* I know the answer.

At the rancho in General Cepeda instructing the children.

I miss my ranchos
July 17, 2010 at 9:35pm

A bumpy eight hour trip is what it took. I don't think I've ever really been in the desert before . . . at least not in the literal sense. The mountains surrounded us for what seemed like hours. And these ***were*** mountains, unlike the small *colinas* we have in Pennsylvania. Between the highway and the mountains, there was sand; hard rocky sand; snakes; scorpions; sand . . . and some short scrubby plants mingled with the cacti as well. We were not in Kansas anymore . . . I wasn't sure we were even in Mexico anymore.

We arrived at our destination after the driver stopped a few times, asking for directions. GPS systems haven't caught on here for the buses yet. We entered the mission, and there were about half a dozen college graduates to greet us. I don't mean they graduated from college 10 years ago and were seasoned missionaries, I mean they graduated last year, and this is what they were doing with their degrees. Right away, I thought I was at a "youth group" convention. These teens, who happened to be in their early twenties, were giving us the rules and regulations before showing us the hand motions to songs for our blessing before meals.

Now please don't misunderstand, I do enjoy praise and worship music; I can appreciate charismatic prayer, I mean that's part of our faith. But it's not for everyone . . . especially when you have college students talking to grown men, four of whom were priests, as if they were the new freshman class who wants to have a "Jesus Party" (I find that phrase offensive if not diminutive). But I digress. I shared a room with the two other priests, while the fourth had his private quarters. I was so tired, I slept deeply. How could you not, with the slight whine of the mosquito in your ear.

All that having been said, it's a missionary house. It ain't the Ritz Carlton, nor is it a barn with beds. It's an old servants' quarters turned into a mission house. The meals are simple, but really very good. Now some more "grown-ups" have arrived, so it's a bit better, although, I had to remind our driver today to keep at least one hand on the wheel and to stop looking at the guy in the passenger seat while speaking with him . . . kids!

I got up early to shower (cold! That'll wake you up) and prayed a holy hour. We then got into our groups to head out to the *ranchos*. There were two different *ranchos* where we were going to in order to celebrate Mass. The first had mostly women, because the men had gone to a different part of Mexico to find work. Some of them even come to the EEUU. This particular one had problems in the past. It was along the highway, and with no way to support their families, unfortunately many of the women had turned to prostitution. These mission folks went in last year and started a sewing ministry with these women, so that now they could support their families through their wonderful works of art, and they have broken ties with that former way of life.

The rancho I went to, with four others (two missionaries and two sems), was mixed with men, women and children, about thirty families. But the men were working during the day. We arrived in the rocky, sandy desert at this small mud capilla (chapel). It had five benches that held about four people (although a few kids fit their six bodies into the space. Along the wall, there was a ridge about a foot deep that worked as a bench around the perimeter.

The *capilla* (chapel) was locked, so we rang the bell in the tower about thirty times. The other ministers went out to knock on doors, and ask people personally to come to Mass and find out if they needed confession. Soon, off in the distance, I saw a woman walking toward the *capilla* with a child clinging to each of her hands, and then a third (an older girl) walking along behind. I greeted her with a kiss, having introduced myself, and the children each gave me a kiss as well. She unlocked the church, and I prepared the altar, and got my written homily ready. It was going to be a short one, written on a file card. It was hard to think what they would most need to hear.

As the chapel began to fill up, I noticed that there were no men. They rang the bell a second time, which signaled that Mass would begin shortly. The only other one that attended was the dog named Tommy.

Twice the owner had shooed him out, but he returned a final time and rested down beneath one of the benches. There were now about twenty-five children and about a dozen women, most of whom were mothers. My homily wouldn't work . . . I would have to change.

The time came, and I walked from behind the altar, and I spoke to the children . . . in Spanish. The Gospel was the story of the Good Samaritan. At the school we attend, they are often very expressive, and so I considered, "Worst case scenario, they might not understand my words, but hopefully with the Gospel they heard and my actions, they'll get it."

I don't know what I was thinking, but I wanted to get my point across. I began. I acted like I was riding a horse, clopping around and the kids were giggling, and I galloped all the way around the capilla until I was in front of the altar again. And then, Pow! I dropped to the ground as though I had been attacked . . . and it hurt on that rocky dirt floor! The moment I said "pow," a baby screamed and started crying. People started laughing (and I said, *lo siento*) and they laughed some more.

I called up a little girl (*Guadalupe*) as if she were the first passerby for the victim. I said in Spanish "Do you see the poor man?" "She said, "*Si.*" Then I couldn't resist. I said, "You do? Where!" Everybody started laughing again. I had joked in Spanish, and they got it! Well, now I was excited, and started in with the second passer by, and then the third. All I did was repeat the lesson of Jesus. "Who is your neighbor?" "*Todos.*" Exactly! That was all it took.

After Mass, we gave them rosaries, and I blessed them, sprinkling the people as well, and they were so gracious . . . so humble . . . so hungry for much more than food. The guys went out and played volleyball. Yeah! I played volleyball in the desert! Never would I have called that one. I then went inside and the girls were gathered with the women and the girl missionary. They sat there in expectation; so what could I do? . . . well . . . I could tell them a story.

At Lebanon Catholic, I had made up some mythological stories that were variations on *Ovid's Metamorpheses* and *The Voyages of Sinbad,* but how would I put that into Spanish? Well, it didn't matter, because it seems everyone, at some point, has heard a story about a hero; a villain; and a princess. That's all it took. The Missionary girl helped out with some words I didn't know, and I used some words she didn't know. At one point (I was becoming animated) and I turned toward the mothers and they were just as captivated as the little ones. Had no one read stories to them? Of course not . . . they couldn't read.

I could've stayed there all day, and they wanted to hear another story, but the van had arrived, and it was time to go. I was pumped. "Let's go to the next rancho," but we needed to return, refuel (the van and ourselves) and get ready for the week. During the week, we would visit two ranchos a day. I had a renewed sense of why I was here. And, although some of the surroundings were the best . . . it wasn't where we stayed that was most important . . . that gave life. It was where we were going in the days ahead. And isn't that what the Christian journey is all about? We're all just passing through. But it's what we *do* while we're passing through, that makes all the difference.

Found a rosary . . . small miracle
July 18, 2010 at 12:24pm

I'm on the ride back now. It was definitely the toughest week here . . . and probably the most rewarding as far as an organized trip. I didn't like staying at the mission at all, and ah! I forgot to take a picture of my room. Next time . . . sure. The missionaries didn't change too much throughout the week, but they really do live the life. I mean, that's how they live. They aren't poor, but they choose to live poor. I give them credit for that. And certainly, over time they will mature as well.

I didn't like taking a cold shower every other day . . . in the afternoon, knowing we would be riding in vans on dirt roads in the evening again, and get coated with dust and dirt before retiring for the night. I didn't like getting back at 9:30 at night, and eating the *cena* (which

I couldn't because it was so late). I didn't like not having coffee when I woke up, and having to make a holy hour in a stuffy upper room. I didn't like having to sing a praise and worship song before every meal, and then a "youth groupy style" prayer that used the term "Father God" more times than really is probably allowable in any prayer, let alone prose. I didn't like having to sit on the spare tire in the back of the van, because we were loading up a ten passenger van with sixteen people. I didn't like the flies at every Mass, or the constant swarm of mosquitoes waiting for an opening to enjoy their *comida*.

So, with all these things I didn't like, how could it possibly have been the most rewarding experience? Because for an experience to be great, and life-changing, and rewarding, doesn't mean it has to be agreeable, or comfortable, or "fun." Where do I start? At the Ranchos; where else.

We decided (or rather it was decided for us), that this week, we would go to the same *rancho* for four days, and then different ranchos every night for Mass and a witness talk by a seminarian or missionary. The method was the same for each of the *ranchos*, as different as each one was. The *rancho* (or *ejido* as they are called) each had a chapel in the middle of the community. Each of these chapels had a bell, and so when we arrived at the *ejido*, and ring the bell thirty times plus two more, the people would know it was time for Mass. That was the signal everyone understood. The sems and missionaries would then go out to houses, knocking on the doors and inviting people to Mass, while I remained in the chapel to hear confessions and greet the people.

This was the longest week ever! And yet, today is already Saturday. We arrived at the *ejido* we were going to be at all week, on Monday morning. I had taken sick the night before . . . must have been the food again. I took my pills that morning, but still was a bit shaky. I didn't eat breakfast, and my stomach was protesting, but it would have to wait. The van ride to the *ejido*, up and down; bumps and holes; sharp turns and dust; all these variables were not helping my duodenal peristaltic spasms. It was not a great experience, because I was sick.

We arrived at the *ejido* and the chapel was open. I ran inside, and there was a bathroom attached to the *capilla*, but it was locked. I looked for a window; another way in, but there was nothing. The sems and missionaries went off to knock on doors and invite people to Mass, while I was asking everywhere for the key to the bathroom. I was getting closer and closer to an emergency situation (if you know what I'm sayin') so I began knocking on doors; introducing myself and then politely asking if they had a bathroom. No one had a bathroom! I know, I know . . . but it's true. Many didn't use indoor plumbing.

I did find out who had the key, and began to walk toward where they had pointed as being the location for her house. *Lupina* was her name (short for Guadalupe) and as I walked towards her house, I saw the school, with a fence around it, and a building with four open doors which looked like a bathroom. The fence had barbed wire strewn along the top, but inside the fence was a *burro* and some goats. I walked around the fence to where the gate was locked with a chain, but the gap was wide enough to pass through (I had lost some weight). I practically ran through the fence, dodging goats and *burros*. I went into the first door and there was no paper! I keep a roll of TP in my truck, but that didn't help me much here.

The toilets were working (because I flushed one to check). I walked into each one, but no paper. Finally, in the last door they were doing construction. There was some fabric there, that had been used to clean up liquid nails and dried cement. They were cleaning rags . . . but that was all I had.

I staggered back to the *capilla* and the people were already arriving for Mass. I felt a bit better, but still unsettled. The young missionary with me asked if she could use the bathroom before I began Mass. "You could, but it's locked," I replied. "No it's not. While you were gone, the lady came by and opened the door." I peeked in to see a nice bathroom, which included even a shower and a small cot. (I won't comment here regarding my reaction.)

The Mass was packed with women and children . . . and one man. I told the story again of the Good Samaritan, (in Spanish) acting it out as before. I called some volunteers to act like the priest, Levite, and Samaritan. The children were very eager in this group to be involved. The children seemed to enjoy it, and the mothers present got the lesson as well. The children were so beautiful . . . and simple. Some of them were wearing American shirts, and asked us what the words meant. I was starting to feel a little unsettled again, and I knew I would have to celebrate Mass again in the evening, so I took two pills, and we drove back to the mission.

When we returned to the mission, we constructed our plans for the three following days we would be at this *rancho*. Our plan was to tell Bible stories to the children and act them out, while the adults would get talks on the Holy Family, with a focus on Mary, because mostly women were present for these sessions.

Monday evening Rancho: We arrived, and the *capilla* was open. Again, the missionaries and sems went out to seek the people, and bring them to Mass. The sems came back and brought with them a woman whose house had collapsed. Apparently, part of the roof caved in, but the rest of the house was immaculate. There were two pigs in the yard and some sheep. Mass was packed with women and children. After Mass, there were to be witness talks, so I walked outside to hear confessions. The children came outside with me and I started talking to them.

Many of them were wearing American shirts with animal pictures, or words. I began to tease them, and they just laughed, either at my words or my comments. I would ask them if this boy was the *mascota* (pet), and they laughed. I asked them about the *cerdos* (pigs), and they called them "*pigitos*." Imagine that! We had a delightful time, and when we finished talking, they asked me for confession. Wow. The missionary came out of the church, and was standing by me while I was hearing this confession, until he realized what was happening and then made himself scarce. He was floored, because the kids never went to confession.

Another gentleman approached me in tears, saying that his house was full of demons and he was scared to death. I walked with him to his house. The door was flanked by two bull skulls that were painted black. I walked into the house, and through it, sprinkling holy water and blessing it; I passed the chicken coop and the *vacas*, (cows) and amidst the garbage that surrounded his house. I told him he should go to confession, because the devil fears a soul filled with grace. I returned from the house, and the missionaries and sems were playing soccer with the kids. We left there at 9:30pm; went back to the mission house and ate. Evening came and morning followed, the second day.

Tuesday: A better day than Monday, as far as sickness. I was still sick, but was taking pills and not eating, so it was better. Today, we would put our plan into action. One of the seminarians would read the bible story I edited for time and content, and I would act it out, while the other group dealt with the women. We rang the bell, but the people had already seen our van come into town and were getting ready for our retreat. We must have had about twenty kids. We sat them at tables and the stories began. We did David and Goliath, but as the seminarian read, I noticed the children were getting antsy. Therefore, for Noah's ark, there was no reading. I just told the story as I could, with my broken Spanish, and acted out the parts. The kids got up and were rocking in the boat; they represented their favorite animals, etc. It was great.

When we had finished, the children drew pictures of their favorite story, and every single one drew the ark of Noah with animals. "*Yo quiero café negra.*" (I want a brown). Everyone needed a brown crayon for the ark. What gifted young children, boys and girls. When they finished the drawings, a parade of pictures was lead through the chapel so the mothers could witness the skills of the children. We ended with adoration, benediction and song. After the last song, they just stayed around, like they were waiting for the next thing! They wanted to stay there forever.

The *rancho* Tuesday evening was about forty-five minutes away. We arrived, and people peeked out of their doors. They started to gather and were so grateful to have Mass. They had not celebrated Mass there for several months. They had no benches in the chapel, only school desks, and everyone sat in a school desk. A little dog came in and lay down under the seat of the desk where her master sat. More and more people were arriving, but everyone found a seat. It was a tiny chapel, but absolutely beautiful.

Again, I preached without notes on the miracles we experience every day that are so subtle we don't see them. Then I told my vocation story and about the sign that the Lord gave me. After Mass, the children were staying outside, sitting around. There was an eighteen year old who asked for confession. She said she had not been since second grade. She was the caretaker of her *primos* (cousins) and *hermanos* (brothers and sisters). We chatted, as I was teaching them English. They just laughed so hard. *Repite* "My Naaame IS . . ." and I would say "*Padre Miguel.*" Then they would say (in parity of me) "*Mi Name is Padre Miguel*" and then I would yell, "*Yo soy Padre Miguel, no ustedes!*" (I am Padre Miguel, not you!) By the end of our session, they could say in English "My name is . . . . What's up dude?" A personal triumph. We returned home by about 10:00pm and ate *cena*. I ate nothing. I fell into bed and didn't move until morning. Evening came and morning followed, the third day.

Wednesday: For today, I switched from the kids to the adults. I wanted to give a reflection on Mary: *Obedience and Trust in God.* Many of these women were husbandless because their spouses were working outside of the *ranchos*. I gave my talk in my broken Spanish, about how Mary was young and pregnant; without a husband; and poor. How Jesus could have been born anywhere, and yet he was born in a *rancho*. That Mary was pregnant and had to ride a *burro* (to which many shook their heads in understanding, having done the same themselves) and that the Roman government was an oppressive one, much like their own. Despite my Spanish, or lack thereof, they seemed to get it.

Meanwhile, without me acting, the sems were improvising. When I finished my talk, I peeked outside, because I heard the laughter, and saw them acting out the creation story with as much vigor and life as they could muster. It was hilarious, and yet their Spanish was good. The kids were loving it. They were supposed to get through two more bible stories, but they never got past creation! It really lifted my heart to see them outside of their comfort level and doing so well. One of them would comment: "I never wanted to teach, or saw myself as a teacher, and yet I feel like these are MY kids!" And I understood EXACTLY what he meant.

We finished up with the Divine Mercy Chaplet. Many of them had never prayed this prayer and didn't really know about Divine Mercy. The missionary did an excellent job of teaching the lesson. This would prepare them for the Mass of Healing we decided to close with on Friday.

We returned to the house, and I was sick again, so I took a nap in the hopes that the sickness would go away. That night we went to a *rancho* pretty close by. The church was large, relative to the others, and beautifully decorated, but . . . there were sparrows everywhere inside. They had made their nests on the rafters of the church and refused to leave. As a result, there was bird poop all over the altar, tabernacle, and floor of the sanctuary. Although there was a statue of St. Francis in the corner, he did not look pleased at this lack of discretion exercised by his feathered friends. But in a moment, there were seven faces peeking through the door.

The sacristy door was locked, but some had brought brooms. The littlest one reached her hand through a hole in the sacristy door and unlocked it. Inside there were mops, and rags, and these children went to work, sweeping and then mopping the sanctuary floor, while the boys took the rags, wet them at the water pump, and wiped down the altar and benches. Now, this lasted for a few minutes with the boys before they started "accidently" snapping their rags at their buddies, but they had finished the job before the people started to arrive.

The birds refused to leave and were a constant distraction. During the Mass, which was packed once again, I kept a corporal over the elements, and yet the birds exercised due discretion during the Mass, and sang part of the opening hymn and the *Sanctus*.

After Mass, there were witness talks once again, so I gathered outside with the kids. There must have been thirty of them in a circle around me, and I tried to teach this group English as well. They were asking me what their names were in English. Some were easy, like *Juana* or *José*, while others were a bit more difficult, like *Guadalupe* or *Jovani*. The oldest one there was eighteen . . . a girl who looked as if she were fourteen. I asked what she was going to do now? She said she was going to the *Universidad* for teaching or administration. "What will you do after that?" I asked. "Come back here and work," she replied. It was only when I had time to reflect, that I finally got what she was saying. I thought maybe, come back to *General Cepeda* and work or something, but I believe she meant to come back to the *rancho*! Like they didn't want to leave, because this was home.

The other girl who was hanging out in front of the chapel was thirteen years old. She had helped sweep out the church. She was a beautiful young lady and shy to boot. I was saddened however, because as we stood there chatting about her family and friends, a truck would pass by, with a few *hombres* (men) stuffed in it. They would gaze on her like a coyote scouting prey. It wouldn't be long, and another truck would pass slowly by, eying up this young *muchacha*. All I could think is, this poor girl doesn't have a chance among these *lobos* (wolves). The one who spoke of the university, had such hope. That regardless of how poor she was, she would be able to make it. I wanted the same for this other girl (*Lisabeth*) and pray that for her.

We rounded everyone up, and headed back to the mission. Covered with dust from the rides in the open window van, I had to wait until the next day to shower. I would have to be satisfied with washing my face and hands in the tub, in the center of the courtyard, where I had hand-washed my clothes the day before. It was 11:00pm before I retired for the evening, and sleep was slow in coming. It was a rough night, before the sun peeked through the small crack in the door. Evening came and morning followed, the fourth day.

Thursday: This was going to be a pilgrimage day to the Cathedral of *Saltillo*. I was sick and decided to do nothing. There were no *rancho* visits today, so everyone took off, and I slept and prayed and read and rested. Evening came and morning followed, the fifth day.

Friday: This was a sad day. The last morning at our *rancho* also happened to be the day that the state was coming by to give free blankets to the people. We would have competition today. There was really only one activity slated for the day, and that was the *Mass of healing*. We got a late start. There would be no evening *rancho* Mass, because we were going to spend the afternoon in quiet reflection in the desert. I was looking forward to that.

The people started arriving and we were preparing for Mass. During the Mass, I explained that we would anoint the people as we do for the sacrament of *Anointing of the sick*. I preached a simple homily on the healing of mind body and spirit, and then conferred the Sacrament. The people approached the sanctuary as if they were coming for communion, and I laid hands on each of them. The second part of the rite directs the priest to anoint the person on the forehead and palms of the hands with a formulary. The problem was that these women were not empty handed. They brought up their babies with them.

The *Rite of Anointing* is only for those people who have reached the age of reason (6 or 7 years). I could not give it to an infant or toddler, because they had not reached the age, so what would I do? These mothers were holding out their hands, and then the hands of their babies. I made a pastoral decision. As I finished anointing the mother, I would simply touch the hands and forehead of the child. It seemed to work fine. The end of Mass was sad because we were leaving. I thanked them for their witness to us and told them I was sad.

There was one little girl the who came to everything faithfully the whole week, and did what she could to help. She happened also to be the daughter of the catechist for the *rancho*. I could see she was very sad that we were leaving. She was the one, the first day, who I had called up to help with my homily of the Good Samaritan. She was lingering after everyone else had gone away, and I called her over. She gave me a little embrace, and said she was sad. When I had lost my rosary in Mexico City, I bought a new one there near *Guadalupe*. It was a nice sterling silver rosary with a JP II cross. I took it from my pocket, and put it around her neck. Her face lit up with a brilliant smile. Her name was *Milagros Guadalupe* (Miracles of Guadalupe) and I thought in a real way, her name represented the people of the *ranchos* . . . all *miracles of Guadalupe*.

I turned to walk away and she yelled, *"Padre."* I turned and she offered me *her* rosary, one of the string and bead rosaries we had given out the day before. I told her to keep the brown rosary and pray for me. She smiled and walked away. I helped put the tables and chairs away that we had used for our mini-reception after the Mass, and got the van packed. We stepped into the van and drove out of the *ejido* for the last time.

Desert day: The plan was to take us out to a nice clearing in the desert with the mountains and trees so we could reflect on the week and pray. As we approached the valley, which was a forty-five minute drive, there were ominous gray clouds forming over the range. As we got closer, the lightening flashed brightly against the blackened sky. This was the desert?

We arrived amidst thunder; no rain; no more lightening, but gray clouds looming over the peaks of the mountains. We celebrated Mass under a grove of small trees. The wind was picking up, and the thunder was getting louder and more frequent. Some had eaten their lunch on the van, knowing that I would preach some, and calculating the allowable time. Most had not eaten all day, because we were at the *ranchos*. As we got to the *consecration*, we had some visitors. A herd of *vacas* (cows) began to circle our group. At first there were only a few, but then others began to arrive. Our backs were to the cows. But as we looked into the eyes of the congregation, we saw an approaching danger. One of the seminarians pressed the button on his umbrella, and it shot out like some kind of bulky baton. That relieved a bit of tension, and two of the missionaries picked up stones and threw them towards the cows.

The cows lost interest and departed, but the storm was becoming a bit more menacing. As we finished the closing prayer, it started to rain. We packed up everything and got into the vans. The rain let up a bit, and I thought to myself . . . today's not my shower day, so I might as well get wet. I was wearing an all white suit with my *sombrero*, so I didn't want to get soaked.

I walked to the other side of a great ravine and made my way across the range. I encountered some vacas of my own . . . and they had babies. They held their ground and then began to move toward me! I just pictured myself being pushed over the ravine. Three mothers with three calves . . . not the best combination.

I lowered myself on the one side of the ravine, and carefully walked over so I would be behind this small herd. I climbed back up the side, now clear of the cows and continued to walk . . . then the skies opened up. The rain felt like bullets, and yet, all I could do was extend my arms and bask in the refreshing water. There were four of us out in the rain, and it was wonderful! The horn from the van began honking, which was the signal to return to the vans. Well, it looked like "Desert day" was over.

We got back to the vans and most were ready to go home. I was bummed, because this was what I really needed. We drove from that area to another where the rain had not yet reached. We disembarked again, and I found a little hollow in the mountain, where I spent some time and began to sketch what came to me as Jesus' own time in the desert. It was a wonderful afternoon; and for the first time in Mexico . . . I heard nothing. There was silence. Even in the mountains, there is not such silence. Nothing moved; the breeze, although cool, didn't make a sound. I felt truly alone; in solitude; and could understand why Jesus sought the mountains and the desert to commune with God.

This was one of the toughest weeks I've had anywhere. The span of emotions, from pity and sympathy, to anger that people have to live like this; to frustration and sadness, that if I saw a dog in these conditions, I would call the police; to humility and love that

I experienced in the hearts of these people, not so unlike us. It's Saturday and we're on the ten hour ride back to *Queretaro*. I can't wait to get back; and yet, I miss the *ranchos*. I have learned to see the little miracles that are often overlooked. Especially all the thousands of *"Miracles of Guadalupe."*

When I packed this morning, I put my vestments in my backpack. As I did, I noticed something in the bottom of the pack, so I reached in, and the moment my fingers grasped the brown beads, I knew what it was. *Un milagro.* A sacred gift, from a wonderful *Miracle of Guadalupe.*

Prepare for Departure
July 27, 2010 at 5:09pm

Just a few observations and last thoughts before I return:

Mexico is loud. I made this observation only several weeks into my stay here. Even without the train, there is the daily barrage of firecrackers. Even without the honking horns, (someone should open a business in car horns here) there are the dogs barking . . . all of the dogs barking. Even without the church bells sounding, (which I like, but not from fifty churches within a fifty-square-mile area) there are those who seem to believe in their hearts that everyone else in the neighborhood wants to hear their music. Even without the car alarms, (which it seems every car has, and those parked feel the need to beep the alarm several times) there are the loud mufflers or no mufflers. Even without the birds, or cats, or whistles; even without the incessant sirens from the police cars; even without the shouts from the revelers; the only place I have found silence, was in the desert of *General Zepeda.*

Second: I just have this inordinate desire to drink water from the faucet. For eight weeks I have been cautious about using the water for anything but washing, and even then, being especially careful about it. We do take a great deal for granted. Even if the water tastes bad, at least we can drink it.

Third: When I first arrived, *Aedes* greeted me immediately. She had tiny eyes and long legs vested in stripes. In fact, the stripes went from her head to her toes like one of those bad dresses from the 80's. She was dainty, to say the least, and her voice a shrill whine I could hear as she neared my *habitacion* (room). She approached me without any inhibition, and yet she moved so gracefully that, I have to admit, I was distracted. And yet, there was malice in her approach. Unlike others I knew like her, she would approach during the day, and before I knew what had happened she was here and gone. I knew that she would not leave empty-handed, for she always approached like that person who needs something and knows what it is. She returned several times, each time more painful than the last. And the last times, she brought her "lady friends."

Her name . . . *Aedes*, well in Latin it's that, but in English they call her the "Asian Tiger Mosquito." Yes . . . the blood-sucking mosquitoes. This one was a transplant from, you guessed it . . . Asia and the Orient, but she adapted very well for the southern US and Mexico. By the time you realize she's on you, she's already gotten her fill and is taking off. But, she returns shortly after for another meal . . . and another . . . and another.

Finally: I will miss Mexico. I will miss the people here terribly. In a special way, I will miss the housemates I have met over the last eight weeks.

I will enjoy, once again, eating without the worry of whether or not my *ADH* will be suppressed or not, because of the Amoeba I ingested. I will enjoy, once again, not needing a *celebret* to celebrate Mass just about anywhere in my country. I will enjoy, once again, those that I miss terribly, never having been away from the country, let alone my town this long. Finally, I will enjoy understanding a bit more, the language and the culture of a population that is growing very quickly in our country . . . a population of faith-filled, hard-working people, who are simply seeking the best for their families . . . something we understand as well.

ABOUT THE AUTHOR

Fr. Michael W. Rothan is the Pastor of St. Joan of Arc Church in Hershey PA since 2011. He is the son of Mr. & Mrs. Richard Rothan of Millersville and one of five children. He attended 12 years of Catholic school in Lancaster County after which he obtained a Bachelor of Science degree from Shippensburg University. Fr. Rothan then received his PA certification in Biology and Chemistry from Millersville University. After having taught in both the Public School system and the Parochial School system, he was accepted into the Program of Priestly Formation for the Diocese of Harrisburg. He attended St. Vincent Seminary where he obtained a Bachelor of Arts degree in Philosophy, a Master of Arts degree in Sacred Scripture, and a Master of Divinity degree. He was ordained a Diocesan Priest, June 5, 2004. He has authored three books: 61 Minutes: Homilies and Reflections from the year of Mark; 61 Minutes: Homilies and Reflections from the year of Luke; and "Home Free", Autobiographical. This book is the last in his "61 minutes" series, but the first to be written partially in Spanish.